Whatever Became of Sin?

Karl Menninger, M.D.

WHATEVER BECAME OF SIN?

HAWTHORN BOOKS, INC.

Publishers / NEW YORK

WHATEVER BECAME OF SIN?

Acknowledgments

A preface may be an effort to supply a raison d'être for the writing of a book, or it may informally introduce the topic or philosophy of the contents. My preface would be of the first type, and as such I think it should properly be at the end of the book. A preface is usually the last chapter written by the author and should be the last one to be read by the reader. You will find it on page 223 if you must look now.

But let me here make my acknowledgment of indebtedness for the help I have received from many people in many ways. My dear wife is a joint author with me of everything I write and would have been so listed here except that she might be blamed for any seeming departures from medical orthodoxy. In addition to her great help, I received encouragement and advice from many colleagues, notably the following:

The Reverend Richard Bollinger, of the Department of Religion and Psychiatry, the Menninger Foundation; the Reverend Gerald Daily, S.J., Rector of Newman College, University of Melbourne, Australia; the Reverend Alfred Davies, of the Kansas (penal) Reception and Diagnostic Center; Dr. Frederick J. Hacker, of the Hacker Clinic and Foundation, Los Angeles, California; Dr. Seward Hiltner, of Princeton Theological Seminary; Dr. Philip B. Holzman, of the University of Chicago Pritzker Medical School; the Reverend Carlyle Marney, of The Interpreters' House, Lake Junaluska, North Carolina; Dr. Gardner Murphy, George Washington University, Washington, D.C., and former Director of Research, the Menninger Foundation; the Reverend Leslie A. Newman, Methodist clergyman of Sussex, England, and Chautauqua, New York; Dr. Paul W. Pruyser, Henry March Pfeiffer Professor, the Menninger Foundation; Dr. Sydney Smith, Editor-in-Chief of the *Bulletin of the Menninger Clinic*; Professor Arnold Toynbee, The Royal Institute of International Affairs, London, England; Dr. Lewis F. Wheelock, my friend and my assistant in the Chicago office of the Menninger Foundation, formerly Visiting Lecturer in History at the University of Kansas.

So many people have helped me that I could not possibly list them all. W. Clement Stone, of Chicago, was interested in the idea of the book and encouraged its development. And I am particularly indebted for help in its preparation to Virginia Eicholtz, Managing Editor of the *Bulletin of the Menninger Clinic*, and to Vesta Walker, Chief Librarian at the Menninger Foundation, and to my secretaries and typists, Berenice Brinker, Marilyn Kollath, Beverlee Hayes, Clara Erdman, Ellen Tebbel, Mary Hooper, Judy Walton, Carole Rosebaugh, and Judy Craig. For their indefatigable general assistance, including much photocopying, I thank Alvin Todd and Willie Foster. For the devotion and help of all these people I am indeed grateful.

Karl Menninger, M.D.
Topeka, Kansas; and Chicago, Illinois

Contents

Whatever
Became
of Sin?

1

A Brief and Biased
Review of Moral History

When, in an apprehensive or deploring mood, we seniors are tempted to dispense to our successors cautionary admonishment and dire prediction, we should first reflect on the moral history of mankind, which can be summarized: They *hang* prophets. Or ignore them, which hurts worse.

Yes, so they do. So they always did. But the urge to prophesy comes upon us, nonetheless, and we must tell it, if not "like it is," at least as it seems to us to be. *Morituri salutemus et crucem manebimus.*

But by speaking out we shall have tossed onto the cenotaph of human history another pebble from the quarry of hope.

On a sunny day in September, 1972, a stern-faced, plainly dressed man could be seen standing still on a street corner in the busy Chicago Loop. As pedestrians hurried by on their way to lunch or business, he would solemnly lift his right arm, and pointing to the person nearest him, intone loudly the single word "GUILTY!"

Then, without any change of expression, he would resume his stiff stance for a few moments before repeating the gesture. Then, again, the inexorable raising of his arm, the pointing, and the solemn pronouncing of the one word "GUILTY!"

The effect of this strange *j'accuse* pantomime on the passing strangers was extraordinary, almost eerie. They would stare at him, hesitate, look away, look at each other, and then at him again; then hurriedly continue on their ways.

One man, turning to another who was my informant, exclaimed: "But how did *he* know?"

No doubt many others had similar thoughts. How *did* he know, indeed?

"Guilty!" *Everyone* guilty? Guilty of what? Guilty of overparking? Guilty of lying? Guilty of arrogance and hubris toward the one God? Guilty of "borrowing," not to say embezzling? Guilty of unfaithfulness to a faithful wife? Guilty only of evil thoughts—or evil plans?

Guilty before whom? Is a police officer following? Did anyone see? Will they be likely to notice it? Does he know about it? But that isn't technically illegal, is it?

I can make it up. I will give it back. I'll apologize. I wasn't myself when I did that. No one knows about it. But I'm going to quit. It's a dangerous habit. I wouldn't want the children to see me. How can I ever straighten it out? What's done can't be undone.

The solemn accuser on the Chicago street corner has had many predecessors. In the eighth to sixth centuries B.C. peripatetic exhorters held forth in thriving Palestinian villages attracting large and attentive crowds. To their listeners these earnest young men likewise cried "guilty" and proclaimed ominously that for all the general prosperity, sin was prevalent thereabouts which, unacknowledged and unrepented, would bring dire consequences. These men were ignored, ridiculed as alarmists, jailed as trespassers, or driven from the country. In the course of time, their predictions were fulfilled and their countries were annihilated.

Later on, remnants of these chastened peoples returned to reestablish themselves as a nation with a morally strict government. Commercial trade and prosperity returned, with fluctuating military fortunes. Seers again appeared, preaching the old refrain of needed repentance.

One of these, John ben Zechariah, lived in a desert area outside the metropolis and attracted considerable attention from the common people. Crowds trekked out into the desert to hear him. He reproached them for their swinging ways in public and private life.

"Desist! Repent!" he cried.

"But why?" asked some. "We never had it so good."

"Why not?" said others and vowed to mend their ways. To signalize their intentions they underwent a public bathing ceremonial. John ben Zechariah was nicknamed the Baptizer and little communities sprang up devoted to bathing, poverty, chastity, and penitence.

This commotion in the desert did not go unnoticed by the Establishment; ben Zechariah was picked up by the police, taken back to the city, and jailed. Soon afterward he was decapitated—without warning or trial—and his severed head was publicly displayed on a platter at a social gathering. Prosperity, with much public construction and international commerce, continued briskly.

Another itinerant appeared from a remote rural area and preached in a similar vein. He, too, pointed to widespread wrongdoing and social injustice and covert despair. He, too, counseled repentance. He, too, was besought by the troubled citizenry and was listened to earnestly. He, too, was irritating to the Establishment, and He, too, was publicly executed. Those of His followers who took Him seriously were harassed and persecuted, but their numbers increased prodigiously and they spread far afield. Various organizations of them evolved, quarreled, and divided. A little later came the Barbarians, and then the Dark Ages.

A thousand years passed. A new continent was discovered. Emigrations and immigrations, revolutions and great discoveries followed. From time to time waves of depression and despair engulfed peoples of different areas, but these alternated with periods of expansion and "progress" and shifting, mixing populations. Local waves of violence succeeded one another, alternating with phases of peace and politics in high circles, industry and trade in lower circles. Civilization and "enlightenment" had arrived.

In one especially favored area most of the people became very prosperous, but they had a bad conscience. They had slaughtered and corralled and dispossessed the natives; they had massacred and robbed and driven the Indians and Mexicans from their own lands (then appropriated them); and they had brought the horror of abduction and enslavement of illiterate natives (American, Canadian, Mexican, and African) to its high point of "success." Having done so for centuries, they regretted it, and turned with ferocity upon one another—brother against brother, region against region—

in a long, bloody orgy of what was regarded as the "only way" to "settle the matter."

Out of the fratricidal carnage and suffering came the martyrdom of an immortal leader with a conscience, and a cessation of commercial slaving and of organized fighting. For the first time in a century the public conscience was clear. People buried their dead, mourned their losses, mended their fences, and pensioned their "veterans." "Public lands" were opened for settlement and many strove to forget the past in a feverish exploitation of the resources of the new land.

The population multiplied and shifted. "The West" and other unspoiled areas were occupied, "settled," and despoiled. The aggressive energies which had been absorbed in warfare were turned now against nature. The prairie was plowed. The forests were felled. The wild animals were shot or trapped or poisoned. An incredibly abundant and useful migratory bird was exterminated completely by mass slaughter; the two most abundant and useful mammals (the bison and the whale), nearly so. The wilderness was ravished; the country was "developed." This was then a good and boastful word and not, as now, one of reproach and horror, meaning squatted upon, appropriated, exploited, and polluted.

So the nation "grew." We glowed; we gloried; we prospered; we preempted; we evicted; we extended; we consolidated; we succeeded! We shut our eyes to all that was unpleasant about these words and these processes. We were too busy to discern the misery created everywhere, too smug to see the devastation we were wreaking, too greedy to recognize the waste and the inequity and ugliness and the immorality.

The Present

Many centuries have passed since the Hebrew seers preached the importance of a moral code—preached and warned and exhorted and died. Human beings have become more numerous, but scarcely more moral. They are busy, coming and going, getting and begetting, fighting and defending, creating and destroying. Many move about now, very swiftly, very far, and in large groups and small. Their numbers have multiplied vastly, spreading over former deserts, forests, and wildernesses. They have learned how to cover the grass with pavement, wash the soil and refuse into the ocean, and besmear the earth with waste. They now communicate with one another in a thousand ways, swift and slow; they transport themselves rapidly on land, sea, and through the air. They also *fail* to communicate in a thousand ways and continue to destroy one another with great effectiveness. They spend most of their wealth on stockpiles of explosives and poisons.

Many of them live lives of great comfort and ease while other thousands die of starvation daily. Millions, barely surviving, exist most miserably, working at monotonous drudgery. Conscripts are coerced to hurl fire, poisons, and explosives at "enemies" whom they resemble but do not know, and have only fictitious reasons for fearing or hating. Those not at war engage in angry dissensions over property, priorities, privilege, policy, and popularity. Fear and uncertainty, even among the prosperous, lead many citizens to rearm themselves with privately owned killing machines, as in earlier days (but with more deadly weapons).

It became the epoch of technology, rampant and triumphant. We boasted of our inventions, innovations, and gadgets. Rugged individualism, acquisition, thrift, boldness, and shrewdness were acclaimed as the great national virtues. Although hard work was admired, luxury and ease were inordinately esteemed. And as we appropriated and accumulated, we bragged and we braved.

Noisy display enticed people in less prosperous countries to rush to our shores and join in the great grab. These newcomers were exploited in order to produce more and more "gross national products" and electrical energy. We dammed up more and more rivers and gouged out more coal and smashed down more forests. Our population increased—too much. Our traffic increased—much too much. Everything was "going great"—but too much.

Suddenly we awoke from our pleasant dreams with a fearful realization that *something was wrong*.

2

What Is Wrong?

The skies darkened over the cities. The lakes turned yellow and the fish died. The rivers were full of pollutants and sediment and the songs of the birds were stilled. The vestiges of wildlife still remaining in remote areas began to disappear—although a few bloodthirsty hunters and poisoners still persisted and pursued. Debris dumped into the ocean for centuries began to appear all over its great expanse. Water levels fell steadily everywhere; wells went dry; vast projects for transporting water long distances developed with squabbles over appropriation of these distant supplies. Experts warned of approaching depletion.

Ninety percent of all the consumable goods produced on the earth were being devoured by the fraction of the world's people who lived in that one country. The water used by each one of its citizens was a thousand times what the average citizen of a hundred other countries received. Debris, detritus, and refuse from these affluent spenders and wasters polluted rivers and lakes and bays and even the ocean. Gold, poisons, and atomic bombs were stockpiled in vaults; used cars, bottles, and other discarded objects accumulated on vacant lots. Poisonous wastes which would remain dangerous for 500 centuries were about to be dumped into old and possibly leaky salt mines in my own state.

More and more of these atrocities—at first kept secret or known only to a few—became common knowledge and a common concern. Each increment of bad news brought an increase of public alarm for a time. "Environmentalists" clamored against the industrialists who reviled the former as sentimental obstructionists. Then, in a surfeit of distress and with an overwhelming sense of helplessness, we began to sink into a posture of apathetic inaction, the old-time sins of acedia and anomie.

6

A chronic, generalized anxiety and gloom began to settle over all. More and more people became worried and puzzled and apprehensive. Bursts of ostentatious gaiety, social exhibitionism, and political grandstanding continued, and there was much bizarre pleasure seeking and restless moving about in all directions, but the bad news continued and a general depression became everywhere evident.

The churches, filled for a time, became preoccupied with schisms, dissensions, and departures. Unarmed protesting students were shot down by armed militiamen. Unarmed protesting prisoners were shot down together with their hostages! The youth for whom we had sacrificed so much seemed to reject their heritage, shaking their fists at their elders for a great betrayal. Small colleges, long the cradles of leadership and cultural nurture, dried up and disappeared, dead of starvation. Huge impersonal state "universities" burgeoned everywhere like ersatz education factories in which vast stadiums were provided for very profitable gladiatorial combats of great violence. The former slave people whom we had encouraged to work and study took an eager and skillful part in these activities as part of their increasing arousal and expression of discontent.

Our government engaged us in a very long, expensive, and bloody program of destruction against a simple people and their beautiful land. Homes and farms were burned, forests defoliated, crops and orchards destroyed, wildlife exterminated, communities wiped out, cities bombed. The alleged purpose of this holocaust was to halt the extension of "communism" at all costs lest it corrupt these simple people and spread to others.

Simultaneously it was also considered necessary in America for all households to be armed in case of an attack by a neighbor and for all policemen to be doubly armed in case of an encounter with a "hippie."

The people of churches and synagogues continued to gather in decreasing numbers to worship, to pray, to fast, and to repent. Their clergy sent out the distress message: "Our nation is sorely troubled. We believe this to be a sickness of the spirit."

People shook their heads and shrugged their shoulders. What to do? What to say? Is this us? Is this our once fair birthplace, our peaceful, prosperous homeland? Our unique and beautiful planet? This dark, foreboding picture—can it be so? Hasn't the author painted a darker-than-life canvas of our troubled world? Is not the doctor overly gloomy?

"What ails the American spirit?" an editor asked of some of our seers.[1] "It is the age of rubbish," answered one.[2] "Religion just doesn't play the role it used to play. . . . Few other things . . . can hold the culture together. . . . Young people don't have anything that they want to do. . . . they haven't decided what they want their lives to say."

"The malaise of the American spirit," declared a professor of government,[3] "cannot be blamed on wrongheaded policies, inept administrations, or even an inability to understand the dimensions of our current discontents. The reasons are more fundamental . . . arising from the kind of people we have become. . . . we cannot bring ourselves to make the personal sacrifices required to sustain domestic order or international authority."

A professor of history added:

> When a growing portion of the nation's youth loudly proclaims its defection from everything; when even the most traditional and conservative campuses seethe with perpetual turmoil; when two successive Presidents worry about a credibility gap (a polite way of saying that a significant number of Americans consider their President a liar); when black people find themselves trapped between failure of a promised integration and white resistance to black control of black communities; when white people generally split between those who feel guilty about the blacks and those who unashamedly hate them . . . when the richest nation in world history cannot keep its water and air clean, much less eliminate poverty; when great cities are acknowledged to be ungovernable, not to mention unlivable; when the country is racked with fear, foreboding, and hopelessness—then we had better declare a state of spiritual crisis, for the alternative would be to declare that irrationality, decadence,

[1] "The Spirit of '70: Six Historians Reflect on What Ails the American Spirit," *Newsweek*, 76: 19–34 (July 6, 1970).

[2] Richard Hofstadter, professor of American history at Columbia University, New York.

[3] Andrew Hacker, professor in the Department of Government, Cornell University, Ithaca, New York.

and disorder constitute our normal and preferred national condition. . . .[4]

Daniel J. Boorstin, director of the National Museum of Science and Technology at the Smithsonian Institution, puts our current situation this way: ". . . we have lost our sense of history. . . . lost our traditional respect for the wisdom of ancestors and the culture of kindred nations. . . . Flooded by screaming headlines and hourly televised 'news' melodramas of dissent and 'revolution,' we haunt ourselves with the illusory ideal of some 'whole nation' which had a deep and outspoken 'faith' in its 'values.'"

Arthur M. Schlesinger, Jr., Albert Schweitzer Professor of Humanities at the City University of New York, declared,

> Improved methods of medical care and nutrition have produced the population crisis; and the growth and redistribution of population have produced the urban crisis. The feverish increase in the gross national product first consumes precious natural resources and then discharges filth and poison into water and air; hence the ecological crisis. Nor can one omit the extraordinary moral revolution which makes our contemporary society reject as intolerable conditions of poverty, discrimination and oppression that mankind had endured for centuries.

Well, that's what some of our prophets are saying today. The reporters wrote it down for all to read. Many others have spoken and written similarly.

And do we believe them? Believe prophets? Oh, perhaps a few people do. But prophets are customarily disbelieved and disregarded. Their forebodings are often fulfilled; we know that. The sown wind reaps the whirlwind. But with time the prophets are stilled and forgotten; the nations disappear. Nineveh and Tyre, Memphis and Persia, Athens and Jerusalem, Carthage and Rome, the Holy Roman Empire, the Empire of Great Britain, the Second French Republic, the Thousand Year Third Reich. . . . The morning newspapers discussing possible peace quoted the President as say-

[4] Eugene D. Genovese, chairman of the Department of History at the University of Rochester, New York.

ing that our country "must always have a strength second to none in the world."[5] The same illusions, the same dangers, the same warnings, the same cycles persist.

Yet *can* we believe our prophets of gloom? They are so often mistaken—at least about some things. Crime is bad but it was far worse a century ago. Wars are fewer. Comforts are greater. Life is longer and health more general. So many things in the course of living are "better" today (for the "better people"). True, the denizens of the ghetto are no more comfortable even with electric lights. The children of the Delta are just as hungry. The Appalachians are still full of hand-to-mouth squatters. The Indians whose land is being scraped or gerrymandered away from them are more miserable than ever.

It is not solely in America that moral tone has fallen. The brave Protestant Federation of France, remnants of the once great Huguenot majority but now numbering only 750,000, issued (in February, 1972) a 26-page document on the present state of French society. It declared therein that *the present economic and political system of our society is unacceptable. The domination and manipulation of the weak by the strong in socioeconomic activities is "radically incompatible with the gospel."*[6] (Italics mine)

Oh, the politicians tell us we are going along in great shape. We read of new triumphs in technology. There is an average crisis but we are going to solve it—by some more destruction. We live in a miracle world. Anything can happen. Once we were fascinated, spellbound, excited at the prospects. But we are no longer amazed; we are not amused. We are not comforted or reassured. It cannot go on like this, we reflect. Yet, what shall we do? How can we turn the tide? How do we mend matters? How can we correct what *is* basically wrong? And what *is* that basic wrong?

Has the sense of morality vanished from the people? Has the rule of expediency, of success, of technological triumph replaced the necessity for moral integrity? Everything was "succeeding" for a while —progress was the order of the day. But now the new gods seem to

[5] September 2, 1972.

[6] Trevor Beeson, "France's Protesting Protestants" (editorial), *Christian Century*, 89:274 (March 8, 1972).

have failed us, while the old God is said (by some) to be dead. Things are all wrong.

Who Is to Blame?

We turn, angrily seeking someone to blame.

Who started the wretched, interminable war? Who ruined our air and oceans? Who filled our beautiful rivers and lakes with filth? Who beggared our paupers? Who crushed our blacks? Who alienated our youth? Who corrupted our business morals, our politics, our judicial system? No one? Who is the evil designer against the welfare of man? Is no one to blame when so much is wrong?

There is a parable in Luke about someone secretly sowing weeds in a wheat field while the master and his servants slept. The servants were all for quickly cutting them out, but the master said that at harvest time one could more effectively separate the wheat from the tares.

A fragment of manuscript has been found (or imagined!) which carries on this parable slightly at variance with the old text. An approximate translation reads:

> And then the servants counseled together saying, "It would be much better to pull out those weeds right now rather than wait, but we must obey the master even when he is wrong. In the meantime, let us look about for the enemy who would do this evil thing to our master, who is kind to everyone and doesn't deserve this treatment." So they quietly inquired and made search in all the region round about, but they could find no one.

> But one of the servants came privily to the chief steward at night saying, "Sir, forgive me, but I can no longer bear to conceal my secret. I know the enemy who sowed the tares. I saw him do it."

> At this the chief steward was astonished and full of anger. But before punishing him, he demanded of the servant why he had not come forward sooner.

> "I dared not," cried the servant. "I scarcely dared to come and tell you this even now. I was awake the night the weeds were sown. I saw the man who did it; he walked past me, seemingly awake and yet asleep, and he did not appear to recognize me. But I recognized him."

"And who was he, indeed?" asked the chief steward in great excitement. "Tell me, so that he can be punished."

The servant hung his head. Finally, in a low voice he replied. "It was the master himself."

And the two agreed to say nothing of this to any man.

3

The Disappearance of Sin:
An Eyewitness Account

In all of the laments and reproaches made by our seers and prophets, one misses any mention of "sin," a word which used to be a veritable watchword of prophets. It was a word once in everyone's mind, but now rarely if ever heard. Does that mean that no sin is involved in all our troubles—sin with an "I" in the middle? Is no one any longer guilty of anything? Guilty perhaps of a sin that could be repented and repaired or atoned for? Is it only that someone may be stupid or sick or criminal—or asleep? Wrong things are being done, we know; tares are being sown in the wheat field at night. But is no one responsible, no one answerable for these acts? Anxiety and depression we all acknowledge, and even vague guilt feelings; but has no one committed any sins?

Where, indeed, did sin go? What became of it?

Lt. William Calley was portrayed to the world as a bloody villain, in both the English and American senses of that adjective. He slaughtered helpless women and babies with the hypocritical justification that they might be carrying concealed explosives. He was formally accused and tried for military disobedience as well as murder before a jury of peers who had been engaged in the same business of military destruction, and he was found guilty.

But a great cry went up from the people. Many sectors of the general public angrily disputed the possibility that what Calley did could be properly labeled a crime. Indeed, many would not concede that he even committed a sin or made a mistake. He had obeyed orders (they said); he had done what everyone wanted done or was doing, and it was for the sake of a great righteousness. Some might (and did) find him technically guilty of a crime, but what he did was right; it was no sin. It was a glorious, patriotic deed.

The Sixth Commandment, "Thou shalt not kill," obviously made a tacit exception of bullocks, lambs, Indians, Philistines, and Viet Cong. Every slayer can find reasons for making his particular violation an exception, a non-crime if not a non-sin. Hitler had his reasons for killing the Jews. Custer had his reasons for killing the Sioux. Our military men had reasons for killing Viet Cong soldiers, and the Viet Cong had their reasons for killing ours. Under certain circumstances purposive killing is frequently declared, by one side or another, to be a non-crime. But is it ever a non-sin? Or, is nothing now a sin?

Avoidance of the Word

The very word "sin," which seems to have disappeared, was a proud word. It was once a strong word, an ominous and serious word. It described a central point in every civilized human being's life plan and life style. But the word went away. It has almost disappeared—the word, along with the notion. Why? Doesn't anyone sin anymore? Doesn't anyone believe in sin?

Congress voted some years ago to require the President to proclaim each year a national day of prayer, and Truman began it in 1952. The following year (1953) President Eisenhower made his first proclamation and in it he made a reference to SIN. He borrowed the words for his proclamation from a call issued in 1863 by Abraham Lincoln, the country's first Republican and most theological President:

> It is the duty of nations as well as of men to own their dependence upon the overruling power of God, to confess their sins and transgressions in humble sorrow, yet with assured hope that genuine repentance will lead to mercy and pardon.

An article in *Theology Today* has this to say about Eisenhower's use of the word "sin":

> None of Eisenhower's subsequent calls to prayer mentioned *sin* again. The word was not compatible with the Commander-in-Chief's vision of a proud and confident people. . . . Since 1953, no President has mentioned sin as a national failing. Neither Kennedy, Johnson,

nor Nixon. To be sure, they have skirted the word. The Republicans referred to the problems of "pride" and "self-righteousness." The Democrats referred to "short-comings." But none used the grand old sweeping concept of sin. I cannot imagine a modern President beating his breast on behalf of the Nation and praying "God be merciful to us sinners" though experts agree this is one of the best ways to begin.[1]

So, as a nation, we officially ceased "sinning" some twenty years ago.

However, there is a vague but strong impression that many believe sin still permeates our lives. The lead editorial in *The New Yorker* for September 23, 1972, conveys this feeling of moral decline.

A Harris poll published last week showed that fifty-five per cent of the American people are in favor of our bombing Vietnam. Thirty-two per cent are against it. The others do not know what they think. In short, it appears that the majority of the people in our country believe it is right, or necessary, for us to go on killing the Vietnamese people—North Vietnamese and South Vietnamese alike—because, according to the poll, "It is important that South Vietnam not fall into the control of the Communists."

No matter that Russia and China, giants among nations, long ago fell into the control of the Communists, and that it is now our government's policy not only to coexist with Russia and China but to attempt to establish friendly relations with them. What matters is not to let this tiny, once obscure semi-nation become Communist. So, in a stupor, with scarcely a thought, we drop our thousands of pounds of explosives every day, and wipe out those nameless, faceless, distant creatures who in our bleary minds are not quite human beings.

And it is not our President who is doing the killing, it is not our bomber crews, it is we the American people. We are the ones—the fifty-five per cent who say yes and the rest who say so little—who keep the bombs falling. Now that our ground troops are withdrawn and our casualty rate is down to almost nothing, now that the lives that are being lost in ground combat are Vietnamese lives (why die if we can pay someone else to do our dying for us?), we blithely take to the air. Just in case we might still have qualms about the bombing, our government tells us, over and over, why we do it.

[1] Frederick Fox of Princeton University, "The National Day of Prayer," *Theology Today*, 29:260 (October 1972).

We seek, the government tells us, some geopolitical advantage in Vietnam; *that* is why we are bombing. We, the most powerful nation in the world, waging a strange, vertical war against one of the world's least powerful nations, seek a balance of power; *that* is why we are bombing. By killing and maiming our friends in South Vietnam, by ravaging their land, by destroying their society, we seek to convince our friends in Europe and the Middle East that they can count on us to stand by them; *that* is why we are bombing. We seek to impress our potential enemies with our might and courage by recklessly spending Vietnamese lives in a fratricidal struggle that could not go on without us and by carrying out air attacks on people who cannot defend themselves or retaliate; *that* is why we are bombing. We are bombing them in Hanoi so that we won't have to fight them in the streets of San Francisco: we seek a generation of peace. We are fighting a token war now so that we won't have to fight the real war, the ultimate war, later: we seek survival.

We draw closer to Russia and China, but we must stop Communism in Vietnam, for it is there that our national security lies, and we seek national security. *That* is why we are bombing.

Why are we bombing Vietnam? As we put off the one day that might bring our prisoners of war home, we seek the return of our prisoners of war. *That* is why. We seek prestige. We seek respect. We seek credibility. We seek honor. *That* is why. And in the course of all this seeking, all this bombing, our souls have withered. Day by day, we are turning into monsters. For a hundred reasons, and for no reason whatever, we are blowing men, women, and children to bits with our bombs, and we can't feel a thing.[2]

There you are. Fifty-five percent of 200,000,000 people is quite a few. For them, given a plausible excuse, dynamiting innocent people is no sin, or it's a lesser sin to avoid a greater one. What greater one?

But, you will notice, even this eloquent, anguished editor does not use the word "sin."

Again, on October 23, 1972, *Time* devoted its cover page and its lead story to the "national disgrace" of spending $400,000,000 to elect one of two leaders. But in none of the text, which excoriates

---

[2] *The New Yorker*, 48:27 (September 23, 1972).

the practice, does the word "sin" occur. It is evil, disgraceful, corrupt, prejudicial, harmful, but—evidently—it is not sinful.

"Now, Dr. Karl. You ought to define that word. What do you mean by 'sin'? All kinds of things have been called sin in times past. It has been used as a scarehead for controlling the ignorant for centuries. But just what have you in mind? What kind of sin do you mean? Carnal sin? Mortal sin? Venial sin? Original sin? Existential sin?"

I could counter with, "What *was* the sin that no longer exists?" I mean any kind of wrongdoing that *we* used to call sin. I have in mind behavior that violates the moral code or the individual conscience or both; behavior which pains or harms or destroys my neighbor—or me, myself. You know—and *Time* knows—what wrongdoing is, and if a better word than sin is available, use it.

So choose your own word and be patient with me if I take several chapters to try to air my views. Meanwhile, before I do, what do *you* think?

Has the reader dismissed the whole sin-and-guilt business from his mind? Can he? And the anxiety and depression, also? Just call it existential, do you, and plod onward? If so, congratulations. Some of us can't do that. It is a burning sore, a deep grief, a heartache for many of us.

Some behavior once regarded as sinful has certainly undergone reappraisal. It is no longer a sin to assert that the earth is round. Tea and coffee drinking are generally allowed, now. Adultery is technically a crime but for many people it is certainly no sin. Lots of sins have disappeared; nevertheless, I believe there is a general sentiment that sin is still with us, by us, and in us—somewhere. We are made vaguely uneasy by this consciousness, this persistent sense of guilt, and we try to relieve it in various ways. We project the blame on to others, we ascribe the responsibility to a group, we offer up scapegoat sacrifices, we perform or partake in dumb-show rituals of penitence and atonement. There is rarely a peccavi, but there's a feeling.

The disappearance of the word "sin" involves a shift in the allocation of responsibility for evil. Perhaps some people are convinced of the validity of the Skinnerian thesis, and no longer consider themselves or anyone else to be answerable for any evil—or for any good. The law does not take this view; instead, for law, crime is the thing.

I am not referring to existential or theological sin, if I may call it that. Not the innate sinfulness of mankind—our natural propensity for transgression. Nor original sin, if it be conceived of as different. I am no theologian, but a doctor. Talking to prisoners in jails and prisons where they writhe in agony from the slow torture officially inflicted to "reform" them has made me realize how much more these miserable sinners are sinned against than sinning.

It seems grotesquely like the child's game of tag. A lad is in various ways wronged and hurt by persons or things in his environment; he retaliates with a wrong against one of them; they hit back. This exchange continues until he (being easier to catch than his environment) is seized by the official grabbers, the human dog-catchers, the police. Sometimes this is a brave act; human dogs go mad, too, and many a policeman seizing desperate fugitives does risk his life. But often arrest is a crude act of bullying or brutality. Once his catch is landed the policeman can bow out, and then official righteousness begins, with excruciating delays, to grind out its dreary ritual.[3]

The captive is hurt, and hurt again—this time officially and devastatingly. He is sentenced and branded, forever labeled a "bad" citizen. He is detained "to do time" ostensibly for repentance and "reformation." To him this is only vindictive torture, hypocritically rationalized. When finally released from it, he is moved to repay it in kind. He does, and he is then recaptured and retortured: the press then decries the prevalence of "recidivism," which is an impressive scientific word for this tit-for-tat-for-tit game, sins for sins for sins for sins. At some point they are called crime, but never— anymore—are they called sins. Two percent of the sins of the city become "crimes" and are thus "appropriately" handled. But what about the other 98 percent?

Definition of Sin

I promised to return to definition. Sin is transgression of the law of God; disobedience of the divine will; moral failure. Sin is failure to realize in conduct and character the moral ideal, at least as fully

[3] This is vividly described by Morton Hunt in *The Mugging* (New York: Atheneum, 1972).

as possible under existing circumstances; failure to do as one ought towards one's fellow man (Webster).

This definition is broad enough to meet the needs of both believers and nonbelievers, but it fails to say why the transgression and disobedience are regarded as "bad," why they are popularly disapproved or forbidden, considered to be "No, no." Sin traditionally does have this quality of taboo, of wrongness, and we can assume it is carried over from the earliest days.

The wrongness of the sinful act lies not merely in its nonconformity, its departure from the accepted, appropriate way of behavior, but in an implicitly aggressive quality—a ruthlessness, a hurting, a breaking away from God and from the rest of humanity, a partial alienation, or act of rebellion.

Standing on one's head is nonconforming, and it is neither aesthetic nor congenial behavior nor expressive of a moral ideal, but it is not likely to be considered sinful. Sin has a willful, defiant, or disloyal quality; *someone* is defied or offended or hurt. The willful disregard or sacrifice of the welfare of others for the welfare or satisfaction of the self is an essential quality of the concept *sin*. St. Augustine described it as a turning "away from the universal whole to the individual part. . . . There is nothing greater [i.e., more important, more desirable, more worthy] than the whole. Hence when he desires [seeks, devotes himself to] something greater, he grows smaller."[4] And sin is thus, at heart, a refusal of the love of others.

Dr. Seward Hiltner reviews three complementary ways in which sin has been conceived in Christian theology: as *rebellion*; as *estrangement* or *isolation*; and as *error* in performance, a missing of the mark (the old Hebrew meaning). One may condense these aspects of sinfulness into defiant withdrawal, supererogation, and self-absorption.[5] These all describe the evildoing which some call sin.

---

[4] *De Trinitate*, XII, 14, as quoted in the Dutch Roman Catholic catechism.

[5] One of my most helpful sources, in reviewing the theological meaning of sin, was the writings and addresses of Seward Hiltner, in particular his essay "Christian Understanding of Sin in the Light of Medicine and Psychiatry," *Medical Arts and Sciences*, 20:35–49 (1966). See also Reinhold Niebuhr, *The Nature and Destiny of Man*, 2 vols. (New York: Scribner's, 1949); Joseph Fuchs, "Sin and Conversion," *Theology Digest*, 14(4):292–301 (Winter 1966), and *Human Values and Christian Morality* (Dublin: Gill & Macmillan, 1970); Louis Monden, *Sin, Liberty, and Law* (London: Sheed & Ward, 1965).

Had I suggested that *evil* had disappeared, word or fact, all readers would demur. The question hinges on the propriety of calling any evil "sin." But if you think sin is hard to define, try defining evil!

Perhaps it is the various implications or *corollaries* of the sin doctrine which are objected to by, for example, the behaviorists. For sin traditionally implies guilt, answerability, and, by derivation, responsibility. For many it implies confession, attrition, reparation, repentance, forgiveness, atonement. I am aware of objections that can be offered to each one of these, but I also know of social values served by retaining them. I shall discuss these later on. But this book is not to be a theological treatise, and I shall proceed on the assumption that the word "sin" *does* imply these corollaries and that I at least find the corollaries acceptable in principle.

I am not deterred by the age-old paradoxes of freedom and predestination or divine will versus what is being called "behaviorism." But I shall not fill these pages with pietistic and anti-pietistic harangue.

How Do You Know?

In some form, all of us repeat the experience of Adam and Eve in the Garden of Eden, seeking to eat of the Tree of the Knowledge of Good and Evil in order to find out for ourselves whether what has been "told" us is the real "right" and "wrong" of things.

For we are not all told the same things; versions differ; actions differ. All rights and wrongs do not seem to be quite the same. For most of us, they were identified for us in word and deed very early. For me, wrong is basically what my mother and father taught me that one should not do, or at least what *I* should not do.

Later, the general soundness and authority of my parents' convictions were increasingly confirmed in my experience by social attitudes generally and I gradually took over in my conscience the responsibility of judgment. In the light of new knowledge, I made some minor modifications and corrections in the code. My teachers and schoolmates seemed *generally*—not precisely or totally—to share my views or rather my impressions of others' views, and I borrowed a few of theirs. And so it has continued through life. As I have grown older, I have increasingly confirmed or rejected parts of the code in the light of experience and reason.

This understanding of good and evil, of right and wrong, became correlated in my mind with other abstract polarities such as love-hate, light-darkness, construction-destruction, social-antisocial, success-failure. The Judeo-Christian tradition had its standards of good and evil, and I learned them first. Later I learned others. In various cubbyholes of my mind are variations and elaborations, but the basic distinctions of my mother and father remain in my conscience codebook.

Let me give an example. My mother was born in slave times among people deeply opposed to slavery. Abolitionists—including her people—were bitterly hated. Thousands were fighting and dying over the question. The Civil War ended, and the "right" view (my mother's, her mother's) prevailed.

Years later when she and her husband moved from their small cottage into an old "mansion" type of dwelling in a new community, I remember my mother being horrified to discover that in this fairly spacious edifice the rooms called "servants' quarters" were cubicles adjacent to the attic, with no source of heat in the winter.

Actually those stuffy little cells must have been more unbearable in the hot Kansas summers than they were in our cold winters, but Mother railed at the architectural callousness that would ignore decent provision for the comfort of servants in winter "just because they are black." In trying to remedy matters, she discovered to her naive amazement that it was not customary to provide such creature comforts as heat and ventilation for "the hired help." For her this was SIN.

Without my clearly recognizing it, this recollection has undoubtedly determined one of my pet prejudices: architectural sins. I was more than a little intrigued by the brilliant Thomas Jefferson's forgetfulness regarding stairs in Monticello. The enslavement of orphan boys for the filthy, dangerous job of chimney sweeping in London for 200 years horrified me as much as it did Kingsley and Dickens. Parliament repeatedly objected to passing control acts on the basis that it would be too expensive to adapt the chimneys for mechanical cleaners, and far simpler and cheaper to drive the miserable waifs up the stacks by scorching and whipping them from below. That they would soon succumb to cancerous erosion of their genital organs or to tuberculous pneumonia was no comfort. The architects knew all this perfectly well when they planned those torture tubes.[6]

Similarly the architectural sins represented by the unspeakable dungeons, cages, and pigpens provided by most cities for the incarceration of persons awaiting trial have long been a horror, a disgrace, and an architectural reproach. Great hideous masses of concrete and steel continue to be erected for this insidious purpose, each more terrible and inhuman than its predecessors. Recently there have been a few exceptions among the 4,000 local jails. The architects still their consciences by saying that this is what the public wants, although the public, of course, almost never sees them and little guesses how barbaric they are.

Conscience

The function of approving or disapproving what the instincts and the occasion impel one to do has long been called the conscience. It was identified as the "superego" by Freud and the "archaic conscience" by Father Mailoux, a theologian and psychoanalyst. It operates partly from the dark past, as it were, using strictures and sanctions from the childhood period, and remaining largely unconscious and inaccessible to new information. Characteristic coping measures used by the parents are taken over automatically and imitated in such manipulations as compromise, mollification, corruption, and implacability. These become the pattern of the child in his moral program. The conscious, rational portion of the superego is in contact with the environment, and it does grow and change with the times and with experience.

In the course of psychoanalytic treatment, a patient's recollection and reinterpretation of the origin of the childish characteristics of the superego enable them to be revised, perhaps superseded. More rational and logical strictures better adapted to the social mores but still consistent with the moral principles characterizing

[6] George L. Phillips, *England's Climbing Boys: A History of the Long Struggle to Abolish Child Labor in Chimney Sweeping* (Cambridge, Mass.: Harvard University Press, 1949). See also *American Chimney Sweeps* (Trenton, N.J.: Past Times Press, 1957).

the individual's ideas are formed. This portion of the psychic apparatus is called by psychoanalysts the "ego ideal."

"Sin" is not a word much employed by psychoanalysts. It is implied in the adjective "aggressive" as applied to behavior, meaning purposively hurtful to others; likewise in "self-destructive," i.e., purposely hurtful to oneself. Both types of behavior are at least tacitly disapproved. The analyst need not say "That is (was) a sin; don't do it." He asks merely, "Wasn't that rather aggressive?" or "Isn't that self-destructive?" It is taken for granted that either quality disqualifies an act, and marks it for elimination in the best interests of health.

Psychoanalysts do not use the word "sin" because of its strong reproachful quality, its vague or nonspecific quality, and its corollaries and implications of guilt, reparation, and atonement. It is not for the analyst to decide what is sinful for his patient or what he should do about it. The psychoanalyst believes that the qualities of aggression and self-destruction are evil, and this he can point out without charging the patient with moral turpitude, or committing him to a specific obligation, or himself (the analyst) to an esoteric or specific code.

Why are aggression and self-destruction *prima facie* evils for the psychoanalyst to single out? Because both are opposed to the life principle, to the healing of the patient's disorganization and distress. If we were to equate sin with self-destructiveness and overt aggression, probably many psychoanalysts would concur. They would say that there is definite, objectively and empirically "bad" behavior (as a rule), whereas sin is indefinite, a value judgment based on a code. In the pages to follow we will pursue this distinction further.

But first I must return to the promise to review the events in the recent rapid decline and disappearance of the word "sin," not because any particular word is so important in itself, but because its obsolescence may be a clue to fundamental changes in the moral philosophy of our civilization.

The Disappearance of Sin

Of course the word "sin" has not *totally* disappeared from our vocabulary. Some of us use it quite regularly every Sunday; some of us use it intensely once a year during Lent or Yom Kippur. In everyday speech many use the word quite frequently, often half-jokingly. If someone says he is sinning, we smile; he seeks the reaction in us, with forgiveness implied. If we speak of our own sins, we are usually being humorously self-indulgent or pretentiously pious; few of us are very shamefaced in any such confession.

And these tendentious uses of the word "sin" are usually only gestures in the direction of general culpability and imperfection. Time was when it was very serious to contemplate that one had an unresolved sin in his heart, or an unconfessed sin on his record. "Sin, although we moderns may not think so, seemed to the ancient Jews a fearful imprudence. The hand of the Lord would descend on it heavily, and very soon."[7]

It is surely nothing new that men want to get away from acknowledging their sins or even thinking about them. Is this not the religious history of mankind? Perhaps we are only more glib nowadays and equipped with more euphemisms. We can speak of error and transgression and infraction and mistakes without the naive exposure that goes with serious use of that old-fashioned pietistic word "sin." But although it has disappeared from serious use in our workaday vocabularies, perhaps it has not gone from the back of our minds. We shall see.

When I was a boy, sin was still a serious matter and the word was not a jocular term. But I saw this change; I saw it go. I am afraid I even joined in hailing its going. And I would like now to recapture briefly the circumstances of its departure as I recall them.

Long before I was born, of course, the *major* responsibility for identifying and dealing with adult misbehavior had been taken over by the State. Much adult sin, in other words, had become crime; it was chiefly youth who sinned. After the reign of Henry VIII in England many sinful acts were formally declared to be not only immoral but illegal. Murder, mayhem, robbery, treason, and scores of other specific transgressions became defined crimes with prescribed punishments. Remaining to the domain of the moralists (churches) were the seven cardinal sins of anger, greed, pride, sloth, envy, lust, and gluttony. Even some of these, in special forms, were preempted by the law.

---

[7] George Santayana, *Winds of Doctrine* (New York: Scribner's, 1926).

Perhaps the transfer of authority for major social offenses from the home and church to the Crown or State was less a matter of seizure than a matter of forcible gift. In colonial days the parish authorities were prevailed upon to enact into law many details of the moral code in order to make sure that there would be a democratic enforcement of virtue in the community. Fossils from this era are discoverable here and there in state legal codes, including one, I believe, in Connecticut, which sets a penalty for the offenses of hanging out laundry on Sunday or for using profanity in the presence of the mayor.

It became very popular—this setting up of rules and regulations about behavior by legislative enactment. In this country, ever since the earliest legislative assemblies, our representatives have met regularly in the various state capitals to add furiously and voluminously to the already overloaded, complicated accumulation of sanctions and penalties borrowed largely from England. Now and then there are moves to revise the codes, and a few states have adopted revisions (including Kansas, I am proud to say). But most of the states still retain mounting heaps of poorly organized, ambiguous, and contradictory enactments.

Converting Sin to Crime

Making what were once dealt with as sins into crimes rendered the designation of sin increasingly pointless from a practical standpoint. Neither church ruling nor priestly admonishment was any longer required either for sanction or for penalty. Sin as sin became a strictly personal matter, an offense contrary to conscience or moral standard, an intimate, wrongful choice of action—predominantly secret, although often visible. Dealing with it was a task left to the pulpit, the confessional, and the individual conscience.

The early Christian church cells were comprised of small groups of people who met regularly—often secretly. The order of worship was, first of all, self-disclosure and confession of sin, called exomologesis. This was followed by appropriate announcement of penance, pleas for forgiveness, and plans for making restitution. A final period of friendly fellowship (koinonia) closed the meeting. This general formula continued until the Council of Nicea, A.D. 325, when Constantine took over the church for all Roman citizens.

To make it acceptable, however, he replaced the requirement of open personal disclosure with private confession to a priest. Private confession to a priest at least once a year was made obligatory in the thirteenth century. Luther dispensed with closed confession for Protestants; the Catholics continued it, but are now discussing open or public confession, while some Protestants are considering the reintroduction of "closed" confession!

Dr. Redmond A. Burke of the University of Wisconsin at Oshkosh has made a scholarly study of the origin of private confession, which he believes was a particular contribution of the Celts. Ireland was the one country known to antiquity that the Romans did not conquer and it therefore never formed part of the Roman Empire, and was not directly touched by Roman influence.

A number of peculiarities separated the Celtic church from the Roman Church until after the seventh century when, at the Council of Whitby in A.D. 664, the Irish were forced to forsake their unique practices for Roman regulations. Yet the Irish, with their unusual zeal for self-sacrifice, were responsible for the introduction of secret confession and penance in place of customary public confession as practiced at large in the Roman Church. It is generally agreed that it first began when Irish monks started to confess their sins privately to another monk.

Once private confession began to replace public confession, the compilation of a manual for confessors became a necessity. These *Manuals for Confessors*, or "Penitential Books," which first appeared in Ireland in the sixth century, were useful guides for the clergy in an age without elaborate treatises or moral theology. Each work sets down all sins in detail, together with fixing a scale of penances to be administered according to the seriousness of each transgression. These manuals were subsequently brought by Irish missionaries to the Continent, where their use became widespread once Europeans adopted such a form of private penance. Roman Catholicism thus became heir of a typical devotion of ancient Ireland in secret confession to which counseling was added.

These manuals have little literary merit, but they did have social implications which helped to popularize them in Ireland and Western Europe. They were in vogue from the seventh century, but were first received unfavorably on the Continent at the church councils of Châlons in 813 and Paris in 819. But their popularity so increased that they were finally adopted. (Today there is a perceptible trend away from private confession in the face of strong opposing statements coming out of the Vatican.)

One hundred years ago there was still plenty of sin and sinning going on. While the law courts were busy and the prisons filled with perpetrators of crime, the clergy, too, were busy in the confessional and in informal sessions with the problems of sin and sinners.

The pulpit was powerful, and public moral condemnation was effective. Elijah Lovejoy, the great abolitionist editor, was not mobbed and robbed and murdered because of the facts he published; it was, rather, his moral denunciations that the slavery people feared and hated. They vigorously and violently disputed his charge that slavery, which was certainly not a crime, was nevertheless a great and heinous sin. This made some of them great sinners which their angry protests and violent demonstrations did little to disprove.

And, of course, there were other sins—thousands of them. The word was in common parlance. It was no joke, or witticism, or euphemism to call someone's act a sin. Sin was taken seriously. One need only read over again, as I did recently, the text of Goethe's *Faust* to realize how profoundly moved and controlled people were by the notion that certain things were SINFUL and that they entailed dreadful and inescapable punishment. Nathaniel Hawthorne's *The Scarlet Letter* deals with similar assumptions. That kind of attitude toward that kind of sin has indeed undergone revolution.

That certain acts are considered by adult society to be improper, indecorous, disapproved, and unacceptable has to be learned by every child for himself. He isn't born with any convictions about morality. These "certain things" vary, of course, in different cultures and ages and with different parents. Most primitive peoples teach their children with patience and kindness a set of taboos and sanctions using myths, rituals, and other methods. So-called civilized peoples are often severe in their discipline, attaching a pain penalty to infractions.

The Role of Punishment

These artificial consequences of sin vary greatly. The American Indians were shocked by the harshness of our forefathers in teaching morality to their offspring, and some tribes referred to settlers as "the people who whip children." The child-whipping we did—and do—was performed both by rough and uncultured parents and by the more educated and sophisticated. "Spare the rod and spoil the child" was considered a wise warning, still conscientiously heeded, we are told, in the private schools of England and certainly in the elementary schools in some of our states.

The pedagogical reasoning is that since it is human nature to seek pleasure and to avoid pain, and since certain antilearning (and hence sinful) activities such as idleness or mischief yield pleasure, they must be constantly counteracted by the addition of a painful component. "Who loves his son will whip him often" (Eccles. 30:1).

This harshness toward childish disobedience—"sins" in the eyes of the parents—came with the first settlers. It still persists in America (and in England, Germany, and other "civilized" countries). Thousands of little children are taken to hospitals daily, even in the year 1973, because they have been beaten, burned, pinched, scalded, and otherwise tortured by their parents, usually in the fair name of discipline and with the ostensible purpose of correction.[8]

"Spare the rod and spoil the child" was long considered wise counsel. And one hears today—over and over—that "permissiveness" is the explanation of our juvenile delinquency. The implied remedy is more punishment, so that a child's "sin" provokes a parental sin of far greater order.

The harshness of some contemporary juvenile-court judges in dispensing to offenders *and to their parents* reproachful "lectures," ominous threats, and long imprisonment for minor offenses is still frequent enough to grieve reflective members of society while delighting the galleries and a certain noisy minority which clamors for circuses and executions.

This points up an important factor in the disappearance of sin, namely, that the punitive rituals—public and private—became too severe. People began to disapprove of the harshness of the penalties assessed against "sins" by parents, priests, and courts. The stocks, the tongue-slitting, the cheek-branding, were too cruel. Imprisonment was substituted in the case of "criminals." The punishment

[8] Parents Anonymous is a recently organized movement to bring together parents who find themselves afflicted with a high degree of irritability and a compulsion to punish overseverely one or several of their children.

repeatedly assessed against the Pueblo Indians for not yielding—
that of being thrown from a cliff, or having a leg cut off—would be
unthinkable today. Children were sent to the gallows for peccadil-
loes; crimes in England punished by deportation to Australia were
often minor offenses indeed, as we would judge today. Life was
sterner in the olden days, and penalties for displeasing power—
parental, civil, economic, or Divine—were stark. And this association of sin and penalty was ingrained. The vanishing of sin has
really been a disappearance of harsh reprisal, a softening not of
moral fiber but of human compassion.

Thus sin, or designating something sinful, began to disappear because it was too expensive in terms of the current standards of
comfort. Instead of reducing the penalty, people merely negated
the sin. Sabbath violation is a clear example.

When my wife and I were consultants some years ago to the
editor of the widely circulated home magazine, *The Household*,
a prize was offered for the best essay letter written by a reader—
parents presumably—on "How I Cured My Child" of some form of
misbehavior such as running away, playing truant, telling lies, stealing, and even bed-wetting. The contest attracted considerable
attention and effort. Some parents had found excellent methods of
corrective teaching and wrote about them intelligently and con-
structively. We published those letters.

But what we didn't expect—and didn't publish—was an astonish-
ingly large number of letters written to us (*contesting to win a prize*,
remember) boasting of the success of cruel methods which had been
"successfully" used! Shocking frights had been arranged for the
child, local police were persuaded to participate in false arrests,
painful exposures and alarming threats were used, in addition to
physical cruelties of various sorts.

The parents who proudly reported these successful maneuvers
considered them "good" ways to solve the problem. They were just
as proud of their "thing" in child rearing as wise, kindly Doctor
Spock's followers are of his. They seemed earnestly to believe that
theirs were the really more effective ways to control evil and block
the development of wrong behavior patterns. They are echoed by
many voices even today who would "beat some sense into the kids,
burn some sense into them, knock out the evil from their constitu-
tions" and similar treatment methods.

This justified usefulness of inflicted pain—what Skinner calls aversive conditioning—has been more than faintly visible in the history of even so ostensibly merciful a discipline as that of medical practice. Analgesia and anesthesia, it must be remembered, are fairly recent discoveries and also fairly recent considerations in the healing art!

Medicine, including psychiatry, was pretty grim through the Middle Ages and on up almost to the twentieth century. Punitive "treatment" of many kinds was used not only without embarrassment but actually with pride, and with claims of great successes. Violent purges, nauseous medication, depleting venesection, emetics, blistering, and switching were among these. I myself have seen (long ago) face-slapping and emetics employed by serious, even professional adults in order to "put a stop to" hysterical behavior, and I have seen children whose convulsive seizures or enuresis had been conscientiously "treated" by the administration of "whippings" after each occurrence.

I read recently—in the year of our Lord, 1970—that one of our colleagues had met with proud success in the treatment of a very disturbed child by the use of "an electric cattle prod"! For centuries the mentally ill were particularly victimized with painful "therapeutic" disciplines. It was thought that their behavior contained a large element of perverse willfulness which was best counteracted by such measures.

This punitive element in medical treatment reflected a philosophy of morals which medicine would have denied. Doctors long ago gave up the notion that illness reflected sin, but their practices often demonstrated the unconscious persistence of the idea. Implicit in news stories in the papers, in articles in the serious weeklies and monthlies, in daily conversations, in sermons and other public addresses was the principle that sin merited punishment, and unless and until the penalty was paid, the sin would continue. For school children the "sins" were telling lies, swearing, stealing ("taking things"), cheating in games or in classroom tests, "copying" the work of other students, immodesty, disobedience, and rudeness in any form to teachers or parents. All "crimes" were sinful, of course, but more relevant to us were "secret sins" such as stealing, cheating, lying, and various sexual activities.

The Great Sin of Youth

Almost no other activity was so regularly condemned and pun-ished as erotic self-stimulation, autoerotism. For centuries, school children, prisoners, sailors, and slaves were savagely punished when detected in or even suspected of "the solitary vice" of "self-abuse."

"Of all the vices and of all the misdeeds which may properly be called crimes against nature which devour humanity, menace its physical vitality and tend to destroy its intellectual and moral faculties, one of the greatest and most widespread—no one will deny it—is masturbation."[9] This moral taboo is thousands of years old and exists in many (but not all) primitive cultures.

In addition to long-established attempts at deterrence by punish-ment there developed in Europe about 250 years ago a strong intimidation curb from the medical profession. A famous book, *Onania, or The Heinous Sin of Self-Pollution* (1716), probably written by a quack, went through 80 editions. Forty years later a renowned and universally respected Swiss physician, Tissot, took up the same theme in a book similarly named: *Onania, or a Treatise upon the Disorders Produced by Masturbation* (Lausanne, 1758). It had a profound effect on medical thought, and medical articles about masturbation became numerous, so that "by the end of the eighteenth century the masturbatory hypothesis for much disease was widely accepted throughout Europe and America."[10]

Some competent writers seem to believe masturbation to have been an important "taboo" only in "Christian" civilization and only in the past 300 years. But the condemnation of masturbation is said to occur in the *Egyptian Book of the Dead* (1550–950 B.C.).

---

[9] Pouillet, 1876, cited by Hare, *v. infra.*

[10] Like so many later physicians. Tissot was incapable of dealing dispassionately with his subject. His book abounds in moral censure; the "flagrant crime" of mastur-bation reduces its victim to a state "which more justly entitles him to the contempt than pity of his fellow creatures" and his punishment by disease in this world is only a prelude to his punishment by eternal fire in the next (E. H. Hare, "Masturba-tory Insanity: The History of an Idea," *Journal of Mental Science,* 108:2 [January, 1962]).

Louis Epstein in his book *Sex Laws and Customs in Judaism* described the Jewish attitude on masturbation as follows: "The Zohar . . . accounts it the severest sin of all. . . . The ethical literature of post-Talmudic days, down to the latest centuries, endlessly harps on the severity of this sin, exhorts its avoidance, points out its danger to health, threatens dire punishment in the day of reckoning, and pleads for penitence and expiation." Masturbation is a major sin under Orthodox Jewish codes and at times in Jewish history has been a *capital offense punishable by death.*[11]

The Christian church has generally taught the sinfulness of masturbation, although the Bible says virtually nothing about it. When its harmfulness was also asserted by the medical profession, who could doubt its great evilness? A skeptic unmoved by these two sources of authority, says Hare, might yet tremble to read the strictures of Voltaire and Rousseau on the subject.

One author, Flemming (1838), so feared that his mild opinions on the subject might expose him to attack that he found it advisable to write, "I hope I shall not be accused of having written an apology for self-abuse." He doubted if masturbation was often the only or principal cause of mental disorder, but he went on to describe it as causing "a downcast or vacant appearance, pallor, easy blushing and so on, to be followed later by a tendency to solitariness, marked vacuity, loss of attention, and a frequent absorption in thought."

Another author, Lallemand (1842), cited by Hare, emphasized the cold and callous qualities of the masturbator: "He has no other interests; he loves no one; he is attached to no one; he shows no emotion before the grandeur of nature or the beauties of art; still less is he capable of any generous impulse or act of loyalty; he is dead to the call of his family, his country, or of humanity."

When a patient of Allnatt's (1843) "entered the room with a timid and suspicious air and appeared to quail like an irresolute maniac when the eye was fixed steadily upon him," that surgeon was left in no doubt of the cause of his patient's complaint (and the patient, "on being directly charged with masturbating," immediately admitted it).[12]

[11] David Cole Gordon, *Self-Love* (New York: Verity House, 1968), p. 19. Italics mine. However, this is denied by Rabbi Louis Finkelstein.

[12] Hare, op. cit.

Pouillet (1876) contributed an essay on "onanism in females." He held that although no single sign was pathognomic of masturbation, yet there were a number of signs which, taken together, "create a strong, even an almost certain, presumption of this vice, in spite of denials." These signs included an unsteady and peevish disposition tending toward anger, an exaggerated timidity in the presence of parents and a surly attitude toward strangers, profound idleness, a tendency to lying, and "finally, a certain aspect, à je ne sais quoi, easier to recognize than to express in words" (Hare). I cite the author's words in order to convey the attitude of hypocritical horror with which this normal and physiological process was described.

In time the alleged physical effects of masturbation began to narrow down to indigestion, acne, and anemia. But worse was to follow. Beginning with no less authorities than our own Benjamin Rush (1812) and Esquirol of France (1816), mental disease began to be ascribed to it—mania, stupidity, marasmus, and death; dementia, melancholy and suicide. Even the early psychoanalysts condemned it, and Freud admonished his own son against it.

> Despite the fact that in his writings he was tolerant of masturbation, listing its helpful as well as harmful aspects, when one of his adolescent sons came · to him with worries about masturbation, Freud responded by warning the boy very much against it [according to one of them]. An estrangement between father and son ensued. While Freud did not consider masturbation a vice [sin], it was nonetheless a "symptom."[13]

The brave, far-visioned Havelock Ellis (1901), however, said that Tissot's book had "raised masturbation to the position of a colossal bogey," and accused Tissot of combining his reputation as a physician with religious fanaticism.[14] But Ellis was one of few. Psychoanalysis has done rather little with theories about masturbation except to identify it as a phase in the normal evolution of sexual expression, usually replaced shortly by interpersonal relationships. It is a basis for fantasy formation including fantasies of indulgence and fantasies of punishment by loss of the genital organs. These contribute to the strength of the taboo against it.

[13] Paul Roazen, *Brother Animal* (New York: Knopf, 1969), p. 41.
[14] *Ibid.*

Freud viewed it, according to his physician-biographer Max Schur, as "the primary addiction." Freud fought a lifelong battle against a compulsive addiction to smoking. He struggled hard to relinquish it, knowing well that it was irritating and eroding the near-cancerous lesions in his mouth for which he submitted to so many painful operations in his last 14 years. He often referred to it unblushingly as "my sin" in speech and in writing. *He related it definitely to the "great sin," the "original sin,"* masturbation (italics mine).

This he considered "the one great habit that is a 'primary addiction.' . . . The other addictions, for alcohol, morphine, tobacco, etc., enter into life only as a substitute for and a withdrawal [symptom] from it."[15]

In America the masturbation taboo has always been, until recently, very explicit. Masturbation was never a "crime" but it was a moral offense of such seriousness that many "authorities" joined hands in insuring its prohibition. To help stem the temptation of evildoing, threats or inflictions of dire punishment were commonly made to children by all and sundry. Parents watched for the slightest evidences of the "sin." School teachers were on the alert for it. The medical profession ascribed to it various diseases, general physical and mental deterioration, and especially "insanity."

The doctors really believed this theory, and of the official adjudications in cases of mental illness, many were officially based on "masturbation." I have examined many old state hospital records in which the etiology of case after case is so ascribed. (Sometimes fright, loss of money, or death of mother were cited.)

The overt threat of this possibility was contained in books and articles prescribed for youthful instruction, e.g., *What Every Boy Should Know.* In the high schools of this country until well after the turn of the century it was widely customary to have "sex talks," made by local doctors once each year, given to the boys and girls separately. The themes were usually the dangers of pregnancy, venereal disease, and masturbation.

I have always been rather proud of the fact that my own father, when doing his turn at this civic chore about 1906, told the boys that while not to be recommended (this would have been scandal-

[15] Max Schur, *Freud: Living and Dying* (New York: International Universities Press, 1972), p. 61.

ous!) masturbation was not as harmful as some books and speakers described and was nothing to worry about. For this audacious affront to the popular and professional code he was much censured.

What was told to the girls by their lecturers I never knew, but I am fairly sure they were *not* told that current research into the sexual response of women suggests that "far more women can (and do?) reach orgasm through masturbation than by intercourse."[16]

Why should this particular physiological experience have been built up into such a great sin? The adolescent's discovery of a new form of intense pleasure in bodily sensation, the discovery of the possibility of bringing about this pleasure at will—silently, secretly, and repeatedly—opens to the child a new world of adventure, ecstasy, temptation, remorse, and fear. Are adults envious of this? How the child senses the adult taboo on this exciting phenomenon has been much disputed, but that he perceives it without words is indubitable. To an extent difficult for the present-day reader to grasp, this was *the major sin* for middle- and upper-class adolescents a century and less ago.

Among high school and college students until fairly recently masturbation was a *bête noir*—indulged in secretly, of course, by all, bragged about by a few, but deplored and denied by most. It was an ever-present, easily reached source of guilt feelings, often exploited by religious leaders. Consider the emotional conflict in a boy (or girl), instructed in the faith, that Jesus, the good man, the Son of God, died "for your sins," whose chief secret preoccupation was his propensity for repeating this dreadful act. I have seen a large room full of university men bowed on their knees in prayer for forgiveness and for strength to resist the temptation of (this) sin.

Even the involuntary nocturnal emissions of adolescence were decried as larval forms of masturbation, and "suggestions for the control of pollutions" (emissions) were offered gratuitously. Any sexual feelings were considered evil, or at least dangerous. "Round dancing" was considered by millions of people in this country and in England and Canada to be immoral and taboo because it "might excite evil passions."

[16] Seymour Fisher, M.D., *The Female Orgasm*, quoted by Norman Lobsenze in *McCall's*, October, 1972, p. 156.

The amazing circumstance is that sometime soon after the turn of the present century, this ancient taboo, for the violation of which millions had been punished, threatened, condemned, intimidated, and made hypocritical and cynical—a taboo thousands of years old —vanished almost overnight! Masturbation, the solitary vice, the SIN of youth, suddenly seemed not to be so sinful, perhaps not sinful at all; not so dangerous—in fact, not dangerous at all; less a vice than a form of pleasurable experience, and a normal and healthy one!

This sudden metamorphosis in an almost universal social attitude is more significant of the changed temper, philosophy, and morality of the twentieth century than any other phenomenon that comes to mind. It is not difficult to see why ALL sin other than "crime" seemed to many to have disappeared along with this one.

This, in a way, now seems regrettable. For masturbation lost its quality of sinfulness through a new understanding, but there was no new understanding of ruthlessness or wastefulness or cruelty. A small amount of the disapproval of masturbation may have been displaced by previously undervalued "sins" such as those mentioned but, in general, it seems as if the great phenomenon of a deadly sin suddenly disappearing—and disappearing "without anyone noticing it"—affected our attitude toward other disapproved behavior.

It is as if we expected those *other* sins, presumably *all* other sins, to vanish or diminish in seriousness in the same mysterious way. It is common knowledge that many younger people do and say things which their elders consider vulgar, improper, or even definitely wrong—let me say "sinful." These are violations of taboos which were very serious for the parents and grandparents. We cannot say that youth *always* did that, for it is not so. There is no new understanding of assaults and rapes and even lesser violence which makes it more acceptable and less sinful. Yet it *is* more acceptable to many people.

"Violence," said Alexander Solzhenitsyn in his speech accepting the Nobel Prize, is "less and less embarrassed by the limits imposed by centuries of lawfulness, is brazenly and victoriously striding across the whole world." In recent years, he notes, there have been new breakdowns in our protection. There once was a time when violence was seen as a means of last resort. Now we begin with it. It is a method of communication.[17]

Whence this change? Is evildoing really no longer taboo, simply because the exaggerated punishments of another adolescent experience were found (and decided) to be inappropriate? Can all sin have been repudiated as such because one behavior once considered evil is now no longer condemned? It is easier to suppose this in regard to sexual "sin" (other than masturbation) than in regard to such "sins," for example, as stealing and lying, although there is a psychological connection between all of these which has long been recognized.

[17] "The Talk of the Town," *The New Yorker*, October 14, 1972.

4

A New Social Morality

I t was about the turn of the century that a new social philosophy
and a new code of morality, as it seemed, began to manifest
itself all over the earth. It was not so much an increase in humane
concern as an attempted purging of all sentiment in connection with
the "control" of behavior, i.e., not merely crime and other sins but
the steps incident to the training of children in the way they should
go. Not only sympathy and affection but also hate and shame and
fear of punishment were to be suppressed in favor of the neutral,
passionless, objective, rational, and normal (i.e., moral). But gradually all social processes and institutions felt the effects.

The new attitude toward behavior developed from several
empirical scientific discoveries: (1) hypnosis (Mesmer in 1775,
Braid in 1841, Liebault and Bernheim in 1880, Charcot in 1886);
(2) psychoanalysis (Freud, 1910 on); (3) conditioned reflex
phenomena (Pavlov, 1900 on, Watson in 1915); (4) new drugs
found to have specific alterative effects on mood and behavior; and
(5) the scientific methodology of research: observation, collation,
hypothesis construction, and comparison of the results with the
hypothesis.

Hypnosis

Of these great factors in the changeover, hypnosis was the earliest
but, because of or in spite of its revolutionary implications, it never
became entirely respectable. For a time—indeed, for several separate times—it was very popular. That one could be induced by
suggestion to do or think what he did not realize he was doing or
thinking, or even remember that he had done so, was a phenomenon

which squarely challenged the prevalent ideas of responsibility. This made it a very significant discovery. It is historically most important as having directly led to the discovery of psychoanalysis.

Psychoanalysis

Certainly the greatest impetus toward the new scientific attitude was Freud's discovery (about 1900) of the psychoanalytic method —the technique of systematic exploration of *unconscious* psychological processes. From what he and others observed in their patients, a new formulation of human motivation gradually developed which emphasized love attachments and hate attachments— conscious *and* unconscious—as basic personality structures. Conflicts between these, with partially buried, partially exposed "memories," were labeled neuroses and regarded as illness.

Theology had long stressed something very similar; consequently it is not surprising that there were, from the very beginning of the psychoanalytic "movement," attempted correlations and intrinsic antagonisms between "soul" doctors and "mind" doctors. The names Carl Jung, Alfred Adler, James J. Putnam, and Oskar Pfister stand out from the days of Freud; in later years many workers continued to debate (and attempted to integrate) these two viewpoints.

For the most part, the psychoanalytic model was applied not as a research tool, in which use it is preeminent, but as a treatment method, in which it is equivocal, but marketable. Freud had shown that the process of examining the psychic apparatus and the multiple components of the motivation of behavior had a certain enlightening or freeing effect.

It is a question whether one should call psychoanalytic enlightenment a "cure," but understanding oneself better often leads to controlling oneself better, and so, in spite of Freud's cautioning, clinical exploration of the unconscious determinants of behavior patterns came to be regarded as a very special kind of medical treatment. To distort somewhat a popular aphorism, it began to be assumed that to understand everything is to be cured of everything.

A part of the power of the psychoanalytic movement derived from its assumption of a noncensorious "scientific" attitude toward all sexual phenomena. Prior to Freud and Havelock Ellis, sexual behavior was looked at romantically, legally, biologically, and morally, but never very objectively. Much "sin" was assumed to be sexual in nature[1]—if not masturbation then the more "adult" forms of deviance: adultery, homosexual activities, and variations in method of sexual contact. Many people still regard these things as reprehensible if not criminal, despite very marked changes in popular standards which have occurred.[2]

Rise of "Talking Cures"

The high priests of the new attitude toward behavior were at first the psychoanalysts because of the Freudian theory of psychosexual evolution. The procedure of "being analyzed" caught the imagination of the public in somewhat the same way as did the heart transplant operations forty years later, and the outcome was looked upon as a kind of miracle.

Psychoanalytic treatment, however, is an extremely expensive procedure, requiring the attention of a trained listener for an hour daily over a period of many months or even years; obviously this was not a solution for the control or modification of the behavior of millions. But the principle had been established that some individuals who suffer from doubt, depression, phobia, anxiety, and hysterical pain can be relieved by being listened to—with interpretations, counsel, and reassurance. Listening began to be a treatment method of great importance, especially in the form of "psychotherapy."

Psychotherapies of various kinds requiring far less time commitment than psychoanalysis began to multiply. The established respectability of seeing and listening to patients a number of successive times without inflicting pain or prescribing pills was a great step forward in the practice of medicine. Psychiatrists and others who applied themselves to these "talking cures" were no longer despised and ostracized but were increasingly accepted and in some instances magnified and overestimated.

[1] See Faust, The Scarlet Letter, etc. See also Chapter 6.

[2] See, for example, Dana Farnsworth, "Sexual Morality and the Dilemma of the Colleges," Amer. J. Orthopsychiatry, 35:676 (1965), and The Wolfenden Report (New York: Stein and Day, 1963).

The word "psychotherapy" was almost totally unknown to our grandparents; to our parents, it was known but held in bad repute. If my father had announced to his colleagues (say, in 1900) that he was treating a patient with "psychotherapy," they would have understood him to be confessing a pious fraud. He would have been patently denying that there was anything medically (organically) wrong with the complainer, that the alleged affliction was imaginary, absurd, "all in his head" and required solely "suggestion" for its alleviation. Such "psychotherapy" might be supplemented by various forms of hocus-pocus—placebos, plasters, faradic stimulation, massage—plus evidence of interest and encouragement from the doctor.

The era of therapeutic nihilism (prior to 1910) was a period of reaction to the overdrugging (polypharmacia) and overoperating (polysurgery) which had developed in medical practice. One must concede that in both there was much fraudulence. Psychotherapy similarly was regarded by some as a form of external deception used to counteract the patient's own self-deception or his attempted deception of the outside world (including the doctor). While some defended this counterdeception as at least harmless, few endorsed it publicly.

This appraisal had been radically changed in principle by Freud's discoveries. First the possibility and then the necessity of scientific criteria for the conduct and evaluation of psychotherapy became recognized. This is not to say that all psychotherapy became immediately purged of its spurious elements; however, it became respectable and widely employed, not only by psychiatrists but also by neurologists, psychologists, internists, and general practitioners —and more recently by clergymen and other laymen. The psychological and evolutionary aspects of sexuality were progressively clarified and the taboos of concealment and shame increasingly removed, not only from masturbatory but from other kinds of sexual acts. Many sexual feelings and acts formerly regarded as sinful were exonerated as normal and proper.

Conditioned Reflex Phenomena

Experimental studies of shaping or "conditioning" the reflex response to stimuli formed the basis of theories by the Russian genius Pavlov, which soon permeated the thinking of psychologists worldwide. A charismatic professor at the University of Chicago and later at Johns Hopkins University—John B. Watson—made "behaviorism" and "conditioned reflex" household words in America. From this start, the psychology of the control and modification of behavior became a topic of general interest and special study everywhere. The recognition that there could be internal determinants of an act—other than instinct, fear, wish, and free will—affected profoundly the notions of "motivation," "intention," "premeditation," and other legal postulates.

Proposals for new methods of child rearing developed from this new conception of "why we act like human beings." The aseptic, hands-off emphasis prevailed for a time and then, in a reaction against it, came various forms of what is pejoratively labeled "permissiveness." This had reference to the degree of external control imposed by persons in power by means of threats and injuries.

New Drugs Found to Have Specific Alterative Effects on Mood and Behavior

Alcohol has been a "permissive" drug for centuries, a relaxant, stimulant, and mild analgesic. Other chemical alteratives of behavior began to be noted. Paraldehyde (1882), arsphenamine (1907), and luminal (1912) were among the first drugs used in psychiatry to produce specific behavior-pattern changes. Then came the new sleep-inducing drugs, and later the whole modern arsenal of mood-altering and tension-altering chemicals. This was followed after a few years by the multiplication and extension of nonmedical drug use, and the addiction of some individuals to the injection or ingestion of some of these chemicals.

Drugs have thus greatly changed the thinking and practice of psychiatrists. But all medical thinking was also changing about that time under the influence of newly discovered therapeutic drugs. The pessimism which had characterized the therapy of the last decades of the nineteenth century began (about 1910) to be replaced with increasing optimism about the possibilities of affecting some diseases. Even mental illnesses were suddenly seen as subject to modification if not complete cure, first by means of "moral treatment," then by the talking cure deriving from Sigmund Freud, and finally by new drugs.

The escape from pain, anxiety, boredom, remorse, and other unpleasant states of being by means of these drugs has become such a permanent feature worldwide that it needs no particular description here, except to point out that it has strongly affected morality, the moral code. I shall have more to say about it later.

Scientific Methodology and Research

The development of psychology as a science, the experimental models of Wilhelm Wundt and others, the Gestalt and field theory of Kurt Lewin and others, the discoveries of the hypnotists and the psychoanalysts, all led to new theories of behavior, theories of motivation, and theories of learning. These departed widely from the simple, good-and-bad, pleasure-pain, carrot-stick stimulus-response formulations of an earlier day. The behavior of all living things began to be regarded as being capable of objective scientific study from many angles other then merely its desirability or undesirability.

The increasing interest in scientifically understanding and modifying behavior tended to diminish the use of traditional methods and to alter the punitive attitude toward "badness." More and more openly it began to be proposed that much "juvenile delinquency," behavior which in adults would have been definitely criminal, was probably better viewed as *symptomatic*, i.e., indicative of underlying pathology for which the offender was not (entirely) to blame or to be blamed.

Child welfare and child health organizations, child guidance clinics and youth groups were increasingly guided by advice based on these assumptions. And in rough, tough old Chicago a special juvenile court was established for the particular handling of young transgressors, the first one anywhere in the world.[3] Soon afterward, in the same city, an Institute for Research in the field of juvenile delinquency was established by the municipality.

Healy's work, and later that of Herman Adler, Vernon Briggs,

[3] This was on July 1, 1899, and came about as a result of the joint efforts of the Chicago Women's Club and the Catholic Visitation and Aid Society.

Lawson Lowrey, David Levy, W. A. White, and Eleanor and Sheldon Glueck stimulated the profession to be more optimistic about the possibilities of changing the behavior patterns of offenders; just as Ernest Southard, Adolf Meyer, Thomas Salmon, Smith Ely Jelliffe, and W. A. White had begun to rekindle hope in the effectiveness of treatment for the mentally ill.

The Effects of the New Moral Philosophy

As a result of all these scientific discoveries, not only did medical practice change, but many social customs and standards changed. New kinds of child rearing and new kinds of teaching developed in which the notion of sin as it had been taught began to undergo erosion. "There are no 'bad' children; only bad parents," we were told. A greatly increased emphasis was put on love and tenderness toward the child. Words like "bad," "wicked," and "immoral," while still employed, began to sound old-fashioned. "Sin" began to be questioned. Magazine articles appeared bearing such titles as "Sin or Symptom?"—the implication of which was that the new view of behavior had translated what were once indications for punishment into indications for maneuvers aimed at healing. The idea that particular behavior was the result of numerous determining events and forces led to increasing doubt about its easy control or modification.

This change was of great practical importance to mothers, teachers, policemen, and prison wardens. Mothers and fathers, for example, had the problem of rearing children and "conditioning" them (to use one of the new words) to favor the right and avoid the wrong. This is simple enough until *inexplicably* wrong behavior appears; then what to do? It wouldn't do to call it sin anymore. Parents didn't like to think of it as a symptom; symptom of what, indeed? "Some maladjustment or affliction developing in my child? Perish the thought!" A symptom, perhaps, of parental mismanagement? Perish that thought also! But the thought often failed to perish, and many parents suffered much undeserved guilt feelings and self-reproach.

The new viewpoint had great appeal for young liberals, literary people, teachers, psychologists, and other "intellectuals" who caught the vision of this new orientation before most doctors did. A few psychiatrists were intrigued with their new responsibility. The general public was intrigued but uncertain. Many stoutly resisted the spread of what they regarded as moral decay or corruption. "Right is right and wrong is wrong; badness deserves punishment, and gets it when sentimentalists do not interfere. To call misbehavior sickness or symptomatic is merely to find an excuse for avoiding punishment—another dodge for the unscrupulous rich or the object of misguided sentimentalism." But many others welcomed it as a more intelligent way to deal with difficulties.

Gradually the effects of "the new psychology," as it was called, began to be apparent and it did seem to many worthy people that morality was being invaded and eroded thereby. Much behavior that would be classed *a priori* as sinful had long since passed into the control of the law. What was considered criminal and so treated was understandably sinful. And now, increasingly, some *crime* was being viewed as *symptomatic*. Sins had become crimes and now crimes were becoming illnesses; in other words whereas the police and judges had taken over from the clergy, the doctors and psychologists were now taking over from the police and judges.

How this latter transfer came about we shall discuss at length in the next chapter. Much "sin" had become identified as "crime" long before our times; what I saw occur was the effect on the concept of sin of this realization that some *crime* was *sickness*. For, if the worst of sins can be nullified of their evil character by closer examination, what about the minor sins that were not even considered criminal? Are they not often the consequences of pathological attitudes of super-piety, prudishness, puritanical oversternness, neurotic inhibition, and "reaction formation"?

Moreover, some of the "sins" which privately gave sensitive minds the greatest concern (guilt feelings) were increasingly seen as really not sinful, nor immoral, nor wrong. The general conclusion seemed to be that if behavior is really wrong, it is a crime—unless it is a disease. Noncriminal, nonpunishable acts might be unpleasant, inelegant, or in bad taste but why the damning categorization of "sinful"?

The Twilight of Sin

Perhaps, however, some forms of behavior might still deserve the name. Hating one's brother, surely; dishonoring one's parents, envying one's neighbor, or "blaspheming the Holy Ghost" (a common delusion of psychiatric patients in earlier times, echoing charges sternly hurled by pietistic preachers).

But no, these offenses were translatable into psychological terms and "explained" by psychological theories. To call them sins had no usefulness. There remained, of course, sin in the sense of alienating oneself from God; for believers this was, is, and will continue to be THE sin. But articulate believers seemed to be fewer in number; their voices were drowned out by the cheers of the new psychologists.

Thus it was that "sin," except for the rituals of the confessional and the prayer chamber, increasingly disappeared from public view —or hearing. Believers continued their beliefs not only in a Creator but in His displeasure at their moral failures. They confessed their sins in their own company—but they did not refer to them in daily life intercourse. Sin was no longer a topic of conversation, debate, argument, accusation, and public remorse—as it long had been. It was no longer a euphemism for masturbation, adultery, drunkenness, smoking, or "gambling." It became a word of mild disapproval, less and less frequently applied—or a jocular word.

But at the same time, sin became for believers and nonbelievers alike a far more dignified concept, a truly serious, ponderable, personal matter. The latter, those of serious and intelligent makeup, are just as concerned as believers with the errors of mankind, and its present increasingly dismal situation. They may talk in terms of immorality and ethics and of antisocial behavior instead of sin, because it absolves them from acknowledging a God to be sinning against. This is a distinction without a difference in my opinion. It is as presumptuous to "know" God as to deny His existence. One believes, or believes that he believes, or he believes that he doesn't.[4]

I believe there is "sin" which is expressed in ways which cannot be subsumed under verbal artifacts such as "crime," "disease," "delinquency," "deviancy." There *is* immorality; there *is* unethical behavior; there *is* wrongdoing. And I hope to show that there is usefulness in retaining the concept, and indeed the word, SIN, which now shows some signs of returning to public acceptance. I would like to help this trend along.

---

[4] Reinhold Niebuhr, *Nature and Destiny of Man* (New York: Scribner's, 1949).

"There is a mysterious fact about the great words of our religious tradition: they cannot be replaced," Paul Tillich wrote. "All attempts to make substitutions—including those I have tried myself —have failed . . . they have led to shallow and impotent talk.

"There are no substitutes for words like 'sin' and 'grace.' But there *is* a way of rediscovering their meaning, the same way that leads us down into the depth of our human existence. In that depth these words were conceived; and there they gained power for all ages; there they must be found again by each generation, and by each of us for himself."[5]

But in the back of the room voices are heard. "Listen, if you will, to that! Comes now Karl Menninger himself, long on the firing line in defense of psychoanalysis, behavior sciences and motivation research, and pointing to symptoms labeled crimes, and attacking the inhumanity and stupidity of "treating" people with prisons and punishment. Comes now this doctor to lend aid and comfort to the enemy, the moral hard hats, the 'punishment and vengeance' people, the prudes and the religiously superstitious. Is he a turncoat? Is he conceding the opponents a point? After fifty years of persistent effort by many of us to annihilate the 'sin' concept, which was used to justify terrible punishments for derelictions, would he go over to the enemy?"

NO! The moralistic bullyboys are no friends or allies of mine. I think I have spoken out against them louder and oftener than most. I say they are wrong. But they are not concerned with sin. They are not concerned with morality, only with legality and vengeance. They advocate practices to halt crime which are often more criminal than the crime they seek to halt.[6]

I was much reassured by a recent letter from my longtime friend and colleague, Lawrence S. Kubie, a pioneer authority and leader in the psychoanalytic movement, whose advice I asked about this book. In his reply he wrote:

> The concept of Sin has fallen into disrepute precisely because it has failed to help people to change and by failing has betrayed human aspirations and culture. Few people realize that the incidence of de-

[5] Paul Tillich, "You Are Accepted," *A.D.*, 1:36 (September, 1972).

[6] See Assertions in *The Crime of Punishment* (New York: Viking, 1966). I mean exactly that, that many crimes are committed in the process of punishing those officially found guilty. The law gives no sanction for their abuse, torture, and medical neglect.

linquencies among the "faithful" is at least as high as, if not higher than, its incidence among non-believers. We need you to make it clear that although the concept of illness is often misused as an excuse and as a device for escaping responsibility, such misuse does not destroy its potential values.

The legal concept of the "irresistible impulse" is not invalid merely because it, too, can be misused. Surely no one need remind us (but perhaps we need to remind the public) that antibiotics or aspirin can also be misused. We do not for this reason attack them. We surely agree that just because the concept of illness has been misused does not mean that it has no value for a deeper understanding of Sinning. Similarly because the concept of Sin has so often been misused as an excuse for brutality and vengeance (masquerading as righteous punishment) does not mean that it has no value, if and when properly used.

I think that you would perform a great service by a critical exposition of the equal tendency to misuse both the concepts of sin and of illness in relation to errant behavior. From this basis you might then point the way towards wiser uses of both concepts.

Thus encouraged by this discerning colleague, and others mentioned in the Acknowledgments, I have pursued the possible usefulness of reviving the use of the word "sin"—not for the word's sake, but for the reintroduction of the concepts of guilt and moral responsibility. Calling something a "sin" and dealing with it as such may be a useful salvage or coping device. It does little good to repent a symptom, but it may do great harm not to repent a sin. Vice versa, it does little good to merely psychoanalyze a sin, and sometimes a great harm to ignore a symptom.

I contend that there is such a thing as moral concern and such a thing as personal responsibility. Freud's hypothesis of a destructive drive within us which we try constantly to control or conceal corresponds to ancient notions of motivation. It may not be wholly correct, but it fits what we see. Arising from it comes a universal and persistent yen for aggression and retaliation, both in the end suicidal. It must be controlled to the best of our ability. What aids may we count on to effect this control?

Is the responsibility for guaranteeing such control entirely that of the parent, the teacher, the clergyman, and the police? Should we expect no help from the psychologist and the physician? Is it not possible that some of their patients, deeply involved in self-destructive or socially destructive activities, are seeking help for minor symptoms which disguise major sins? Is it possible that some thus attempt to atone with money and suffering for the sins they are —or are not—confessing? We would condemn clergymen for offering only pastoral counsel as therapy to a man suffering from brain syphilis or "schizophrenia." Would we withhold all censure from a psychiatrist who is giving psychotherapy for "neurotic" symptoms of sleeplessness or sexual inhibition to a man involved in rascality and wickedness of notable degree?

Psychiatrists have finally demonstrated that there is an effective treatment for certain conditions which doctors formerly ignored or mistreated. But do we not repeat the error if we ignore appropriate help available for some individuals whose sins are greater than their symptoms?

5

Sin into Crime

M any former sins have become crimes. A few former crimes have become sins. Crimes are infractions of the law—federal, state, or local. The responsibility for dealing with them passed from the church to the state. The policeman replaced the priest. In this way much "sin" has seemed to disappear by having been given a new name and a new monitor.

Time was when the state was concerned chiefly with maintaining the king's peace and his property. Disturbing or threatening the former or taking or damaging the latter were punishable by the king's guards. Such offenses were the crimes, such offenders the criminals. Offenses of the peasantry against one another were disapproved, of course, and, later, punished systematically under the Codex Justiniamus and Codex Theodoramus in Rome. These punishments were codified in various ways, and the codes amended from time to time.

In early Judaism sin was synonymous with breaking the law—not state law but God's law. Specific forms of sin-crime were named in the Ten Commandments, in the Book of Leviticus, and in the Talmud. Later the Roman Catholic Canon Law took over many of the Hebrew and Roman law sanctions. But in time it, like the Ten Commandments and the Hebrew code, was abandoned as undemocratic or inappropriate for political use, and civil law assumed the responsibility for identifying and dealing with many offenses which had at one time been considered sins, with the sinner answerable to the priest, the church, and God.

After some centuries of exercise in the role of police, judge, and executioner, the church and the clergy were increasingly willing to relinquish their responsibilities for dealing with these ugly matters. Transferring them to the state diminished ecclesiastical power, but it also relieved the church of great burdens of responsibility and expense. Cotton Mather, Torquemada, and others come to mind who are better remembered for their harsh moral judgments and punishments than for their positive contributions.

Morality transgressions thus became split into the merely sinful, regarding which the clergy might still mediate, adjure, and assess penances, and the criminal, for which the soldier, policeman, judge, and jailer were made responsible. Wise lawyers and jurists have often counseled against the trend to extend the area of attempted coercion of virtue, but their counsel goes unheeded and the breadth of control extends.

"There ought to be a law," says someone, and before long, the law has been enacted and another old "sin" has become a new "crime." This is where many sins have gone.

It would take us far afield to review all of the factors that entered into this transformation. It was not done suddenly; nor is the process at an end. Each year thousands of new laws are passed, and thus thousands of new crime possibilities created. The basic prohibitions have been related to generally agreed upon taboos: killing, robbing, mugging, cheating, stealing, and the other felonies. To these were added the "misdemeanors," many of which were subsequently repealed. At the time of their official establishment as crimes, appropriate (?) penalties for violation were agreed upon—widely disparate in different states and nations, but all of them originally very severe.

Once the state had taken over this additional responsibility, it had to do the policing, the investigating, and the charging, trying, and judging of the "sinner." It could fine, it could inflict pain and humiliation, it could merely detain, or it could do all of these and more. But to do this the state had to have rules of procedure, and these it set up. It also erected a new set of penalties differing from most of those formerly used by the church.

At the expiration of the sentence pronounced on him, including the parole period, the offender ceased to be an official sinner, i.e., a "criminal" or "convict," and became again a partial citizen, an ex-convict, with numerous legal and social appurtenances and sanctions and handicaps. It has been said that "we forbid, we arrest, we coerce, we incarcerate, we counsel, we parole, we treat, not infrequently with success—but we never forgive."[1] Although we speak of changing the offender, we continue to damn him for what he had been or what he had done.

That's how it has worked out, this displacement of morality enforcement to the state with its new machinery. The machinery was a long time in developing into the present proud, mighty, and monstrous structure. It is slow, cruel, destructive, ineffective, and tremendously expensive. As a controller of crime it is a massive failure. And since it "processes" only a small percentage of all offenders (2 percent) it serves chiefly as a morality play, a symbolic device rather than a practical control of misbehavior.

Not only is its inefficacy increasingly apparent, but its gigantic costliness in money and human life is also beginning to be recognized. Vengeance and contempt for the poor and friendless are conspicuous motivations for its operations. Very few offenders of means or position go through its maw. There are, in short, plainly two kinds of justice: one for the poor and one for "us."

In recent years many moves to reform, repair, remodel, replace, or otherwise deal with the machine have been made. This is not the place to deal with this subject *in extenso*, but in essence the spirit of "catch 'em, convict 'em, lock 'em up, and let 'em stew" still dominates the system as applied to the poor.[2]

[1] Quoted from Professor Paul E. Wilson, "Collateral Consequences of a Criminal Record," address presented to faculty and Fellows of the Menninger School of Psychiatry, May 31, 1972.

[2] See, for example, James V. Bennett, *I Chose Prison* (New York: Knopf, 1970); Walter Bromberg, *Crime and the Mind* (New York: Macmillan, 1965); Leonore L. Cahn, ed., *Confronting Justice: The Edmond Cahn Reader* (Boston: Little, Brown, 1966); Paul Chevigny, *Police Power* (New York: Pantheon, 1969); Daniel Glaser, *The Effectiveness of a Prison and Parole System* (Indianapolis: Bobbs-Merrill, 1964); Sheldon and Eleanor T. Glueck, *Five Hundred Criminal Careers* (New York: Knopf, 1930) and *Criminal Careers in Retrospect* (New York: Commonwealth Fund, 1943); Karl Menninger, *The Crime of Punishment* (New York: Viking, 1966); Norval Morris and Gordon Hawkins, *The Honest Politician's Guide to Crime Control* (Chicago: University of Chicago Press, 1970); Louis Nizer, *My Life in Court* (Garden City, N.Y.: Doubleday, 1961); Clarence H. Patrick, *The Police, Crime and Society* (Springfield, Ill.: Charles C Thomas, 1972); Lawrence P. Tiffany, Donald M. McIntyre, Jr., and Daniel L. Rotenberg, *Detection of Crime* (Boston: Little, Brown, 1967); Joseph Wambaugh, *The New Centurions* (Boston: Little, Brown, 1970); William A. Westley, *Violence and the Police* (Cambridge, Mass.: MIT Press, 1970); Fred T. Wilkinson, *The Realities of Crime and Punishment* (Springfield, Mo.: The Mycroft Press, 1972); *Juvenile Delinquency*: Hearings Before the Subcommittee to Investigate Delinquency

The average citizen does not realize this, or care much to find out about it. He thinks that, in general, "criminals" deserve what he supposes they get, and plenty of "rights" and safety devices will protect them if they are not guilty. He doesn't realize that their "rights" are of little protection. People who can't afford representation by a skillful lawyer and who—unable to "make bail"—are incarcerated helplessly in horrible jails pending the long-delayed trial have few realistic "rights."[3] It is cheaper and easier to find scapegoats than solutions, and the taxpayers are all for the "cheaper" way. The average taxpayer assumes—correctly—that the nightmare of legal entanglement is extremely unlikely to involve *him*. It's for those "other guys"—the poor and the ignorant, the blacks and browns and reds.

The Triage Process

The process of sorting out the kinds of human difficulties that lead a troubled person to a doctor, or to a clergyman, or to a lawyer is a very complicated one. It is easy to say where a man with a visible wound should go, or a thief with stolen goods in his hands, or a sinner manifestly penitent. But at the beginning, when a decision has to be made, none of these look the way they will appear later when they can be more carefully examined and classified.

For example, if a man with a sore throat or a severe headache were to go to a physician, we all know the process that would ensue. He would be given an examination and then appropriate medication. But suppose the same sufferer were to go to a clergyman. Instead of aspirin or penicillin, he might be given a long interview. In it he might be asked if his headache could reflect preoccupation with a moral conflict, or his sore throat be an expression of regret over bitter words directed at someone. Some might condemn this minister for presumption, yet there have been many psychosomatic studies which have borne out exactly the implications of these questions.

---

of the Committee on the Judiciary, U.S. Senate, 91st Cong., 1st sess. (Washington, D.C.: U.S. Govt. Printing Office, 1971); *Working Papers of the National Commission on Reform of Federal Criminal Laws*, 2 vols. (Washington, D.C.: U.S. Govt. Printing Office, 1970).

[3] See Anthony Amsterdam, "Crime and Justice," *Intellectual Digest*, 2:49 (August, 1972).

Or suppose a man had been arrested for driving his car recklessly, and suppose the police, for some reason, instead of their usual procedure, were to take him to a doctor. Suppose, further, that instead of rejecting him *a priori* the doctor were to ask the man when he last had a neurological examination or a blood test and insist that those procedures be carried out. Many might think this an absurd handling of another "drunken driver." And yet there are many demonstrated instances in which such behavior proved to be a reflection, not of intoxication, but of brain disease, one which just these procedures—and only they—would reveal.

In general, the lines of procedure are well established and, in common parlance, the distinction between sin, symptom, and crime *is* the professional management the subject receives—i.e., what rescuer is chosen, which *somebody* is supposed to know best what to do about it. To this "somebody" is then assigned the responsibility for bringing about the desired change; e.g., doctors give medicine; surgeons do surgery; policemen arrest people; lawyers "defend" them; judges order people locked up in iron cages; clergymen sympathize or counsel or suggest penance. (They also preach, an underestimated function to the discussion of which we shall return later.)

The Police

In a sense it is the policeman rather than the judge or the jailer who typifies the methods of the state as distinguished from those of the church in dealing with transgressors. In the policeman the state has a mobile mechanism for detecting, detaining, and accusing offenders—a traditional occupation of which the church long ago divested itself. The police function is, in a way, the crucial feature of "law and order," although this importance has not been reflected in the selection or training of officers.

The policeman has the delicate and difficult responsibility of making a quick presumptive decision. When a dereliction is observed and presumably recognized—both of which often require considerable effort—what happens next is an extraordinarily complicated, unpredictable matter. It depends upon many intangible variables. Here are a few of them:

1. The intelligence and experience of the police officer who observes the offense or to whom it is reported.

2. His emotional state at the time of observing the offense and attempting to follow up on his observation.

3. The moral philosophy or code of this officer and his department.

4. His susceptibility to dissuasion or corruption and the current police practice in that community at that time.

5. The demeanor, clothing, general appearance, hair grooming, and speech of the suspect.

6. The color of his skin: white, yellow, brown, red, or black!

7. The reaction of the accosted offender to the encounter, including the verbal facility and clarity with which he explains or defends his action or predicament.

8. Inferences or evidence regarding the arrested man's connections—social, financial, political.

9. The time of day, the place, the surroundings, the witnesses, the availability of help for either party.

10. The wisdom and the state of mind of the police court judge or other authority before whom the offender is taken by the arresting officer.

11. The availability of space for detaining the suspect.

12. The general state of mind of the people everywhere at the time of this arrest.[4]

13. The stage of the sin-into-crime shift, and the degree of zeal of coercion-to-virtue prevalent in that area at that time. These vary greatly from city to city, from precinct to precinct, from city to country, from agricultural to industrial communities, and from year to year.

This partial list of the determining variables of a decision throws light on the incredible difficulties of the policeman's task. It partially explains why he is so constantly exposed to criticism and hostility for blunders of omission or of commission. He must decide in a few minutes whether to take an offender in charge or release him, where to take or send him, and how to get him there, and what to accuse him of.

[4] I recently read a review of the long prison torture endured by a poor stagehand whose work assignment had been the menial task of shifting scenery in a theater. He was doing so on the night Abraham Lincoln was shot! Someone in the alley called his name; he went to investigate, was picked up, and from that moment on was assumed *prima facie* to have been a part of the terrible conspiracy.

He has some guidelines, to be sure: crime is something which shabby, strange, foreign-looking men do, ugly men, men with hairy faces, long-haired and strangely garbed young "hoodlums," black men, brown men, red men "prowling" (or just standing or walking) in white men's neighborhoods. Crime is not something in which courteous, well-dressed, white gentlemen get involved; if they are seen somewhere—anywhere (unless they are noticeably furtive or fugitive)—they are "probably going about their own affairs." The prototype of the criminal in the public mind is likewise fixed in most policemen's minds, reinforced by many actual samples.

We know, when we stop to think about it, that the whole cops-catch-robbers ritual is just another part of our inherited folkways, important for its symbolic value. Instead of priests presiding over our morals, armed, uniformed officials function in a constantly publicized morality play. Scapegoats are necessary for the spectacle. The "goat" may be innocent; or he may be (and very likely is) guilty of something other than the alleged offense. But it really doesn't matter; he is, for the moment, an available villain captured by skill and daring, booked, locked up, and now "awaiting justice." He must look the part, and he must be found in a vulnerable situation. Arresting him, transporting him, charging him, judging and convicting him, finally making him officially a *criminal*—and as such, he is herded into a cage and locked in with bed and board, of sorts. The public can heave a sigh of relief. This dangerous man won't be around again for a while.

I wouldn't insist that this morality play with its unlucky scapegoats has no value. But it is mostly sham; it is expensive, inefficient, and misleading and it results in cruel suffering. The unfairness of the seizure, the mercilessness with which the culprit is often treated, the heartbreaking delays in trial and decision are deplorable.

True, someone—perhaps this man—has been merciless with *his* victims—including some of us. Remember the accusation of demagogues that "nobody seems to care about the victims." If you are going to give the criminal "rights," remember the victims have "rights," too. They should be repaid and helped. But we're too busy punishing.

This morality play has been running a long time. It used to be more publicized—even paraded in the streets. But what with jails and lockups instead of the brandings and floggings behind the cart, it has lost its old medieval excitement. Too much of the show has gone underground. Too many villains and suspects are stewing in dungeons *unseen*, gnashing their teeth, nursing their hate and plotting revenge. Others, meanwhile, continue their "criming" without being intimidated, warned, captured, tried, sentenced, or "punished" in any way. Fifty percent are never arrested; 20 percent are never found guilty. It suits them just fine to have the morality play go on with a few of the careless and incompetent bunglers "selected" for the kill as scapegoats.

The late J. Edgar Hoover declared year after year that crime was continuing to increase and ever more rapidly (in the face of repeated scholarly reports that crimes were proportionately fewer today by 50 to 200 percent than a century ago).

Admittedly, our streets continue to be unsafe. Homes and hotels continue to be burglarized. Proscribed drugs are being peddled. Rapes and murders still occur. The *visibility* of crime continues to increase, and hence more scapegoats are needed. The police are given more money for equipment and are kept busy searching nervously for long-haired youth smoking marihuana and for intoxicated and deteriorated derelicts stumbling about or sitting idly, and for black drivers making improper left-hand turns! Meanwhile, rape, skyjacking, dishonest political and business exploits, and the artificial crimes incident to the laws regarding drugs are daily headlined in the press and television.

So it is understandably reassuring to some people that our prisons remain crowded. A goodly number of villains are caught daily and fed into the machine. Ninety percent of them have done no violence, and 80 percent could be handled more cheaply and more effectively by other methods. But many of these wretches have illegally taken someone else's property, and this is a cardinal sin tremendously important in a capitalistic society.

We no longer cut off their hands, but we willingly spend $25,000–$50,000 each to "punish," make miserable, and detain in idleness thieves whose illegal acquisitions—television sets, second-hand cars—could be bought for a few hundred dollars. The estimated national tax bill for making captured token offenders *suffer* (not for the arrest or trial or probation—just the squeeze) is over $1 billion annually! I doubt if the public is having that much fun out of it. But that's what it is spending.

In the minds of some people the solution for all of this is to appropriate more money (or get hold of more Law Enforcement Assistance Act funds) to hire more policemen to ride more cars and helicopters and operate more crime detection machines and buy more Mace and riot control hose nozzles to intimidate more disturbed protesters and catch more scapegoats to put in more iron cages. That's law and order.

Yes, I am being sarcastic. I regard this sort of bullying and saber-rattling and boondoggling with government money to pacify an artificially alarmed public—as *sin*, and a big *sin*. It is the sin of politicians, of officeholders, of newspaper and television reporters, of voters—indeed of a great many consenting people, some of them no doubt persons of goodwill and purpose. But to use the sinning propensity of mankind—especially of underprivileged, maneuverable, exploitable mankind—as a ploy in the profitable game of collecting and spending public monies for making jobs to give "punishment" and "protection" is an evil which needs to be identified and condemned. It is *our* sin, a sin of participation in an immoral, antisocial attitude and practice.

Some men involved in these efforts are sincere, earnest (however ignorant) public servants or "politicians." Most of them know there are more appropriate, effective, and economical ways to control "crime" and criminals, better ways to handle drug abuse. But it would be unpopular for them to propose or espouse those methods.

Just leaving crime to the police is like turning over the coach horses to the hostlers, while the rest of us sit down and enjoy dinner and listen to the speeches. This simply won't work. It used to work in medieval manor days when the king's peace was all that mattered. Police are not priests, prize fighters, thugs, yardmen, psychologists, saints, or supermen. They can't possibly do what some expect them to, aided by all the revolvers, billyclubs, cattle prods, and tear gas bombs on earth. And some of them are poor, weak, corruptible human beings who commit more crimes than they correct. Some honest, competent police really patrol the cities properly, alert for the desperate and furtive outlaws who threaten and molest and injure and kill citizens or damage their property, and alert for people in trouble whom they can befriend and assist, and these officers are far too busy to perform duties of escorting drunks to repulsive lockups, making phony traffic arrests, and harassing blacks and long-haired eccentrics.

Jails

The ambiguities and abuses in the police function and the interminable trial delays pale into insignificance in the crime war beside the atrocities of our local jails. The public refuses to abandon its pleasant fantasy that jails are just little local lockups where miscreants and suspects may spend a night or even a week and be the more wary of sin and police thereafter. People refuse to believe that jails are almost without exception horrible, destructive, ruinous, hideous atrocities of which every citizen should be ashamed.

I say the public refuses to believe it in spite of thousands of reports, because if they did, jails would be outlawed tomorrow by popular demand. If every minister would visit the local jail twice a year, and urge his congregation to do so, there would be a similar revolution.

The average citizen goes along in his thinking with those ignorant, lazy, or cruel judges who say, "A few weeks or months in our little jail may do you some good. Then, if you persist in your wicked ways, you will be given the severe treatment of the state penitentiary!"

Actually the worst penitentiary is less harmful to most young offenders than the best of jails! Jails *ruin* young men. Can't the public grasp this indisputable fact? How can a decent prison attempting a rehabilitation program do anything for a boy who comes to it from a jail where he has been raped, battered, vomited and urinated upon, mauled, and corrupted by some of the old-timers in the bullpen?

Even without the abuse and harassment of other inmates, the horrible confinement in hot, stuffy, crowded, dark, vermin-infested iron cages is a terrible experience—literally a form of torture. When one considers that this is all illegal, since the law does *not* stipulate these iniquitous concomitants of detention in *any* sentence, our sinfulness in permitting the situation to continue in our society, and *at our expense*, seems very evident and very great.

On many a hot, sultry night I have lain awake thinking of the misery of millions of naked, sweating men and boys locked in hot, airless, overcrowded, overheated cages where only utter boredom and ennui face them in the coming days. Aching teeth, chronic intestinal infections, gonorrhea, headaches—mostly these are borne in silence—are their constant lot. True, the misery of the millions of poor in their ghetto apartments and farm hovels is not to be forgotten. But most of these latter unfortunates can at least move about or walk in the night air or speak with other family members. Not so the felons and suspects in our jails.

No one in the know doubts that jails must go. They are gradually being closed, condemned by authorities or abandoned by the communities. But it is all happening too slowly. There are still about four thousand of them in this country, 90 percent of them abominable. It is a startling fact that today, 1973, almost anyone in almost any city can observe torture being administered to young men, boys, even children, almost any day. All he has to do is visit his local jail, grope his way into the "tanks," and talk freely with the prisoners in the murky, still, and stinking air.

Judges and Courts

Closely associated with the iniquity of the jail system is that of the criminal court system. I know of this primarily from the reports of competent observers,[5] but also from my observations in many jurisdictions. Presumably innocent people who have no money to buy bail remain caged in misery for months and months awaiting official disposition of charges brought against them by police or others. These charges are often being played off like poker chips behind the scenes in deals between prosecuting attorneys and defending lawyers. In most cases the prosecutors rather than the judges decide the guilt and the sentence.

The penalities for sins converted into crimes tend to be punitive and vengeful, although these motives are denied by the law. They are remnants of tradition somewhat modified by legislative enactment and bargaining procedures. They are nearly all senseless and

[5] See Leonard Downie, Jr., *Justice Denied: The Case for Reform of the Courts* (New York: Praeger, 1971).

cruel, expensive and futile. No intelligent person believes that they deter or change anyone. Detention has a proper rationale—for investigations, for protection, or for temporary holding prior to transfer. But people are not "cured" of the propensity for writing bad checks or picking up cars by being made to sit idle in an iron cage for five years while their families disintegrate. No thief is rehabilitated by having a hand cut off, as in some countries, or by being subjected to rectal rape and tedious boredom, as in our country. George Bernard Shaw wrote an essay 50 years ago on the *Crime of Imprisonment*. Some way or other this message has never reached the ears of the public.

The whole thing centers around our senseless sentencing practices based on class legislative enactments. Sentences are handed out by the judge by rule of thumb often at the virtual dictation of the prosecutors. Absolute monarchs assumed the authority to pronounce the destination and disposition of offending citizens, and the state took over this prerogative within prescribed limits. The Babylonians limited the retaliation to an equivalent loss, e.g., in the case of mayhem (Hammurabi), and this was followed by the Israelites. Other jurisdictions were less merciful.

Several law codes older than that of Hammurabi (1750 B.C.) have been found (e.g., that of King Lpit-Ishar, 1900 B.C., and nearly a century earlier King Bilalama). But recently a law code was discovered that had been promulgated by Ur-Nammu, a Sumerian (i.e., non-Semitic) king, who began his reign about 2050 B.C. The talon law of "an eye for an eye" and "a tooth for a tooth," which later prevailed, had—in his kingdom—already (2050 B.C.) given way to a far more humane philosophy in which a money fine was substituted as a punitive sacrifice.

This King Ur-Nammu, says Professor Samuel Noah Kramer, showed himself by other acts to be a most enlightened man. He instituted social and moral reforms, removing the "chiselers and grafters" (as described in the code, "the grabbers of the citizens' oxen and sheep and donkeys). He then "established and regulated honest and unchangeable weights and measures." He saw to it that "the orphans did not fall prey to the wealthy," and that "the widow did not fall prey to the man of one mina (sixty shekels)."[6]

---

[6] Samuel Noah Kramer, University of Pennsylvania, Chief Research Professor of Assyriology, *History Begins at Sumeria* (Garden City, N.Y.: Doubleday, 1959).

The Quakers thought they were acting in a humane and Christian way when, in 1789, they sought to substitute quiet (solitary) incarceration for the floggings, brandings, tongue slicings, ear amputations, and the uncomfortable and humiliating stocks. But these old-time punishments, while painful, were public and relatively brief. Intentionally fearful hardships of incarceration were gradually added and the duration of the imprisonment became longer and longer. Six months was once considered a very long sentence (as indeed it is!). All American sentences are far greater than in English and continental practice.

An adolescent was recently sentenced by a Texas judge to 30 years' imprisonment for possessing two marihuana cigarettes, presumably for sale. It costs Texas many thousands of dollars to cage this fellow for 30 years. What does it accomplish?

Undesirable behavior should, of course, be forbidden and if possible prevented. But how will 30 years of a prison regime do that? Will 30 years do it any better than 30 months? Indeed—can it? The real question is, Can this man be deterred or not? *Can* he be changed? *Can* he be realigned and made again self-supporting and community conforming? If so, how? If not, then what can we do? How can he be returned safely to society and self-support as swiftly as possible?

How can the judge decide on any sound criteria whether a man before him is dangerous—or will continue to be dangerous—whether he has an affliction which can be treated, or ignorance which can be subjected to education, or whether he is feeble-minded, or even mad? Information on these matters should be, but rarely is, available to judges before the sentencing.

Presentence diagnostic studies are available to judges in only a few states. I am proud to say that Kansas is one of them. Our state diagnostic center (under George W. Thompson and Dr. Karl Targownik) to which all offenders are sent before final sentencing is one of the great satisfactions of our courts, and the pride of our informed citizenry.

Many judges are sorely troubled by the unenviable task of blindly assigning the miserable villains before them to 5 or 10 or 20 years of futility when 5 or 10 or 20 months of intelligent direction might restore them to useful and peaceful social functioning. Sentencing seminars (in a few of which I have enjoyed participating) are increasingly provided for the more conscientious and truth-seeking judges, and revised criminal codes are being enacted to correct some of the more glaring defects of the old laws (Kansas, Illinois, and others). The effect is to make the process more elastic, more appropriate, more likely to assist the extension of a peaceful society. But thousands of courts (backed by their state legislature's antiquated actions) still operate in a medievally cruel, cramped, and futile mold.

Are not some crimes so shocking, so evil, so pointless, that the public would feel very disturbed if the culprits were given anything but prolonged confinement? Yes, indeed. I think any rational analysis of the potentialities of many offenders would indicate the desirability of not a 5-year sentence—although that is hideously long and horrible punishment—but of a *much longer* sentence in a safe and comfortable but secure environment. This might be a blessing to the man himself and to many others. He would resent the loss of freedom, but he would not be tortured by temptation.

Offenders are constantly being released from prison who any competent psychiatrist or warden could predict will hurt people again. Meanwhile the prisons are compelled to retain thousands of able-bodied men who are not dangerous, never were dangerous, and never will be dangerous, who could be useful but are being made useless, supported in expensive misery by the taxpayers.

This is being done by you! You ordered it, you permit it, and you are paying for it—far more heavily than you realize. All because we have elected lawmakers and officials who go along stolidly pretending to believe it effective to have scapegoats for public spectacles, no matter how unjustly, ineffectively, or how expensively, rather than risk an intelligent improvement.

So long as the compulsion to make the offender suffer and remain "secure" hangs over the penal system, no matter how high the ideals of the administration, the actual process will be destructive rather than constructive. One sin becomes the basis for a long list of sins, *and crimes.*

In January, 1972, the mother of Wilfred Hardman protested to officials in the state prison in Trenton, New Jersey, that her son was showing signs of being drugged by Thorazine.

In a letter to Governor Kahill, Mrs. Hardman wrote:

> My son was seated on a stool swaying back and forth so sedated
> that he could hardly raise his eyelids. I went out to the other room and
> asked to see a doctor. One of the guards told me to go into the
> deputy's office. I asked him what was wrong with my son, that I was
> a registered nurse and that it was very obvious to me that he was
> heavily drugged. The deputy became very indignant and said, "If he
> is drugged, he got it from another patient."

Later she was told that he was "emotionally disturbed" and had
been "trying to eat garbage." She questioned how her son could get
garbage in his cell and insisted that he be treated. She was
informed that her son would see a psychiatrist. She objected to this
procedure because she believed he was too drugged for psychiatric
evaluation to be valid.

Eight days later this message was received by the Fortune Society of New York from Mrs. Hardman:

> My son was found dead in his cell last night.

An autopsy subsequently revealed that Hardman had died of a
brain tumor.

About a week later a letter about the Hardman case was received
by the Fortune Society from Merrill Speller, another prisoner at the
Trenton prison. A few days later a second letter came from Merrill
Speller saying:

> I was severely beaten about the head and body with clubs right
> after writing to you.

A third letter reached the Society from another prisoner stating:

> This morning they almost killed a prisoner [Speller]. They kicked
> him in the face and all over . . . for about fifteen minutes.

A very brief fourth letter came on March 16 to the Fortune
Society:

> Merrill Speller committed suicide.

Who is guilty here? And of what crimes? You are hiring it done!

Crimes into Sins

Prohibitions with respect to the eating or drinking of certain things replaced with legislative enactments the food taboos imposed on our ancestors by superstition, religious law, and tribal taboos. Pork, beef, fish, meat of any kind, tomatoes, tobacco, salt, and many other foods have all been unlawful for some people to eat at some time for some "reason."

The reasons given today for legally prohibiting the consumption of various substances is that they are believed by some to be injurious. Their use is, in short, partial (incomplete) suicide—and suicide is, of course, for unclear reasons, a crime. There was a time, says Troy Duster, when

> anyone could go to his corner druggist and buy grams of morphine or heroin for just a few pennies. There was no need to have a prescription from a physician. The middle and upper classes purchased more than the lower and working classes, and there was no moral stigma attached to such narcotics use.
>
> Suddenly there came the enlightenment of the 20th Century, full with moral insight and moral indignation, a smattering of knowledge of physiology, and the force of law.[7]

Twenty years later, namely by 1920, the purchase of narcotics was considered not only immoral but criminal. Duster says that from 1865 to 1900 addiction was probably eight times more prevalent than now in proportion to the population!

The use of certain drugs is only the most recent general class of offenses (sins) which have been made crimes by legislation. While gambling has always been frowned upon and considered a sin in the eyes of most churchmen, it passed from moral to canonical and then to civil law control, and today it is officially and most stupidly and unfairly a crime.

It is a crime which millions of Americans boast of committing, while the poor, more millions—the shabby, the nobodies of the cities —are daily jailed for being seen doing it. In 1969, 24 times more Negroes than whites were arrested for gambling, yet everyone

[7] Troy Duster, *Coercion of Virtue: The Legislation of Morality* (New York: Free Press, 1970).

knows that poker and roulette and football betting (which are just as definitely gambling as is crap shooting in the alley) are very, very widely practiced (with immunity).

The movement to transfer victimless crimes *back* into the category of sins is gathering momentum, urged on by actual need.

"Vice: Should it be a crime?" reads a caption in the Chicago *Tribune* (March 26, 1972). No, it should not. Why? Because unenforceable moral laws have encouraged corruption and crimes of violence, undermined civil liberties, encouraged police brutality and bribery, overtaxed police forces, overcrowded courts and jails, and, in general, overburdened our system of criminal justice. But attempts to repeal these laws—i.e., to treat the offenses as sins or symptoms and not as crimes—is met with outcries from two quarters: (1) moralistic but mistaken citizens who fear these offenses would increase and (2) the racketeers and truly "criminal" individuals and organizations for whom the present system guarantees big profits.

Aside from philosophical and moral reasons why these "crimes" should be seen again rather as sins, there is the sheer wasteful and extravagant costliness of the present practice. The FBI statistics for 1969 reveal that nearly one-fourth of all U.S. arrests were for public drunkenness. In addition to the expense of finding, trying, and confining these sinners, labeling them criminals, holding them for a while and sending them forth to sin again, there is the great assistance this gives to satellite crimes which are real and great crimes—blackmail, extortion, smuggling, crime syndicate action, police corruption, and pimping.

A similar burlesque of correcting undesirable behavior takes place with regard to prostitution, except that here the usefulness of retaining the law for the furtherance of police corruption is even more evident. Not 5 percent of the women engaged in prostitution are ever arrested and less than 1 percent of the men involved in the racket are ever arrested.

There can be no doubt that the hysterical persecution and witch-hunting that has gone on for the past decades has set up many millionaire criminals while incarcerating and ruining for life a few luckless youth. The penalties for possession of and handling some of the stronger drugs has made them so expensive that theft, robbery, and prostitution to pay the advanced costs have become absolute necessities of existence for many. Hence the punishment of little crimes induces the committing of many more bigger crimes.

Let us assume, for example, that you are a "junkie" in need of a "fix." I am paraphrasing an article by Charles McCabe in a recent issue of the San Francisco *Examiner*:

> You have a connection from whom you can get a $20 bag which will keep you straight today. But there has been a "bust" on dealers. This does not stop the flow of dope. It merely raises the price or, instead of raising the price, dealers cut the heroin content from 7% to 3% at the same price as before. Which means in essence that the junkie has to rob or rip-off or burn twice or three times as many people as has been his custom to keep well; and believe me, as one who knows, keep well he will. For $100 worth of stolen merchandise, the addict can get about $20 worth from the fences. That's scarcely enough.

Summary

It became the civilized custom to attempt to legislate morality and to coerce virtue by law. The law took over not only the great destructive sins—murder and mayhem and rape—it took over the Ten Commandments, then it took over the lesser sins and vices. They were all made into crimes and were constantly augmented. They were prosecuted by clumsy machinery which has become more and more unusable; it commits more crime than it punishes. Most of the crimes involve acts that do not injure anyone but the offender—through self-destructiveness.

There is a trend now to cancel them out as crimes and return them to their status as sins—or to use the now common word, vices. They are called vices, but many of them are not vicious in any sense —but punishing them is. It makes vicious men and women out of merely overtaxed and troubled ones.

"Nothing can be more certain," wrote Oliver Goldsmith, "than that numerous written laws are a sign of a degenerate community, and are frequently not the consequences of vicious morals in a state, but the causes."[8]

[8] Quoted by Andrew Sinclair in *Prohibition, The Era of Excess* (Boston: Little, Brown, 1962).

Goldsmith's Puritan contemporaries in the United States held an opposite opinion. For them numerous written proscriptive laws were a sign of a godly community and were an appropriate means for curbing vicious morals in a state. Much of the writing on the effects of alcohol, narcotics, marihuana, homosexuality, and other "immoral" activities has been colored by the underlying value position of the writers on the relationship between law and morals.

Does the use of alcohol, marihuana, or opiates weaken moral fiber? Does it "lead" to crime? Does it encourage sexual indulgence? Some writers on this subject feel obliged to respond to such questions, even though they may be unanswerable or irrelevant. For example, suppose one were to ask whether marriage leads to wife-beating. The only possible answer is "Yes," but this answer implies that there is something wrong with marriage, which determines the beating. The same bias appears time and again in literature on marihuana, homosexuality, and drug use.

It is very difficult to describe the effects of some ingested substances in objective terms that do not deprecate the activity in question. Objective descriptions typically describe the actor in the third person. We say that the marihuana smoker, the user of opiates, the user of beverage alcohol does certain things or experiences certain feelings. To the extent that we ourselves have not shared his experience, words like "high" or "intoxicating" take on a disparaging connotation. Thus, an "objective" description may invoke subjective feelings in an observer or listener that would not be invoked in those who have experienced the phenomenon.

Suppose we were to ask, "What are the effects of playing tennis on an individual?" In response, we would have to describe a heightened pulse rate, facial flushing, sweating, and marked adrenal activity. In many cases, we would observe loss of breath followed by feelings of dizziness and nausea. There are reliable reports of death following the activity, especially among the middle aged who neglect exercise. For some reason, we could hint, this insidious "sport" tempts otherwise responsible men to participate in a deadly game. This description would not be untrue, but out of context it would have a far different effect on our reader than on a tennis player. Thus, the very "objectivity" of a clinical description may result in an unintended distortion for the purpose of assessing social policy.

In addition to these difficulties, our capacity for understanding is impeded by those who utilize and distort facts for political purposes, attempting to frighten people away from the behavior in question. For example, one of the posters issued by the press of the Anti-Saloon League in 1913 advertised The Effect of Alcohol on Sex Life:

> Alcohol Inflames the Passions, thus making the temptations to sex-sin unusually strong.
>
> Alcohol Decreases the Power of Control, thus making the resisting of temptation especially difficult.
>
> Alcohol Decreases the Resistance of the Body to Disease, thus making the result of disease more serious. The influence of alcohol upon sex-life could hardly be worse. AVOID ALL ALCOHOLIC DRINK ABSOLUTELY.
>
> The control of sex impulses will then be easy and disease, dishonor, disgrace and degradation will be avoided.

In bold black type it declared that sex life was dominated by a compelling instinct as natural as eating and drinking and that the laws of custom and modern civilization demanded that sex life be under the control of reason, judgment, and will. Since alcohol made all natural instincts stronger and weakened judgment and will, all drinks of which *alcohol formed even a small part were harmful and dangerous.*

While such literature contains some truth, it is also misleading. It suggests that the physiological effects of alcohol may be generalized to apply to all people under all social conditions. That implication is clearly not true. Alcohol may be a "dangerous" substance—sometimes, for some people, under some circumstances. But, in fact, it is difficult to distinguish the effects of physiological, psychological, and sociological variables. The issue for the scientist is to determine when and for whom it is dangerous. The scientist must also determine degrees of dangerousness.

For many years now, research has been conducted on the effects of alcohol, research which could only be attempted after the prohibition amendment was repealed. Still proceeding, this research has not yet given us completely definitive answers. It has, however, suggested that the physiological and psychological effects of alcohol are mediated by the personality and the cultural backgrounds of those who use it.

A review of the literature in this area reveals not a single social scientist who supports the theory and policy of the Federal Bureau of Narcotics, i.e., the theory that increasingly stringent punishments and law enforcement will solve the problem of narcotics addiction.[9] There are various difficulties with assumptions of the theory, but only one overwhelming conclusion—*it does not work*. It makes the problem worse.

Over ten years ago the problem was excellently put in a statement by Senator Thomas J. Dodd during the 1962 proceedings of the White House Conference on Narcotic and Drug Abuse.

> In 1956, as a result of widespread national dissatisfaction with the growth of narcotic addiction, especially among juveniles, and because of deep frustration over the apparent failure of existing legislation to deal with the problem, a new Narcotic Control Act was passed into law. This law contained three major innovations that were expected to have a tremendous deterrent effect on narcotic racketeers.
>
> First: It removed from the hands of judges all discretion in the sentencing of convicted narcotic offenders by providing a mandatory minimum sentence of 5 years for the first offense and 10 years for subsequent offenses, with maximum penalties of 20 years for the first offense and 40 years for subsequent offenses.
>
> Second, it removed all possibility of parole for narcotic offenders, thus putting them in a special category in our nation's Federal prisons.
>
> Third, it emphasized the concern of Congress over juvenile drug use by providing up to life imprisonment or even death for adults convicted of selling narcotics to a juvenile under the age of 18.
>
> To demonstrate the severity of this law, it should be pointed out that an illegal narcotic transaction normally involves several violations of the act, each of which could be punishable by a mandatory 5-year sentence. Thus, a first offender could be, and frequently has been sentenced to 20 or 30 years for a first offense.

[9] See, e.g., I. Chein, *The Road to H: Narcotics, Delinquency, and Social Policy* (1964); W. Eldridge, *Narcotics and the Law: A Critique of the American Experiment in Narcotics Drug Control* (1962); L. Kolb, *Drug Addiction: A Medical Problem* (1962); A. Lindesmith, *The Addict and the Law* (1965); E. Schur, *Narcotic Addiction in Britain and America: The Impact of Public Policy* (1962).

When Congress passed the Narcotic Control Act of 1956 it radically departed from the existing trend in state and Federal criminal legislation, a trend toward the individual treatment of convicted offenders with a view to their eventual rehabilitation. Congress made this departure because it felt that the peddling of narcotics was so vicious, dangerous, and contagious a crime that unusually severe and rigid methods were necessary and justified in dealing with it. If the passage of several years under this act had been accompanied by a marked decrease in narcotic crimes, we might say that the law could have justified itself. For, after all, the primary purpose of law enforcement is the protection of the public; the care and rehabilitation of criminals, however important, must be subordinate. But has the law been effective?

We have now had several years of experience under it. Its degree of effectiveness is a matter of dispute. The 1956 law has proved helpful in the jailing of several large-scale narcotic racketeers. Yet the growth of drug traffic continues.

The dispute is heightened by the fact that available information on the spread of narcotic addiction is completely contradictory. The Federal Bureau of Narcotics tells us that there are 46,798 drug addicts in the entire country. But testimony before the Senate Subcommittee to Investigate Juvenile Delinquency by responsible city and state officials indicates that there may be as many as 50,000 addicts in the city of New York alone, and from 15,000 to 20,000 addicts in the State of California alone.

Only last week the executive director of the New York City Youth Board told our subcommittee that 25 per cent of the children studied by the youth board are involved in the use of drugs ranging all the way from heroin to marihuana, pep pills, goof balls, and other varieties. He told of entire neighborhoods where children were exposed to narcotic pushing "as part of their daily life." In his opinion and in the opinion of countless people with whom I have talked, who deal with this problem on a day-to-day basis, there are more narcotics illegally available today then ever before.

Therefore, I think it is clear that the severe mandatory sentencing provisions of existing law have not had the deterrent effect that was hoped for.[10]

[10] White House Conference on Narcotic and Drug Abuse, Washington, D.C., 1962: *Proceedings* (Washington, D.C., U.S. Govt. Printing Office, 1963), pp. 229–230.

Experience everywhere has confirmed this view in the decade since it was written. Nevertheless, in 1973 the estimable governor of the most populous of the fifty states came out with the outrageous proposal that stronger punitive measures should be enacted, including a sentence of irreversible life imprisonment!

John Stuart Mill made a famous basic declaration on the philosophy of regulating private morals:

> [It was the] very simple principle . . . that the sole end for which mankind is/are warranted, individually or collectively, in interfering with the liberty of action of any of their number, is self protection; the only purpose for which power can be rightfully exercised over any member of a civilized community, against his will, is to prevent harm to others. His own good, either physical or moral, is not sufficient warrant. He cannot rightfully be compelled to do or forbear because it will be better for him to do so, because it will make him happier, because, in the opinions of others, to do so would be wise, or even right. These are good reasons for remonstrating with him or reasoning with him, or entreating him, but not for compelling him, or visiting him with any evil in case he do otherwise.[11]

Mill believed a man to be entitled to live his life in his own way without the state making decisions for him as to what is right and good.

Mill's most articulate modern critic, Sir Patrick Devlin, argues that society is, nevertheless, entitled to prevent the harm that would be done to it by the "weakness or vice" of too many of its members. Mill did not overlook this consideration; he overrode it in the interests of individual freedom. Thus, one dilemma regularly faced by society when it employs state power to prevent or reduce immorality is, according to Devlin, to what extent does individual freedom override societal interests to prevent widespread harm?[12]

> The line between drunkenness that creates a social problem of sufficient magnitude to justify the intervention of a law and that which does not, cannot be drawn on the distinction between private

[11] J. S. Mill, *On Liberty* (London, 1859) in *Utilitarianism, Liberty* and *Representative Government 72*, p. 7. (Everyman ed., 1910.)

[12] Patrick Devlin, *The Enforcement of Morals* (New York: Oxford University Press, 1970), p. 113.

indulgence and public sobriety. It is a practical one, based on an estimate of what can safely be tolerated whether in public or in private, and shifting from time to time as circumstances change. The licensing laws coupled with high taxation may be all that is needed. But if more is needed there is no doctrinal answer even to complete prohibition. It cannot be said that so much is the law's business, that more is not.[13]

And so, since Mill recognized the right of society to institute laws for self-protection, and since Devlin acknowledged that each citizen is entitled to the greatest measure of personal freedom, what really is the "right" portion between the two? How do we find the "width" or the "spread" of drunkenness; and just what is meant by "drunkenness"? How do we know that the measures taken to suppress "drunkenness" (prohibition, for example) will not only reduce the use of alcoholic beverages—but will also avoid producing undesirable side effects?

[13] *Ibid.*

6

Sin into Symptom

We have seen what became of some former "sins" which
seemingly disappeared. What had been the business of
the priests became the policemen's business, assisted by lawyers and
judges and jailers. Between them they seek and seize, detain, hold,
humble, hurt, deport, execute, or discharge their "sinners," now
called criminals. The violence of crime is met with the counterviolence of law and order, called "punishment," righteous violence
versus unrighteous violence.

Around the turn of the century public attitudes regarding the
handling of misbehavior began to veer away from the traditional,
legalistic mold. It was whispered that there might possibly be more
effective ways to manage *some* of these errant individuals, with an
eye to achieving change in them and returning some of them to
useful and nondangerous lives. Not humane reasons, primarily, but
pragmatic ones were determinant; it might be cheaper. Besides, the
prisons were overcrowded!

Then, too, along with the discoveries and movements described
in the preceding chapter, the possibility that some of the behavior
manifested by these offenders was "the product" of illness began to
be seriously considered. If one *can* be *treated* effectively by medical
science for a propensity toward certain behavior, it would be absurd
to *punish* him for this same manifestation. It would be an unnecessary duplication of labor, an inappropriate handling, and an extra
expense.

Diseases are not crimes. Hence, no matter how reprehensible or
offensive a piece of behavior may be, it cannot be called a crime if
it is a symptom of disease. A man may murder his best friend or
his worst enemy during a delirium and yet commit no crime. (Silly,
isn't it?) The demonstrated presence in the offender at the time of

74

his criminal act of a condition called "mental disease" which impairs discretion and control cancels the legal guiltiness of the offender. Likewise, discernible illness (physical or mental) in any criminal awaiting execution is a *prima facie* legal basis for deferring the execution! (Only the sane and healthy merit this grand exit!)

Degrees of Voluntarism

The nubbin of the matter is simply this: Unless a man is sane, he cannot have criminal intention nor the capacity to profit from any prescribed punishment. The presence of this intent or "*voluntas*" or "*mens rea*" is essential to definitively labeling an act "criminal." A crime, as with a sin, even when serving the same dynamic psychological function as a symptom, is assumed to be largely a voluntary act. As the symptom of an illness, on the other hand, the act must be largely "*involuntary*."

In practice, the distinction between voluntary, *partially* voluntary, and totally *involuntary* action can rarely be made with preciseness. Yet it is the important issue distinguishing the legalistic from the scientific position in regard to behavior control. "He can't help it," says one. "He does it on purpose," says the other. "He is trying to control it," says one. "He could and must stop doing it," says another. "He can't." "He must." "He should." "He won't." "He could have." And on the argument goes.

"That boy of yours, that woman they caught yesterday, that fellow who raped the girl—don't tell me those people are sick. The boy is disobedient and willful and impudent and needs a thrashing. That woman is a silly, self-pampering, lightweight who just loves to run to doctors. She's not sick; she's a fool as well as a villain, but she's not crazy. And that rapist is a vicious criminal; why, he is a sex fiend! He is a wretch who ought to be punished severely, put in jail and kept there. Let him groan; let him sweat. This business of calling these people sick and calling their behavior 'symptoms' is an indication of the impaired fiber of the nation.[1] Permissivism! The integrity of the law is being subverted."

"Free will" is a notion understood in three different ways by the

---

[1] Worse than murder or rape, one gathers from recent gubernatorial declarations, is taking any part in distributing some drugs. Compulsory life sentence with no possibility of revocation of parole is recommended.

legalist, the behaviorist, and the moralist. The variable overlap of
the voluntary and the involuntary in human behavior is a perennial
mystery. It is masked or distorted by fluctuating correspondence
between the felt and the seen, and between the seen and the
unseen, between the conscious and the unconscious, and between
the intentional and the inadvertent. Unconscious motivation and
biological determinants are always present in every act and yet
they are rarely considered in explaining most behavior.

"Don't breathe!" shouts the X-ray technician as a chest plate is
being made. The dutiful subject stops breathing. "Now you can(!)
breathe again," calls out the technician, as if he had restored the
control of this physiological function, or given permission for its
continuance.

But suppose the technician should forget to give this permission
to resume breathing! Within narrow time limits we can hold our
breath, but beyond that interval, even with the most earnest desire
to commit suicide, we cannot greatly prolong our exercise of will-
power. *Within limits* one's will and wish can control his pulse rate,
bowel movements, eyewinking, blood pressure, and some other
physiological functions. *Within limits*—and narrow limits they are—
these functions are indeed voluntary. But everyone knows there are
deeper controlling mechanisms which cannot be resisted. *The same
is true of much so-called "voluntary" behavior.*

Each man bustles forth to work in the morning thinking he will
perform certain activities, perhaps specific duties he planned at last
night's conference. He makes appointments and schedules. He proceeds under the assumption that the acts of his day are his planned
choices, without reflecting that every one of them is predetermined
by a million circumstances, over *most* of which he had no control!
Thousands of intercurrent events are in progress; unexpected inter-
ruptions are certain. But even these he thinks he "controls" in a
measure. He will rearrange his plans. He must believe that he controls what he is doing; otherwise he succumbs to a frightening sense
of helplessness and tension leading to rebellion, paralysis, or even
panic.

Without knowing it, he lives largely upon illusion. All of us do.
But usually it is only when the process breaks down that the illusion
is recognized and the truth appears.

For some individuals the very suggestion that "voluntary" behavior is never *entirely* voluntary arouses anxiety and provokes vigorous rebuttal.

"Improper behavior," they assert, "is willful wrongdoing." (They may or may not call it sin.) "It must be controlled, if not by the individual, then by someone in authority. Each of us must try, and that effort must be supported by firmness, by threat, by force, and if need be, by fierceness. Success will be rewarded; failure must be punished. There is right and there is wrong; there can be no compromise."

We all know exponents of this simplistic, hard-core super-moralism. Some of them are just ignorant, some are fanatical, others are political rightists, still others are bigots. But some are (also) earnest, honest, and very sincere people. Some of them are even intelligent! What is more—and this may astonish you coming from me—I think they have a point!

The law and the church were so sure of themselves, and so fixed on the position that all behavior is conscious and voluntary (unless accidental), that when scientists began to assert themselves about involuntary and unconsciously motivated behavior, some of them simply carried their thesis too far. Their absolutism is just as offensive and misleading as that of their opponents.

Even if we concede that some—perhaps most—behavior is essentially involuntary, automatic, or reactive (symptomatic), we know that no behavior—or very little of it—is *entirely* involuntary. We *can* hold our breath for a short time! We *can* take a new breath.

The Research Department of the Menninger Foundation has demonstrated that a degree of voluntary control over what are ordinarily considered involuntary body processes can be exerted by intention by many individuals who were not aware of their ability to do this.

Dr. Elmer Green and his colleagues have shown in a series of research projects that normally unconscious psychosomatic processes, such as those involving vascular behavior, can be brought under voluntary control by autogenic feedback training.[2] Physiological

[2] See, for example, Elmer Green, Alyce Green, and E. D. Walters, "Voluntary Control of Internal States," *Journal of Transpersonal Psychology*, 2(1):1 (1970); Elmer Green et al., "Feedback Technique for Deep Relaxation," *Psychophysiology*, 6:371 (November, 1969); Elmer Green, Alyce Green, and E. D. Walters, "Self Regulation of Internal States," in *Progress of Cybernetics*, J. Rose, ed. (London: Gordon & Breach, 1970), p. 1,299.

"self-knowing," as enhanced by presentation of information on meters or dials (biofeedback), is proving to be a powerful new tool for self-regulation of psychosomatic disease.

Dr. Joseph Sargent, an internist at the Menninger Foundation, has completed research in which more than 80 percent of 150 migraine patients have brought improper blood flow in the head under voluntary control to a significant extent. Results ranged from a little relief to essentially complete relief. Most of Dr. Sargent's patients had been on drugs for many years and in some cases had sought psychiatric help without relief. It seems quite clear in retrospect that the power of self-regulation has been seriously neglected in medicine.

Other researchers across the country using biofeedback to inform a person of his own inside-the-skin behavior have demonstrated the possibility of self-regulation of tension headache, blood pressure, and heartbeat irregularities. Even epilepsy, an electrical storm in the brain, is yielding in some cases to self-regulation of brain-wave patterns through biofeedback training.

The value of taking part of the responsibility for one's own psychological well-being has never been more clearly demonstrated than by this recent upsurge of "biofeedback training for voluntary control of internal states," and as people learn that their emotional patterns are reflected in physiological states, a potent attack by self-regulation methods on genetic defects and adverse cultural conditioning can perhaps begin. Migraine, for instance, seems to run in families and is triggered by stress, the conditioning pressure of life. The effects of training for voluntary enhancement of psychosomatic health could be far reaching in counteracting the depressing idea of impotence in handling the problems of living.

To admit the notion of *any* "voluntary" control is to acknowledge that such intangibles as idealism and conscience and "will" do play a determining role. My intention here is to resist the *total* translation of all "sins" and "crimes" into the category of symptoms. Some criminal behavior may be the result of an expression of sickness, but not all criminals are sick. Indeed, few of them are, in my experience.

To admit of voluntarism is to deny the absolute positivism espoused by B. F. Skinner, who believes that even what is apparently voluntary behavior is completely determined, i.e., "predetermined."[3]

The disciples of Skinnerism can be just as bigoted and as stubborn as the moralists and legalists who believe that everything not accidental is voluntary. The latter view makes everyone responsible for everything while the Skinnerian position discards all "responsibility" as a myth. (Its adherents are [nevertheless] forever exhorting the rest of us to *voluntarily* cast aside our ignorant superstitions and *voluntarily* concur in their views!)

Most people—including many scientists—are ambivalent, indecisive, and inconsistent about this. Some of my colleagues will reproach me for conceding any ground to either party, for the issue has long been a "hot" one in psychiatry. Those of us who pioneered in behavior research, who championed the view that misbehavior had explanations other than sheer willfulness, aggressiveness, and evil intent, who insisted, for example, that sexual activity was not something "dirty" and shameful but something physiological and natural, suffered much for our position in the early days. We were denounced as materialistic and pornographic. We were berated, threatened, vilified, scorned. We were called "radicals," "bleeding hearts," "atheists," "immoralists," "criminal coddlers," "do-gooders," and many other names.

Yet empirical studies of "cases"—problem children, adult offenders, neurotic misbehavers—yielded convincing results, and intriguing confirmations of theory. The explanations of behavior offered were plausible, intelligible, and afforded some hope for reconstructive intervention. Unfortunately, the examination of motivation and behavior control had its best public airing in the courtroom, where the ridiculous performances of psychiatrists made it newsworthy.

The law allowed the exception to its absolutistic rules and consequences in what is called "the insanity defense." An accused with adequate financial means could hire a psychiatrist to explain to the court and jury how illness had involved and obscured his will or his judgment and diminished his capacity for self-control and "responsibility." True, another psychiatrist could then be employed by the prosecution to deny what his colleague had said, deny the disease, or deny its alleged effects.

[3] B. F. Skinner, *Beyond Freedom and Dignity* (New York: Knopf, 1971).

The two scientists would appear to differ diametrically. Actually, with a little different wording, they might be substantially in agreement, but the battle over words would go on, to the mystification and disgust of the judge and jury. To the public it appeared to be the attempted substitution of a "sickness" explanation for a "wickedness" explanation; the former was usually (not always!) more palatable to the defense, the latter to the prosecutor.

Operationally the issue was whether an offender should be dealt with by scientists seeking to "cure" (at least, treat) or by jailers seeking to "punish" or at least detain. Both forms of handling are ostensibly intended to bring about a change in a dissident, and the assumption is that in certain cases this is more likely to occur with medical (psychiatric) treatment than with penal, i.e., moral, sanctions. The element of "rehabilitation" was added to the purposes of penal detention, although it was never taken seriously by the prison officials, and rarely accomplished in any offender.

But to receive treatment instead of punishment, one must exhibit or demonstrate illness. And what is the nature of that illness the symptoms of which are not the familiar ones of fever, pain, headache, paralysis, and the like? What are its manifestations and who detects and determines and defines it? This all seemed too recondite for the average person, and both judge and jury turned eagerly to hear the word from experts.

What Is Illness?

Illness can be defined in many different ways—none of them very satisfactory. Operationally it is a condition of being in an individual for which relief is customarily solicited from a member of the medical profession. But since a physician is defined as one skilled in the diagnosis and treatment of illness, our operational definition of illness as a motivating condition for going to see him tends to lead to circular thinking.

Everybody knows, or thinks he does, what an illness is. It is pain, disability, bodily deformity or disintegration. It is an adventitious state of being which impairs or hurts or threatens to destroy us. It is, indeed, a condition we hope doctors can alleviate or cure.

Two centuries ago illness was relevant in criminality only if the subject exhibited behavior resembling that of "wild beasts" or inanimate objects. The M'Naghten decision (1843), medieval and archaic as it was, constituted a lumbering forward step toward the notion that some illnesses were manifested by aberrant behavior.

Some forms of criminal behavior were so obviously connected with deranged mentality that the public identified them in everyday speech and long before either the law or medical science accorded them appropriate management. Some displayed sudden, explosive, pointless, destructive rage attacks. Mothers observed (with horror, no doubt) that a child seemed irresistibly bent on setting fires with no concern for or even knowledge of insurance fraud, vengeance, or political protest. Merchants learned that repetitious pilfering of certain unusual objects was characteristic of a few customers who had little obvious need for the stolen material (in contradistinction to run-of-the-mill shoplifters).

Consider exactly what was meant by saying that such behaviors as these were symptomatic of illness. What quality makes one instance of fire-setting or stealing really different from another? We are back again, as one can see, to the definition of illness or symptom of pathology. So let us try to pin it down.

All conditions to which the designation of illness is given (by the public, or by physicians) have this in common—that the condition is adventitious, which is to say unexpected in arrival and alien in character. It interrupts, to some extent, the ordinary, "normal" course of life. It impairs or threatens to impair comfort, effectiveness, and even life continuance. Illness is always an unwanted, feared, dreaded, detested, avoided "thing," a state of being for which palliation or removal is imperatively desired.

Illness usually makes itself known by the appearance of various supervenient phenomena called "symptoms and signs." These parts and pieces of the "clinical picture" occur singly or in clusters, sometimes consecutively, sometimes simultaneously. Some are as familiar as coughing, vomiting, and sore throat. Others are as strange as sudden blindness, sharp internal pain, localized motor paralysis. Still others are so recondite and technical in nature as to be quite unknown even by name to most people, e.g., parapraxia, eosinophilia, hypoglycemia. Most of the symptoms of psychological disorganization (mental illness) are of this latter type, although some of them, such as phobias and depression, are common knowledge and of almost universal experience.

The Functions of Symptoms

Symptoms are the unit of clinical experience. They are the basic building blocks of medical practice. Symptoms are produced and manifested in many ways—physiologically, chemically, neurally, hormonally, and psychologically. They are grouped together in many different clusters. Neither symptoms nor syndromes are synonymous with disease, but they signal its presence and make themselves a part of it. They always have several functions, *some of them useful!* A symptom is a notice of something "wrong" in the usually autonomous operation of the bodily processes, tissues, organs, and framework. It is a warning, a red flag, a message to the individual that something in his body which ordinarily operates in autonomous silence is not working properly.

If a wheel begins to squeak, experience has taught us that worse can come about unless we apply grease to the axle. The squeak is an incidental consequence of the increased friction, and has no intrinsic purpose, but it does have a meaning and a value. Symptoms have this warning value.

But symptoms also serve other functions. For example, the symptom of pain will alert attention to an inflamed joint, but it will also tend to bring about enforced rest of the impaired part, unassisted. The symptom thus becomes not only part of the affliction but part of the cure.

Again, in civilized countries the symptom is a ticket of admittance to the doctor's office, a ticket that today is usually promptly utilized and promptly honored. One may remember that in ancient days only a privileged few ever got to consult a doctor, even with most valid justification, and this after considerable delay. Sufferers sometimes waited months for attention.

Once in the doctor's office or clinic or hospital, the patient or his relatives describe to the doctor what they consider to be wrong; i.e., they describe the symptoms and their developmental history. We have learned over the centuries that there are significant sequences of pathographic events, and the doctor is attentive to the beginning of the symptom and to its evolution, the events preceding and accompanying its appearance, the changes in its character.

Along with the subjective account given by the patient and the objective accounts provided by observers, the doctor seeks visible or otherwise detectable indications of adventitious change in function or body structure, which he calls "pathology." A flushed face, an area of tenderness, an increased pulse or blood pressure, a diminished hemoglobin count, a small fluctuant tender mass are noted and compared with the patient's complaint. (These data are technically called "signs" but will be discussed here—as often—as if equivalent to symptoms.)

Symptoms (and signs) are apt to combine together in various groupings to form a *disease picture* or a *syndrome*, already mentioned. An increased body temperature, or fever, is one indication that something is wrong, but taken together with various other symptoms—let us say cough, sore throat, prostration—the picture can be identified as a familiar one, a recurrent condition which we have seen before or learned about from colleagues who have witnessed it. We know how it usually develops and involutes. We don't always know the precipitating injury or irritation or type of bacterial or viral invasion. But we say we know this disease and what to do (or not to do) about it.

Symptoms may also convey messages other than merely warnings. The symptom of blushing or flushing of the face may, for example, betray a pleasure at being looked at, embarrassment for suspected detection, anger or guilt feelings aroused, or other unspoken emotions. The heart was once considered the "seat" of our emotions, and such expressions as "heartsick," "hardhearted," "courageous," "brokenhearted," and "chickenhearted" are derivatives of this association.

Centuries ago, in the course of discussing a condition he considered to be mental disease(!), Avicenna, a famous philosopher and physician of Persia, used these words to describe being in love: "It is possible, even though the patient may deny his feelings, to identify the person loved, and to base on this knowledge a mode of treatment. The method consists in repeating certain names while the patient's pulse is being read. As soon as the pulse shows any irregularity, the trial [test] is stopped and one begins again. I have tried this method more than once, and discovered through its use the name of the person loved by the patient."

My brother Will and I cited this case and reported several others in which the symptoms of cardiac distress were actually also expressions of great emotional conflict based on other anxieties.[4] They were overt messages of confession, or perhaps we should say of the feeling of need for an opportunity to confess.

For example, one patient, long a cardiac invalid living in dread of recurring anginal seizures, reluctantly revealed that he had long been subject to secret homosexual temptations, which rushed upon him unexpectedly and gave rise to great conflict and terror lest he yield to them and be forever damned. His confession and subsequent rational discussions of the matter led to a better understanding and control of his feelings, whereupon the heart symptoms almost entirely disappeared. Here, then, symptoms were clearly a substitute for sin, or crime—as he saw it.

"Twenty Million 'Cardiacs' Without Heart Disease" read the headlines of an article from a talk by Frederick A. Whitehouse.[5] For twelve years Dr. Whitehouse was director of rehabilitation for the American Heart Association. He called heart trouble "the world's most useful neurosis, the most useful, flexible, socially acceptable, mentally justifiable, physiologically demonstrative, interpersonally appealing and controlling neurotic mechanism available to human beings."

Heart trouble is often misdiagnosed for a number of obvious reasons, said Whitehouse. One is the fear of being professionally embarrassed by a mistake. "The physician can't tell a patient he does not have heart disease, have him return joyfully to his family —and drop dead the next day. So he plays it safe by reducing the chance." Some patients who fail to seduce one physician into authenticating their heart trouble continue on their way until they ensnare another with an "awe-inspiring display of symptoms" to make the pronouncement. After that they are certified!

In addition to warnings and confessions, symptoms often tangibly express aggressive inclinations toward persons or objects, usually but not necessarily close at hand. Symptoms of many kinds can be perceptibly offensive to others in the environment. Who has not been aware of this at times in caring for a sick friend? What clergyman has not thought about it when his sermon was repeatedly interrupted by loud, hacking coughs?

[4] Karl A. Menninger and William C. Menninger, "Psychoanalytic Observation in Cardiac Disorder," *American Heart Journal*, 2:10–21 (January, 1936).

[5] *Geriatric Focus*, November, 1967.

It is just because of the ever-present—although often not recognized—aggressive function of the symptom that we physicians have to train ourselves to "be patient with patients." They are apt to be cantankerous, irritable, uncooperative, and generally disagreeable —not merely because of their illness, but as a part of it. Sometimes they feel they have a "right" to be unpleasant because they are sick and resent being so. This aggressive component of their sickness may *cause* people to have a negative attitude toward them, and this may, indeed, be the unconscious purpose of the aggressive behavior. Control and exploitation of family or relatives by the aggressive use of symptoms and illness is very familiar.

Sometimes symptoms may be not only aggressive and offensive to others, but definitely *pleasurable* to the afflicted one. And sometimes he is the only one who is unaware of this! Even painful, alarming, or crippling symptoms may have this other side.

In addition to their (secret) aggressive and/or satisfaction-giving functions, all symptoms *also* serve the function of self-administered punishment. This is usually not deliberate or even conscious any more than the aggressive and pleasurable components of the symptom are. The afflicted Job, it will be remembered, proudly asserted that he had no guilt to be assuaged.

Constructive Values of Symptoms

Not every symptom can be saddled with all of these functions —warning, immobilizing, inciting to the search for relief, confessing, defending, indulging, attacking, and provoking or enacting punishment. Some symptoms are obviously not useful warnings; some are not provocative or pleasurable or aggressive or punitive. But some of these (usually unconscious) functions are, at one time or another and in various proportions and combinations, served by every symptom. And while one swallow does not make a summer nor one symptom a disease, every illness has its symptoms and every symptom its meanings.

What "causes" symptoms? What initiates a disease process? External events and objects can impinge on the human organism in a damaging and symptom-producing way—as in the case of a broken leg, a brain tumor, the loss of a loved one. Some of the consequences of these invasions or traumata are direct mechanical changes—the loss of a body part, for example. But most symptoms are not of this nature; they are secondary, compensatory reactions which may be the only basis upon which to form a conclusion that an invasion or injury has been sustained.

The symptom of sore throat, for example, is a local reaction to a local irritation (or a systemic toxemia with local effects). The symptom is first a signal of injury and then a compensatory process of neutralizing and repairing the injury. This process of combating the irritation goes on in the tissues and in the bloodstream and on the inflamed surfaces simultaneously although imperceptibly.

For all its secondary functions listed above, the main purpose and function and meaning of the symptom—let us say of *most* symptoms—is a *constructive* one. The layman thinks of the local discomforts as being the affliction, the disease. But the symptom is itself a part of the attempted corrective process. It is a salvaging device, a readjustment process, a reparation, a lesser-of-two-evils compromise. These words all relate to a picture of organismic functioning as a balance-maintaining, system-regulating process. This is how the human organism is seen from the general-systems-theory standpoint to which more and more of us now subscribe.[6]

"All our lives long," wrote Samuel Butler close to a hundred years ago in *The Way of All Flesh,* "every day and every hour, we are engaged in the process of accommodating our changed and unchanged selves to changed and unchanged surroundings." And this process produces threats, injuries, stresses, and strains which threaten to disrupt the system and have to be dealt with—neutral-

---

[6] See Ludwig von Bertalanffy, *General Systems Theory* (New York: Braziller, 1968); Walter Buckley, ed., *Modern Systems Research for the Behavioral Scientist* (Chicago: Aldine, 1968); George L. Engel, "A Unified Concept of Health and Disease," *Perspectives in Biology and Medicine*, 3:459–485 (1960); Graydon L. Freeman, *The Energetics of Human Behavior* (Ithaca, N.Y.: Cornell University, 1948); Roy R. Grinker, ed., *Toward a Unified Theory of Human Behavior*, 2d ed. (New York: Basic Books, 1967); William Gray, et al., eds., *General Systems Theory and Psychiatry* (Boston: Little, Brown, 1969); George J. Klir, ed., *Trends in General Systems Theory* (New York: Wiley, 1972); Karl Menninger, et al., *The Vital Balance* (New York: Viking, 1963); James Miller, "Living Systems: Basic Concepts," *Behavioral Science*, 10:193–237 (1965), and "Toward a General Theory for the Behavioral Sciences," *American Psychologist*, 10:513–531 (1955); Emanuel Peterfreund, *Information, Systems, and Psychoanalysis*, Psychological Issues Monograph 25/26 (New York: Basic Books, 1971).

ized, counteracted, called off, or otherwise absolved into the system. What we call the "symptom" and the "disease" are usually only the evidence that the stresses and strains set up by an injury are being dealt with and controlled. This process, as I said before, may be a very expensive one, or it may be quiet and inconspicuous and economical.

Long ago (three years before I was born!) my father, Dr. C. F. Menninger, was intrigued with this view and described it in eloquent words which I am proud to quote because they supplement the description of the process as seen from this standpoint, which we have thought was so new!

"Life in all of its forms, physical and mental, morbid and healthy, is a relation; its phenomena result from the reciprocal action of an individual organism and of external forces. Health is the consequence and the evidence of a successful adaptation to the conditions of existence . . . while disease marks a failure in organic adaptation and leads to disorder, decay and death." (Note that the author says that disease *marks* this failure; he does not say it *causes* this failure or causes death. It is an expression of the battle going on furiously, and we know that the battle may be lost.)

"The harmonious relation existing between the organism and its environment, which is the condition of health, may be disturbed. . . . Great mistakes are often made, even by men of culture, in fixing upon supposed causes of disease in particular cases. A single event is selected as in itself effective to explain the whole disaster, when that event alone was merely one of a whole train of causes. A series of external events in concurrence with steadily operating conditions within—but not a single event—an accident, a sorrow, or need, or adversity—can all be regarded as adequate cause for insanity. . . ." And, indeed, for most of what we call disease.

Let me restate it. Each individual exists in a complicated balanced relationship with other persons and things externally, and with intricate parts of himself within. These internal and external parts also attempt to maintain *their* internal and external balances, with constantly changing relationships. Stresses of various kinds bear upon and develop within all of them. All of us make the best possible adaptations to the mishmash of biological and social existence by constantly rearranging ourselves, externally and internally

—and sometimes rearranging someone else! Externally we make friend and foe; we give and take; we approach and retreat. Internally, the many interacting parts and processes of the human organism try to adapt themselves to the outside situations and events and to the other internal parts and maintain a fluctuating balance.

All these complicated processes go on under a certain optimal tension or "stress." Understress results in a slowdown or retreat. Overstress results in a temporary speedup, even a sally forth. If the overstress increases, emergency compensatory measures get called upon to correct the tendency to extreme imbalance. This prevents the threatened annihilation. The sacrifices made to avoid this are always as conservative as possible, but the stakes (or rather, the penalties, the dangers) are very high, and hence the sacrifice may have to be considerable.

What we call illness and what we call crime are often just these sacrifices. As such, then, they are not the unmitigated evils they seem but actually life savers. Many a crime is committed to avoid committing suicide; many a theft is a substitute for mayhem.

The incessant urge to make the best of a bad bargain leads to many a choice of the lesser evil. The choice may seem unwise to the outside view, but each man does the best he can with what he has and what he perceives and what he knows *at that moment.* Murder *is* (for the ego) less destructive than being murdered; slander or mayhem is less destructive than murder. Back of any violent act is the overstressed, overburdened ego struggling to cope with a complex and changing world, making many decisions under many pressures.

This is well stated in a verse written by a colleague[7] of mine during a seminar which he entitled "Apology For Murder":

> You came near as I was falling
> And I—threw you down to right
> Myself. I threw too hard. Now,
> I have you on my conscience
> As a counterweight.

The automatic salvaging process can, of course, be overwhelmed. If the tension and disorganization become too great, the pain will be unbearable, and functioning seriously impaired. On the other hand,

[7] William R. Boniface, M.D., of Cincinnati.

if inner tension becomes too low, growth and adaptation become sluggish and the organism succumbs in another and more terrible way. Even the most "normal"[8] individual has his limits of tolerance, his unexpected and disturbing encounters, his hard-to-bear disappointments, and his inconsolable griefs. As John Cowper Powys wrote: "even the toughest and strongest among us may be sent howling to a suicidal collapse."[9]

Emergency Coping Devices

The emergency readjustments which are made in an effort to maintain the integrity of the organism can be arranged according to their "expensiveness," in a sequence from the least "costly" ones considered "normal" to the very "abnormal" and extremely costly ones. The various coping devices used in everyday living, the *normal* processes of increased tension relief, are such things as resting, talking things out with people, thinking about a problem, having a cup of coffee, or listening to a symphony. There are scores of these ways of living and getting along, variously elected and used by different people as their life styles.

Because it ties in with our topic of sin, I would like to cite one of these coping devices which in my childhood, and for centuries prior to that, was looked upon in many circles as an unqualified sin, even a crime. Swearing is a form of behavior interdicted since the days of the Ten Commandments, yet it may serve the same useful purpose as laughing and crying, which are such obvious and effective reliefs and correctives.

Swearing is a tension-relieving device easily and often abused. If it becomes a habit, it loses its usefulness as an escape-valve device and may even become a symptom[10] (if not also a sin!).

[8] A "normal" person will possess a relatively healthy and intact ego, one whose "elasticity" is not reduced too much by scars and weaknesses and tender spots and blind spots. Such an ego will have established a system of relationships with love objects, a network of intercommunication, a program of work satisfactions and play satisfactions. He will have learned to channel his aggressiveness in the least harmful directions and toward the most suitable objects. He will have found ways to be creative within the limits of his talents. He will have developed a love-and-let-love attitude toward the world.

[9] John Cowper Powys, *The Meaning of Culture* (New York: Norton, 1929).

[10] Raymond Hollander, "Compulsive Cursing," *Psychiat. Quart.*, 34:599–622 (1960).

The great English neurologist Hughlings Jackson said oaths and ejaculations in general were all parts of emotional language which, when uttered by healthy people, restored equilibrium to a greatly disturbed nervous system. He quoted the following passage from an unsigned review:

> The value of swearing as a safety-valve to the feelings, and substitute to aggressive muscular action, in accordance with the well-known law of the transmutation of forces, is not sufficiently dwelt on. Thus the reflex effect of treading on a man's corn may either be an oath or a blow, sometimes both together. The Scotch minister's man had mastered that bit of brain physiology when he whispered to his master, who was in great distress of things going wrong: "Wad na an aith relieve ya?"[11]

"Swearing is like pimples," wrote Barbellion, "better to come out; cleanses the moral system. The person who controls himself must have lots of terrible oaths circulating in his blood. Swearing is not the only remedy. I suppose you prefer the gilded pill of a curate's sermon; I prefer pimples to pills."[12]

And Laurence Sterne:

> "Small curses . . . upon great occasions," quoth my father . . . "are but so much waste of our strength and soul's health to no manner of purpose." "I own it," replied Dr. Slop. "They are like sparrow-shot," quoth my Uncle Toby (suspending his whistling), "fired against a bastion." "They serve," continued my father, "to stir the humours, but carry off none of their acrimony; for my own part, I seldom swear or curse at all—I hold it bad, but if I fall into it by surprise I generally retain so much presence of mind . . . as to make it answer my purpose, this is, I swear on till I find myself easy."[13]

Except in children, and in excess, swearing like the other common coping devices of everyday life was not regarded as a *symptom*, since it is usually not indicative of anything wrong with the organism requiring medical attention. But all these minor devices

---

[11] Erwin Stengel, "Hughlings Jackson's Influence in Psychiatry," *Brit. J. Psychiat.*, 109:348–355 (1963).

[12] W. N. P. Barbellion, *The Journal of a Disappointed Man* (New York: Doran, 1919).

[13] Laurence Sterne, *Life and Opinions of Tristram Shandy, Gentleman* (New York: Boni and Liveright, 1925).

are indications that what *threatens* to become something wrong is being—for the time—adequately taken care of and the tension is probably returning to more comfortable if not optimum levels.

But worse things may ensue. Storms may blow in, accidents and incidents occur, injuries be sustained, threats made. Just the repetition of minor irritations and frustrations may be cumulative in their effects to a disturbing degree. The tension level may begin to rise again, imperceptibly at first. We have all experienced days when we don't feel quite right, not up to par, mildly uncomfortable and uneasy. This is rarely an indication of gross disorder; these are usually temporary derangements and rearrangements within one of the many systems of the organism. But they can, of course, get worse.

When the normal devices for tension management are not adequate to handle the stresses which develop or accumulate in our daily routines of life, there is a series of increasingly powerful emergency measures available which are automatically employed by the organism. Many of these are somatic, and if they become visible as "symptoms" they lead to medical attention and repair. But they may also be psychological symptoms.

One man reacts to increased tension with a headache, another with high blood pressure, and still another with sleeplessness, irritability, and depression. On an empirical basis, these psychological reactions to overstress, these automatic emergency management devices, can be grouped into five levels[14] or degrees of severity. They are all *symptoms* or groups of symptoms. Some of them are certainly *crimes* (as well), and many of us would opt for calling some of them sins.

It would take too long to list all of them, for they are many. They include such things as anger (one of the cardinal sins of old, you may remember) and depression, anxiety, and excessive daydreaming. They include phobias and delusions and hallucinations. But they also include the bad judgment of drunken driving and the incorrigible impulsivity of child-beating, and the distress and pain of stomach ulcers. They include kleptomania and obesity; they include bizarre sexual activities of various kinds; they include drug addiction and self-mutilation and check forging and convulsions— these, and many more.

[14] See Karl Menninger, *The Vital Balance,* op. cit.

Some might consider, as I just mentioned, that some of these coping devices are properly classified as sins. They are aggressive, expensive, unpleasant, hurtful, even obnoxious, but *they are all to some degree lifesavers* for the actor! Whether sin or crime or symptom, every one of these devices represents *an automatically* chosen lesser evil, and an attempt to make the best bargain possible. Given the experiences of the particular individual, the set of psychological structures in his personality, the environmental situation as he perceives it, the stresses felt and the choices open to him, his strange act seemed to him "a good thing at the time"—indeed the only right thing at the time. But *most* of these compromises and decisions are made without much involvement of consciousness or reason.

Motivation, we have said, is never simple, clear, and direct—and never entirely conscious or unconscious. Self-preservation is everybody's motive every minute, all the time, but so is a trend toward self-destruction. These two drives are in constant operation and opposition. Because of them we are constantly and continuously trying both to self-destroy and to self-preserve, to stay alive in spite of ourselves. Each of us develops a life style which is an accumulation of little patterns fitting into a big pattern, but all directed toward a solution to this continuous conflict, and its fluctuating tensions.[15]

Summary

What I have tried to say in this chapter is this: To stay alive in this hectic world, every individual is constantly calling upon resources to cope with stress and overstress, internal and external. Constantly exchanging with his environment, he tries to make the best bargain possible with it, with its threats and demands and opportunities and dangers. Most of the time most people do fairly well—with a little "sinning" here and there, a few symptoms now and then, a minor concealed crime, perhaps—a good deal of worry and fear and regret and wistful hope for smoother waters. Minor surges of stress are handled and we manage to survive.

But overstresses come to all of us, from accidents, deaths, injuries,

[15] See Karl Menninger, *The Vital Balance, op. cit.*; and Karl Menninger, *Man Against Himself* (New York: Harcourt, Brace, 1938).

great disappointments, surprises, mistakes, and other uncontrollable events and from our own deep self-destructive and self-punishing tendencies. These overstresses may exceed ordinary controls and threaten to upset the internal balances.

This situation evokes emergency coping measures with which we survive and go on, but with a limp. We are seen by our neighbors as lame, "nervous," unpleasant, aggressive, impulsive, peculiar, withdrawn, or rude. We may (or we may not) be regarded (or regard ourselves) as sick or as sinful. Our flounderings may even come under the banner of crime.

Usually we right ourselves before we get into more complications —but sometimes a misstep occurs and we are caught in a trap, a feud, a resignation, a commitment, an arrest. Then we may be fortunate enough to get an assist from a friend or pastor or physician who helps to reduce the tensions by his love or his wisdom or his technical devices.

What the manifestations of the imbalances are *called* determines which type of help the sufferer receives—medical, legal, social, pastoral. Some behavior once called "crime" has been relabeled "illness." Some "sins" which never became proscribed by law and labeled "crimes," are also regarded now as symptomatic.

7

Sin as Collective
Irresponsibility

There is yet one other way in which acknowledgment of personal responsibility for wrongdoing eludes our attention and seems to make sin disappear.

Once the population of the earth was such that there was still ample room for individuality for all the millions of diverse groups and communities of people scattered over the face of the earth. Individuals presumably had latitude for self-expression within the confines and sanctions of the groups in which they had a loose membership. "Rugged individualism" began to be described admiringly just at the time when the organization of society made it increasingly difficult to assert.

This is one way to look at it. Historians do not all agree. Some—for example, Jacob Burckhardt[1]—felt that only in the Renaissance did the individual emerge as such, and then gained leeway to express himself uniquely. In primitive cultures the restrictions and demands of taboo are very strong and conformity to tribal norms is strongly enforced.

At any rate, there can be no doubt that the multiplication of human beings on the earth resulted in a multiplication of groups and subgroups with a corresponding restriction of individuality. As society has grown in size, it has grown in complexity of organization. Persons tend to become the people. Multiple dwellings replaced single-family homes; groups and groups of groups absorbed individuals in work and in play. Villages became towns; towns became cities (or disappeared); cities became metropolises.

[1] Jacob Burckhardt, *Civilization of the Renaissance in Italy* (New York: Macmillan, 1908).

94

Defined by language affiliation, geography, food accessibility, and no doubt many other factors, grouping became organized and consolidated. Within nations, states, counties, clubs, associations, societies, universities, parties, institutes, corporations, unions, and fraternities have evolved and thrived; some of these have grown larger, split up, and gone on growing and multiplying. Facilitated by improved transportation and communication, the multiplication of political, social, economic, and scientific clusters of human beings has proceeded with a speed and complexity comparable to that of the population explosion.

The Group vs. the Individual

All of this we know well enough, but we seldom think about its consequences with respect to moral standards. If a group of people can be made to share the responsibility for what would be a sin if an individual did it, the load of guilt rapidly lifts from the shoulders of all concerned. Others may accuse, but the guilt shared by the many evaporates for the individual. Time passes. Memories fade. Perhaps there is a record, somewhere; but who reads it?

Groups are not formed solely for avoiding responsibility. They exist for giving and receiving information, education, enjoyment, assistance of various kinds, or for fighting against other groups or against individuals. They are organized for good deeds and for evil deeds. And the deeds may reflect credit or blame on the individual members of the group, but with considerable dilution.

Some groups aim primarily at self-benefit—both of the group and of all its members. Others aim just as steadfastly at achieving benefit for others. They may or may not be legally incorporated—for profit or not for profit. But whatever the purpose of the group, its methods of thinking and planning are similar because they involve the cooperative endeavor of several people acting to direct other people. This makes a group within a group.

Professor Irving Janis of Yale University coined the word "groupthink" for a kind of self-deception that groups of people working together fall into under the shadow of the sin of group pride, discussed in Chapter 3. The desperate drive for consensus at any cost suppresses honest discussion among the mighty in the corridors of power. Janis uses as examples some of the blunders in the Presidential office, particularly the Bay of Pigs invasion.

"How could we have been so stupid?" President Kennedy is said to have asked.

Professor Janis attempts to answer this question. In spite of all the advantages of group decisions which are extolled by so many, there is also the great danger that group thinking can produce prodigious blunders that any individual member might have avoided.

Symptoms of Groupthink

Janis believes that general agreement becomes so important that it tends to override the realistic appraisal of alternatives. He lists some of the symptoms of groupthink in his study of high-level governmental decision makers. Prime among these is the sharing of an illusion of invulnerability which leads to overoptimism and causes planners to fail to respond to clear warnings of danger and to be willing to take extraordinary risks. *Secondly,* the participants in groupthink ignore warnings and construct rationalizations in order to discount them. *Third,* victims of groupthink have an unquestioned belief in the inherent morality of their ingroup actions, inclining the members to ignore the ethical or moral consequences of their decisions.

Fourth, victims of groupthink hold stereotyped views of the leaders of enemy groups. They are seen as so evil that there is no warrant for arbitration or negotiation or as too weak or too stupid to put up an effective defense. *Fifth,* victims of groupthink, says Janis, apply direct pressure on any individual who momentarily expresses doubts about any of the group's shared illusions, or questions the validity of the arguments.

Sixth, unanimity becomes an idol. Victims of groupthink avoid deviating from what appears to be the group consensus; they keep silent about their misgivings and even minimize to themselves the importance of their doubts.

Victims of groupthink sometimes appoint themselves as "mindguards" to protect the leader and fellow members from adverse information. Janis quotes Robert Kennedy as having taken one of the members of the group aside and told him, "You may be right or you may be wrong, but the President has made his mind up. Don't push it any further. Now is the time for everyone to help him all they can."[2]

Janis also lists some of the symptoms of the resulting inadequacy of problem-solving. Among these are the limitation of discussion to only a few alternative courses of action, the failure to reexamine some of the initially preferred and now discarded courses of action, and the failure to seek information from experts within the same organization who could supply more precise estimates of possible losses and gains from alternate courses of action.

The tendency of groups to split into subgroups and sub-sub-groups, to form new "tribes" and new nations, reflects some of the characteristics of primitive tribalism. The lingual separatism in Quebec, the black nationalism (and antiblack attitudes) in America, the tribal revivals in Croatia and Yugoslavia, the chronic feudings in North Ireland, the various splits and fighting in India and Pakistan, Biharis harassed by Bengalis, the destructive quarreling of the already beset and belabored American Indian—these are only a few of the well-known contemporary splits. The vicissitudes of denomi-nationalism in the Protestant church are only too well known.

"Civilization is developing into a multitude of micro-societies springing up within the productive and distributive frameworks, where each cell, sect, clan, or fraternity attracts its members on the basis of specific but varying criteria pertaining to lifestyles, taste, beliefs and customs."[3] The hippies, Quakers, street people, gay people, John Birchers, Chicanos, Young Republicans, Irish Americans, and a thousand others are such groups.

This splitting into smaller and smaller groups may be a constructive or a destructive process; it may reduce internal tensions—or it may increase them. Unspeakable and unforgivable as was the treatment of the American Indians by the people of this country, it must also be conceded that in nation after nation, in tribe after tribe, internal dissensions greatly weakened the tribes' resistance to

[2] Reference for above material is Irving L. Janis, "Groupthink," *Psychology Today,* 5:43 (November, 1971), and Nevitt Sanford and Craig Comstock, *Sanctions for Evil* (San Francisco: Jossey-Bass, 1971).

[3] Romain Gary, *The Nation,* January 10, 1972, p. 36, quoting from *The Guardian* (London), December 18, 1971, p. 12.

external pressures and attacks. The collapse of the 6,000,000 (perhaps many more) Incas before a handful of Spanish conquistadors has been attributed in large part to the civil war and internal dissensions among them which just preceded the arrival of the Spanish.[4] The lamentable removal of the Cherokee Indians from the Great Smoky Mountains along the Trail of Tears could not have been accomplished if it had not been for the schism within the tribe.

In this respect, the Indians were (and are) no exception to all groups, and intergroup hostility and competition and realignment and coalescence are in the very nature of social dynamics. In all this a certain code of morality prevails. What a group decides to be right is right for its members. Another group may be in agreement or may hold to notions quite the contrary. But "might" decides. So "divide and conquer!"

Group Guilt

For a time the guilt of a group for aggressive action toward another group is painfully shared by all. But it passes quickly. Do the Campbells still deplore their massacre of the McDonalds in Glencoe? Have the people of Spain today any sense of guilt for the Inquisition? "Our overzealous ancestors," they sigh, if reminded. The people of France do no penance for their massacre of the Huguenots. "A sad blunder, which took from us some of the glamour and brains of France." The Germans may soon have forgotten Auschwitz and Buchenwald in spite of the pensions paid and the memorials erected. "Our misguided forebears!"

The people of the United States have almost no sense of guilt for the enslavement of blacks, the mass murder of Indians, the dislodging of the Cherokees, the lynching of blacks, the exploitation of labor, or the theft of the Southwest from Mexico. "Those were rough, impetuous days," we explain. "So romantic! Picturesque but rugged. Our individualist ancestors had to win. Conquer the wilder-

---

[4] G. R. Wiley, *An Introduction to American Archeology*, vol. II (Englewood Cliffs, N.J.: Prentice-Hall, 1971), p. 3; also E. P. Lanning, *Peru Before the Incas* (Englewood Cliffs, N.J.: Prentice-Hall, 1967).

ness, break out the prairie and win the West." And dare we mention Hiroshima?

The bombings of Japanese, Germans, and Vietnamese have their defenders. "Other Americans have condemned these actions and have worked to make America in many ways a humane society. But just as the army has not established an effective sanction system which would prevent My Lai and the many small My Lais that take place every day, so more generally in America we have not been able to establish effective controls over aggression against a variety of powerless out-groups."[5]

Genocide is a word much used since the campaigns of the Turks against the Armenians, the Russians against the Ukrainians, the Nazi regime against the Jews, and, more recently, the West Pakistanis against their relatives in the east. Of course these national massacres have occurred all through history, but the ones mentioned were actually witnessed, at a distance, by many of us still living.

Only a little earlier we Americans had a big and active part in it. In the fair, rich land of California, for example, between 1820 and 1850, our fellow citizens infected, starved, burned, hanged, raped, kidnapped, enslaved, or more usually, simply gunned down more than 100,000 inoffensive and defenseless Indians whose only crime was being where the johnny-come-latelies wanted to be. These Indians were hunted like game—male, female, adults, children. They were exterminated with incredible brutality, some of the recorded details of which are too horrible to print.[6]

Armies, of course, are groups formed with the purpose of carrying out on behalf of the larger groups the intimidation, destruction, slaughter, torture, massacre, rape, and terror desired by the individuals of the larger group. No one disputes the evilness of the dreadful acts of war, but who is guilty? Not I, I obeyed orders. Not I, I merely transmitted the orders. Not I, I issued the orders on the basis of command decisions. Not I, I was only the executive of the managerial group. Not we, we specified a general objective in keeping with the national purpose.

[5] Nevitt Sanford et al., *Sanctions for Evil* (San Francisco: Jossey-Bass, 1971), p. 185.

[6] See William E. Secrest, "Massacre," *Frontier Times*, November, 1972.

As groups multiply, the individual seems to grow less and less significant, certainly less and less clearly accountable for his actions or those of his group. The paradigm came out clearly in the Calley case referred to earlier. This man was clothed and fed and armed by the officials of one group—ourselves. He was trained and ordered to kill some unknown foreigners similarly armed and instructed. He did so, as instructed, shooting dutifully some unarmed "enemy," who were not ordinary armed warriors but helpless, hungry, beseeching women and crying children. For this, he was tried by a judge and jury of his peers, who found him guilty.

But "No! No!" screamed thousands of fellow citizens. "The verdict is unjust. He is not guilty of any wrongdoing."

The President of the United States promptly reduced Calley's relatively mild sentence. Another judge intervened and reduced it further.

> . . . Even if he is guilty . . . there were others at My Lai, others who killed and there were those who gave Calley his orders. Why should only Calley be punished? . . . and those who committed the greatest atrocity of them all—those, the Lyndon Johnsons and Richard Nixons, the Robert McNamaras and Melvin Lairds, the Dean Rusks and McGeorge Bundys and William Bundys and Henry Kissingers, the William Westmorelands and Creighton Abramses, who brought this country to this obscenity of a war, who developed the policies and the use of the weapons that have destroyed Viet Nam, that led inevitably to My Lai, that gave Calley and the other Calleys the weapons and the opportunity to vent what was in them upon the innocent, and who then sanctimoniously proclaimed their devotion to peace and democracy and freedom—will face no trial as war criminals, will face no Nuremberg for their crimes against peace and against humanity! They will go unpunished, too, and will end their careers honored and celebrated.[7]

So the crime, it seems, was only a technicality. Calley is a martyr, not a sinner.

[7] Richard Hammer, *The Court-Martial of Lt. Calley* (New York: Coward, McCann and Geoghegan, 1971), pp. 388–394. See also the long analysis of this problem in Hannah Arendt's *Eichmann in Jerusalem* (New York: Viking, 1963).

Sinner? Sin? Who mentioned sin? Whether or not the judge and jury or the clamoring public were correct in regard to the ethics of butchering civilians being a *crime*—does anyone seriously raise the issue of Calley's personal morality? A sin? Whose sin?

Lt. Calley was one of those millions of marching men equipped with killing machines and told by us to use them. He did. He herded women and children and old men into a group and mowed them down—then pushed them into a ditch. But how can this be called a sin? Not distinguished for his intelligence, good judgment, culture, kindness, or social concern, Calley was nevertheless a "good soldier," i.e., a killer who obeyed orders, not a sinner.

The Sin of War

War is surely the great, prototypical example of group sin. It is a massive, organized violation of all ethics and all laws, a purposive and sanctioned campaign of destructiveness. All behaviors ordinarily regarded as criminal and/or sinful are suddenly sanctioned— murder, mayhem, arson, robbery, deceit, trespassing, sabotage, vandalism, and cruelty. Nearly always the decision to "declare war" is made by a few persons, heavily committed to the "groupthink" just described.[8] Then it is put into effect by another larger, subordinate group, supported probably by still another large, silent group. To compensate all these, heavier taxes are levied on the total population by another small group.

The majority of the people controlled by this oligarchic decision-making subgroup rarely concur in the conviction that military action is the only or best method of obtaining a desire or of endorsing a principle. Often the majority of the people who pay for the guns, ammunition, and hired combatants do not even agree regarding the desirability of the end sought by the means which they so deplore. And as the late President Eisenhower, himself a general, solemnly declared: "Every gun that is made, every warship launched, every rocket fired signifies, in the final sense, a theft from those who hunger and are not fed, those who are cold and are not clothed."

[8] Janis, *loc. cit.*

The whole war business is a horrible, irrational, despicable business, an archaic and traditional method of deciding a disputed point, whose survival is a disgrace to and refutation of civilization. There is always talk of pride and victory—but actually there is no victory; no one ever wins in the long run. One group of fighters and its backers finally decides to quit risking, quit charging, quit dying; that its sufferings are too great to be extended. This side is then said to be defeated. But the other side has suffered, too. And the whole business is disguised in a cloak of romantic glory and sentiment which makes it palatable and even marketable, as fiction, drama, etc.,[9] and spoken of in terms of "pride" and "glory."

Most people never see the awfulness of war; they only read about it, or hear about it from reporters or survivors. War continues to be a deputized human activity; some citizens are sent out to do what the total citizenry couldn't and wouldn't do. The rest of us stand (or sit) a long ways off—and watch or listen, occasionally. And we are so accustomed to receiving reports in prosaic words, in statistics of "body count" or bombing "missions" (sic) and metaphorical phrases such as "punished," "cleaned up," "resistance met with," and "right on target" that the horror, the awfulness, the reality of the total event become totally denatured. The pain, the terror, the sorrow, the blood and filth and mud, and the loss of all that is loved are squeezed out of the reports, leaving dry husks of unassimilatable "facts" in endless heaps.

The picture of one screaming, burning child or of one half-dismembered or disemboweled woman shocks and revolts us, although we are spared the sound of the screams and groans. We are not witnesses to the brokenhearted mother's sorrow. We know nothing of the despair, the hopelessness, the loss of everything. We don't go with them into the hospitals and observe the hideous wounds, the agonizing burns, the shattered limbs. And all this is only one tiny dot on a great map of millions. It cannot be described. It cannot be grasped. It cannot be imagined.

But who is responsible for this evil? Surely it is sinful, but whose sin is it? No one wants the attribution of responsibility for this. Someone told someone to tell someone to tell someone to do so and

---

[9] See Ernest Hemingway's *A Farewell to Arms*, Stephen Crane's *The Red Badge of Courage*, and a thousand others.

so. Somebody did decide to launch it and somebody has agreed to pay for it. But who? And how did I vote?

One wonders whether the superstition that war is inevitable will ultimately disappear like the many others which have yielded to science and civilization. *Why don't we outlaw war, just as we have long since outlawed cannibalism?* How infinitely more horrible it is than cannibalism, which so shocks our sensibilities.

Can't the peoples of the world, with all our present means of communication, quietly agree to agree on this permanent taboo? Is anyone really in doubt about the suicidal course of continued military preparation and prowess? Does it move no one that Dwight Eisenhower, the most famous military general of recent times, after two terms as President of the United States, warned the people of his country against the growth of the military-industrial complex? Who is warned? Who heeds?

Sometimes I think the only completely consistently moral people are those who refuse to participate either by service or by tax revenue. Of course, that means go to jail, or to Canada. But a completely clear conscience on this topic might be worth even these sacrifices. Few of us have one.[10]

As a psychiatrist who regards clergymen as co-workers, I ask whether either their profession or mine has done all that is possible to try to change this situation, this immoral irrationality? My colleagues in Holland—psychiatrists and psychologists—became very seriously concerned about this half a century ago. They made it a matter of group discussion and reflection. The persistence of war, its vast destructiveness, its futility, its injury to the human race, its dreadful wastefulness—they reflected on these things, on the *wrongness* or *sinfulness* of war, you might say. These earnest colleagues composed a position paper which could still be a model for the entire world.

But is it? Has anyone even read it? Has it been brought up and reendorsed at any of the 51 annual meetings of the American Psychiatric Association which I have attended? No. In fact, I would scarcely know where to look for a copy of it, except that I myself

[10] The study of conscientious objectors in prison made by a colleague is highly relevant. Willard M. Gaylin, *In the Service of Their Country* (New York: Viking, 1970).

recorded portions of it in a book I wrote a third of a century ago.[11]
Some things have been quoted from this book occasionally by my
colleagues, but never, so far as I know, this forthright document of
the Dutch psychiatrists.

Freud expressed himself about war in his correspondence with
Einstein: "There is but one sure way of ending war and that is the
establishment by common consent of a central control which will
have the last word in every conflict of interests." That was long
before the United Nations; perhaps it contributed to the germ of
the idea of that great idealistic institution.

Toynbee explains war this way:

> When man got the upper hand over nonhuman nature, he took to
> worshiping his own collective power. This worship did meet man's
> need for dealing with his self-centeredness by getting out of himself
> but at the price of enslaving his soul by telling him to love nothing
> beyond his own tribe's power. To my mind this is an evil form of
> religion. In Christian, Jewish and Islamic terms, it is a form of
> idolatry. The transfer of man's worship from nature to his own collec-
> tive power seems to me to be a great spiritual regression. . . .
>
> Nationalism is the real religion today of a majority of people. [It]
> has been superseded only nominally by the higher religions, each
> of which aims at converting the whole of mankind to its own prescrip-
> tion for putting the individual in touch with ultimate reality. Almost
> all of us are nationalists under the skin.
>
> How can we arrive at a lasting peace? For a true and lasting peace,
> a religious revolution is, I am sure, a *sine qua non*. By religion, I
> mean the overcoming of self-centeredness, in both individuals and
> communities, by getting into communion with the spiritual presence
> behind the universe and by bringing our wills into harmony with it.
> I think this is the only key to peace, but we are very far from picking
> up this key and using it, and, until we do, the survival of the human
> race will continue to be in doubt.[12]

But has any alternative or better idea been offered by psychiatrists? Psychologists? Neurologists? Other doctors? Other behavior
scientists? With the aid of television and other new devices for pub-

[11] Karl Menninger, *Man Against Himself* (New York: Harcourt, Brace, 1938),
p. 466.

[12] Arnold Toynbee, "Is Religion Superfluous?" *Intellectual Digest*, December, 1971,
p. 60.

lic information, have we proposed a solution or taken a stand? Have we urged any recommendations? Or are we leaving this entirely to politicians with whom, of course, we are too dignified to have any truck. We deign to study violence in many forms and make all sorts of reports and analyses and recommendations. Why not about war?

I am trying to make the point that perhaps our neglect, as scientists, of intensive, concerned study of this great social evil may itself be a plain, unvarnished group sin, a sin of ours; a sin of omission in which each individual has his share of responsibility. One of us (not a psychiatrist) has said:

> We professors of science and technology are given to wringing our hands about the carelessness with which "someone else" has allowed these things to happen. I think that we, perhaps more than anyone else, are to blame for the mindlessness of a runaway technology. . . .
>
> . . . I have heard that at the University of Zagreb, in Yugoslavia, it is now required that each student take an oath when he graduates. I do not know the exact wording, but it is something like: "I will use the knowledge I have gained only for the benefit of mankind, and never for any harmful purposes." The ceremony of taking such an oath by scientists and engineers (perhaps by all university graduates) is only a symbolic act, but it means that each student will have to give this problem a little thought, at least once before he leaves school.[13]

The case of the war hero Claude Eatherly shatters the myth that the brave soldier who does his duty will feel no guilt. He was one of the American pilots who took part in the bombing of Hiroshima and Nagasaki. Upon his return to the United States, the military authorities wanted to make a "national hero" of him. But . . .

The story of what is behind that "but" is told by Robert Jungk in his "The Unending Nightmare of Claude Eatherly, Hiroshima Pilot," published serially in the Brussels Le Soir, February, 1961:

> Claude Eatherly came back to America a changed man. His friends could hardly recognize him. He had become taciturn and reserved, shunned the company of his fellows. He began to suffer periods of

[13] Charles Schwartz, "The Movement vs. the Establishment," The Nation, June 22, 1970, pp. 750–751.

dark depression. In 1947 he received his discharge and returned to his home in Van Alstyne, Texas, refusing the pension he was entitled to. He even wanted to send his medals back to the Pentagon but his friends prevailed upon him to refrain. They could not, however, keep him from expressing his shame and fear at the least mention of Hiroshima. To be called a "war hero" caused him to blush, turn sharply on his heels and walk away. When he was asked about Hiroshima and Nagasaki, his face worked with painful emotion. . . .

Eatherly began sending money to the mayor of Hiroshima . . . to be used for the children who had lost their parents in the explosion. He wrote a letter to the municipal council of Hiroshima recounting his part in the bombardment and explaining that it was he who had given the "go ahead" signal and therefore considered himself guilty of the destruction of Hiroshima. . . .

He wandered about the country from job to job, started to study but gave it up and took to drink and cards. Nothing could drive out his memories. The "voices" of the Hiroshima victims pursued him incessantly. He would wake up at night crying out for the burning children to be saved. Early in 1950 he tried to commit suicide. Then he decided that he must get himself punished in order to ease his conscience. If society refused to recognize him as a criminal for his part in the bombing of Hiroshima, he reasoned, he must commit some crime recognized as such in the United States. By suffering punishment for that he would expiate his real crime.[14]

Several times, then, he committed crimes and was captured, tried, convicted, sentenced, and then ordered released or sent to an asylum. He refused an offer of $100,000 for the film rights to a story of his life.

The Eatherly case illustrates how the individual caught in the command of the group and forced to commit crimes cannot escape guilt feelings. Some, perhaps, let them rest lightly on their consciences or are able to assuage them—as all of us do—by various social devices and mental tricks. We can rationalize, deny, repress, project, and do all the other human things for which Freud found names. And we can join in various celebrations of the scapegoat ritual—I am tempted to call it the scapegoat *festival* because it is done so jubilantly—which is designed to take away the sins of the world.

Slavery

One of the primary objects of war in olden times was the acquisition of slaves. One great sin thus fed another. Both were taken for granted as being among the necessary facts of life. And it is disturbing to reflect that less than three generations ago the 5,000-year-old slavery business was still "going strong."

In its eighteenth- and nineteenth-century version, whole villages of primitive, defenseless people were surrounded, seized, dragged, driven, tortured, chained, frightened, and packed together in their own vomit and excretions, kept crowded and imprisoned in the dark for weeks, then unloaded and "seasoned" (allowed to recover), auctioned off, chained up and transported again, beaten, whipped, kicked, cursed, prodded, burned, starved, overworked, dehumanized, terrorized, demoralized, romanticized, corrupted, and killed. This was standard operating procedure. This was the business. And these were human beings!

They were sold and resold to great men and small, churches and churchmen, priests and nuns, farmers, cotton growers, gamblers, criminals, good men and bad—anyone with the price! Not a few dozen; thousands! Can you believe it?

It was no one man's sin; it was not even a group action! It was "everybody." Well, nearly everybody. (Actually it is estimated that only a small percentage of the citizens of the southern states owned slaves. But the nonowners, although in the majority, supported the system.)

Terrible, you say, but it all happened a long time ago. We punished ourselves for that. We know better now.

But do we? Less than one life span ago, 6 million unoffending people were rounded up like cattle, pushed into boxcars and shipped off to be systematically worked, starved, and tortured to death, in one of the most educated, civilized, and Christianized nations on earth. Possible? Various forms of slavery continue in many less-civilized countries to the present day.

The great sin of it was not the buying and working and beating of slaves. It was the right of man to exercise ownership and complete power over a fellowman.

The wish to wield absolute power over fellowmen and become absolutely corrupt in doing so is by no means limited to hard-boiled plantation overseers, cruel Nazi storm troopers, and old-fashioned penitentiary wardens. There are people all about us— people we all know, friends of ours, indeed—who "love it, God forgive me, *love* it" (to paraphrase a line from a recent movie in which an arrogant, tough-minded, tough-talking army general is gazing on a vast expanse of ghastly, human slaughter).

Indeed, one of the deceptive illusions about sin is the fact that even the worst sinners are often such "nice people." Well, after all, sinners are *us*, and in most things we do try to be "nice."

"Wherever I move in society," comments Ronald Sampson, "be it among teachers, soldiers, churchmen, criminals, housewives, police-men, workmen, politicians, foreigners, doctors, I have never met anyone who struck me as essentially an evil man. Men who were weak and pompous, who dissembled and were evasive, who were self-important, vain and ambitious, who were self-contradictory, self-deceiving, unreliable, acquisitive—these I have met in plenty at every level of society; but nowhere was it my misfortune to find an unmistakably evil man."[15]

Yes, nice people ran and used and profited from the slavery racket;[16] nice people bought slaves and whipped them and exploited them; nice people operate the migrant labor slavery. Nice people build those monstrous plants that belch black, defiling smoke into the formerly clear air of Arizona, where many of our Indian captives have been corralled.

The attempt to reconcile the beliefs of Christians with acts of war and slavery was taken seriously by early theologians who tried to substitute for the goals of temporal power, glory, and aggrandize-ment, the goals of reestablished peace (St. Augustine), the defense of just causes, the vindication of social wrongs, and the resolution of disputes between sovereign powers.

The Spaniards in justifying their conquest of the Indians in the New World recorded long disputes and legal efforts to reconcile

[15] Ronald Sampson, of the University of Bristol, author of *The Psychology of Power* (New York: Pantheon, 1966).

[16] See Kenneth M. Stampp, *The Peculiar Institution* (New York: Vintage, 1965).

warfare and slavery with Christian ethics. A document drawn up in 1512 to be read to the Indians before war was launched against them informed them that the invaders' right to their islands came from God, through St. Peter, thence to the Popes, one of whom had donated to the King and Queen of Spain the isles whereon these (the natives) had been living. The authority this established, it said, was to be used to *Christianize* (*sic*) the Indians by the priests. The document seems to have been more effective in assuaging the conscience of the conquerors than in persuading the Indians.

That guilt feelings were troublesome to the priests, to royalty, and even to the soldiers, is evidenced by many statutes and records of the time. Ordinances from Philip II (1573) forbade the use of the word "conquest" in official documents and ordered the word "pacification" to be substituted.

Since the Indians did not conform peaceably in many instances, the conscience of the conquerors required more defenses. For example, Cortez explained to his soldiers that their principal motive must be "to root out idolatry and to save souls" for if the "war" were fought "with any other intent it would be unjust." (The "war" meant raiding the Indians.)

Theory about war in modern times has more and more abandoned themes of morality and justice. Thus a war may now be justified on the ground that the growing power of another nation constitutes a threat, or because of competition for territory or trade or other imperialistic motives.

Wars were fought for similar motives in the Middle Ages, and rationalized as "holy" wars by Islamic or "just" wars by Christian people. But the agonized and heated attempts in national councils in Spain to reconcile Christian theory with the facts bears witness to a troubled consciousness of duplicity and sin. One Spanish nobleman is quoted as saying that nothing is more difficult in war than to respect Christ and Mars with equal discipline.[17]

An Unsung Hero of the Cloth

That the attempts were not successful was pointed to forcefully by a Dominican friar, Antonio de Montesinos, in 1511, preaching

[17] Silvio Zavala, *New Viewpoints on the Spanish Colonization of America* (Philadelphia: University of Pennsylvania Press, 1943).

on the island of Hispaniola to the "nice people," indeed the "best people" of the first Spanish town in the New World. He roused a storm of protest with these brave, direct, memorable words:

> In order to make your sins against the Indians known to you I have come up on this pulpit, I . . . am a voice of Christ crying in the wilderness of this island, and therefore it behooves you to listen, not with careless attention, but with all your heart and senses, so that you may hear it; for this is going to be the strangest voice that ever you heard, the harshest and hardest and most awful and most dangerous that ever you expected to hear. . . . This voice says that you are in mortal sin, that you live and die in it, for the cruelty and tyranny you use in dealing with these innocent people.
>
> Tell me, by what right or justice do you keep these Indians in such a cruel and horrible servitude? On what authority have you waged a detestable war against these people, who dealt quietly and peacefully on their own land? . . . Why do you keep them so oppressed and weary, not giving them enough to eat nor taking care of them in their illness? For with the excessive work you demand of them they fall ill and die, or rather you kill them with your desire to extract and acquire gold every day. And what care do you take that they should be instructed in religion? . . . Are these not men? Have they not rational souls? Are you not bound to love them as you love yourselves? . . . Be certain that, in such a state as this, you can no more be saved than the Moors or Turks.[18]

In the anger directed against Father Antonio by the colonists, his monastery stood firmly behind him and permitted him to continue his preaching, warning the colonists that the friars would no more receive them for confession and absolution "than if they were highway robbers."

Word of this went back to the King in Spain, and eventually the courageous friars were—what do you think? Commended and thanked? No! They were rebuked and silenced for their "error, an error previously condemned by the canonists, theologians and learned men ten years before." Lewis Hanke calls Montesinos' sermon "one of the great events in the spiritual history of mankind."[19]

[18] *Ibid.*

[19] Lewis Hanke, *The Spanish Struggle for Justice in the Conquest of America* (Boston: Little, Brown, 1965).

Don't you agree? Yet how few of us even knew it was preached!

It is a curious illustration of the blindness of the conscience to some facts that while some Spaniards were supporting and some bitterly attacking the enslavement of the Indians throughout the sixteenth century, nearly a million African slaves were being sent to Latin America (partly to replace the extinguished natives!). That infamous trade increased from then until the beginning of the nineteenth century.

Bartolomé de las Casas, a theologian, at the junta at Valladolid in 1550, a generation after Montesinos, stood up bravely and denounced the inhuman, immoral torture and exploitation'of American Indians, and the Aristotelian principle by which it was justified! Indians, he told his opponent spokesman, Ginés de Sepúlveda, in their two-year debate, are truly men capable of becoming Christians. "All the peoples of the world are men," he said. Las Casas finally won the debate, but the victory came too late. Greed, sadism, opportunism, hypocrisy, and "business as usual" had established a beachhead, and Indian exploitation took over the continent.

Modern Slavery

Neglect and oppression of the poor was one of the great sins of that early, compact group, the children of Israel, for which their prophets most emphatically and repeatedly reproached them.[20] And the poor are still with us, as it was long ago predicted they would be: "The poor shall never cease out of the land" (Deut. 15:11). Surely one does not have to be a doctrinaire communist to concede that we have always oppressed them—and that we have continued the practice of slavery in disguised and attenuated forms since it was legally terminated.

We don't call it slavery anymore, but our economic system pro-

---

[20] Amos was perhaps the most specific in regard to the sins of the people for which he warned that punishment loomed. His demand for righteousness and justice implied a demand over and beyond the elimination of particular sins, but he enumerated some examples—and how modern they sound! The cruelties of war, the ostentatious affluence of the upper classes, the slave traffic, and the general harshness toward the little fellows of society—the poor, the shabby, the lowly. All of these stem from the iniquity which comes from a hard and wicked heart. (Abstracted from p. 56 of *The Symbolism of Evil* by Paul Ricoeur [New York: Harper & Row, 1967].)

duces and permits and exploits a kind of slavery, slavery of the subproletariat.[21] Fr. Paul Furfey refers by this to the poor in general and to the extremely poverty-ridden sections of the country—some of it urban and ghetto, some of it rural, some of it on the Indian reservations. There are millions of people in our rich country who go to bed hungry every night, whose lives are pinched, harsh, meager, drab, miserable, and dangerous, and who rise in the dark to drag themselves to another dreary round of arduous toil. I say it is "dangerous" because I don't think we realize how threatened poor people are by their neighbors, especially embittered, resentful, frustrated, borderline characters—nor how threatened we are by the continuation of this evil.

"Doctor Karl," said a black city official of high rank as I rode recently with him through his home neighborhood, "do you see these 'nice' urban renewal apartments? Nothing crummy about them, is there? I live in one. But in one way I'm no better off than the poorest slum dweller on the West Side. Let me tell you that every black household in this city is pervaded with terror! All the time! Most of them have guns—but little good that will do them. They are scared, scared, scared—all of them—all the time. Scared of one another, scared of gangs, scared of the police, scared of losing their jobs, scared their kids won't get home from school alive. And the poorer they are, the scareder they are." Slavery!

The recently reported life and death of Virgil White in Chicago dramatizes this area of misery, poverty, prejudice, persecution, and group warfare:

> Virgil lived in the West Side area; he was caught by a gang and killed at 18. He lived with his mother, stepfather and five brothers and sisters in a flat. His family was a progressive one and worked hard to maintain standards of civilized living.
>
> Two gangs were competing to recruit every youth on his block and to involve him in crime by intimidation and assault. The black community lives in daily terror of the gangs' extortions, violence, and victimization of their children. White parents cannot imagine the despair and fury of black mothers like Virgil's, who had struggled for years to protect her family and teach them values and standards of living.

[21] Paul Hanly Furfey, *The Respectable Murderers* (New York: Herder & Herder, 1966).

This is a kind of slavery!

To enable her children to stay at home and avoid the gangs, Virgil's mother had built in their basement a recreation room where Virgil and the others could bring their friends and give parties. Uninvited boys sometimes crashed these parties. . . .

Then it happened. Virgil was shot in the back on October 27, 1971, on the street near his home. [Ridgely Hunt: Chicago *Tribune Sunday Magazine*, January 23, 1972].

Our society is so organized that most of us don't encounter poor people except on the television screen. In his various books depicting the Mexican folk scene, Oscar Lewis has unforgettably conveyed the misery of poverty and the sufferings of the modern poor.[22] The pictures Lewis paints for us among the Mexican proletariat could be seen in various parts of our own country, in city ghettoes, in rural wastelands such as the Mississippi Delta, in Appalachian Mountain valleys. In addition, Dr. Robert Coles, one of the greatest of all American psychiatrists, has written feelingly of all these poor folk with whom he has lived and worked for a decade.[23]

The living conditions of migrant agricultural workers in numerous midwestern and southern states has been a national scandal for thirty years. Despite child labor laws, children of tender years still work in factories in these United States of America. Domestic labor achieved such a bad reputation as a form of peonage that it has become almost impossible to obtain household employees at any price. That women employees are underpaid for their services as compared with male workers in similar positions is known to everyone. The sharecropping system of the South continues to be a device for extorting labor by economic pressure.

All this we know. But, you say, we readers are not sharecrop landlords. We are not child labor employers. We are not ghetto property owners. We know there are "bad" men doing these things; we deplore it. But what can we do about it? Why, those men never

[22] Oscar Lewis, *Five Families* (New York: Basic Books, 1959); *The Children of Sanchez* (New York: Random House, 1961).

[23] See especially *Children of Crisis: A Study of Courage and Fear* (Boston: Little, Brown, 1972); *Children of Crisis: Migrants, Mountaineers and Sharecroppers* (Boston: Little, Brown, 1972); *Children of Crisis: The South Goes North* (Boston: Little, Brown, 1972); *Uprooted Children: The Early Life of Migrant Farm Workers* (New York: Harper & Row, 1971).

bring the subject up in our hearing! They seem to be nice enough when we see them. Should we denounce them and make a scene? To what end?

The Sins of the Corporation

The words of a distinguished professor in my class in economics at the University of Wisconsin, sixty years ago, come to my mind vividly. "We begin today," he said, "the study of the corporation.

> Man is created individually by God; the corporation is an individual created by man. Like a man, the corporation has a body. It has arms and legs; it has not four but thousands of members. It has a mind and purpose. It has eyes and ears and a kind of brain; it thinks and plans and remembers. And it can grow to be huge and strong. But it has no conscience!
>
> Thus the corporation never suffers from a sense of guilt. It can kill and it can be killed; it can do evil and it can do good; it can be sick, and it can die. But, on the other hand, it has no pity and, no matter what suffering or damage it causes, it suffers no remorse.

Of course, what my teacher was saying about the corporation—as I was later to discover—applies in large measure to the state, the political party, the medical society, and other organizations. In one respect my teacher overstated or actually misstated the case. All groups, even business corporations, develop, if not a conscience, at least a moral code, one usually strictly adhered to, with certain placating exceptions. But the code of one group—society or corporation—rarely conforms in all respects to that of others or to that of society at large. The result is a multiplication of conflicting codes. These presumably comply with the law. The corporation, however, may hire expensive legal talent to guide it around bothersome restraints, to show the management how they can accomplish a desired end without breaking the law.

The sin of the corporation has been analyzed by many people many times, because these sins, even when obvious, so often go for a while unchallenged and unpunished. Four times, for example, the Supreme Court has ordered the El Paso Natural Gas Company—ninth largest of U.S. corporations—to divest itself of connections which are illegal; first in 1962, then in 1964, then in 1967, and again in 1969. The Supreme Court's various orders were each printed and neatly bound in law books for future legal scholars but, as Michael Green says in an article in *The Washington Monthly*,

> . . . for all the practical effects these orders have had, the justices might as well have kept their opinions to themselves. It is now 1971 and El Paso has divested nothing. There seems to be every chance moreover that Congress will overturn the four landmark decisions and award El Paso an *ex post facto* exemption from the antitrust laws which it was held to have violated. This will elevate the gas company to a position of primacy and prestige somewhat exceeding that of the federal government and the Supreme Court.[24]

This sort of thing, declares Eugene McCarthy, is typical of the corporation in America today.

> It has developed into a separate center of power, a center of power which was never anticipated by or provided for in the Constitution, a center of power which has not been subject to the general laws dealing with business and financial practices, a center of power which gradually has taken to itself functions that go far beyond its original economic purpose.[25]

I have many folders crammed with illustrations of the absorption of guilt by the group and its evasion of responsibility for evil action. For example, the ITT scandal of 1972, involving two attorney-generals of the U.S. and officers of the Republican party organization, brought out that the ITT was an enormously large and powerful conglomerate that has "gobbled up" many smaller companies, some of them against the will of their stockholders. It apparently eludes effective prosecution for its acts by the use of various devices which look like bribery—things for which an individual could be sent to prison.

There have been numerous recent public national scandals reach-

---

[24] Michael Green, "The Unnatural Gas Case," *The Washington Monthly*, 3:49 (November, 1971).

[25] Eugene J. McCarthy, "Corporation: New Feudalism," *National Catholic Reporter*, November 5, 1971.

ing clear up to the White House, based upon "leaks" of information regarding the activities of large organizations. Some of their participating employees think or know these activities are against the public interest and are immoral if not, indeed, illegal. There is an unpleasant conflict about this dilemma in which loyalty to the community and the general public conflicts with loyalty to an employer. One must live, but one dislikes being party to a crime (or at least a sin) against society, especially his "own" society.

Naturally no company likes to think that it is being betrayed by its employees. But if large organizations are going to do things which hurt their employees' consciences and make them feel that the public is being wronged, certainly some of them will feel obliged to give the public an insight into what is happening. *Time* calls such people "whistle blowers," likened to the referees in athletic contests, and it lists a number of examples where conscientious, moral-principled employees had to speak out, even at the cost of appearing to be disloyal and losing their jobs and good reputation.[26]

True, some conscientious employees will resign and may then say what they feel, or they may keep silent. But others can't afford to resign, or believe that it solves nothing for them to do so. They will cling to their jobs if they can, and hope to find some means of bringing about a change. How grateful conscientious employees must feel for the courageous exposures by such people as Ralph Nader and others who have fought secret sins of big companies.

One case of a conscientious employee versus a conscienceless corporation was reported at length in *Harper's Magazine*.[27] The renowned B. F. Goodrich Company has a subsidiary plant which profitably manufactures wheels and brakes for airplanes. A brake was being manufactured which failed fourteen attempts to pass the required tests. Some of the testing laboratory technicians insisted that changes in design should be made rather than attempt to "pass" an inadequate model for public use.

"But what can we do about it?" asked their senior executive. "It's none of my business and it's none of yours." It was *finally* corrected, but the complaining employees were asked to resign.

[26] *Time*, April 17, 1972, pp. 85–86.
[27] Kermit Vandevier, "The Aircraft Brake Scandal," *Harper's Magazine*, April, 1972, pp. 45 ff.

What Can Be Done? By Me?

Surely these are considerations to be borne in mind by clergymen when they speak on Sunday morning. But they are no less considerations to be borne in mind by myself and my colleagues when we listen or speak to our patients on Monday morning, or when we talk to our colleagues Monday afternoon and to our social friends Monday evening, and Tuesday and Wednesday and Thursday. They must be borne in mind by every businessman. They are things that affect every one of us. To change them will cost us all, but will profit us all—and our children and grandchildren.

"Few executives can afford the luxury of a conscience," writes Dan Miller. He goes on to say:

> A business that defined right and wrong in terms that would satisfy a well-developed contemporary conscience could not survive. When the directors and managers enter the board room to debate policy, they park their private consciences outside. If they didn't they would fail in their responsibility to the company that pays them.
>
> The crucial question in board rooms today is not "Are we morally obligated to do it?" but rather "What will happen if we don't do it?" or "How will this affect the rate of return on our investment?" No company employs a vice president in charge of ethical standards, and sooner or later the conscientious executive is likely to come up against a stone wall of corporate indifference to private moral values. In the real world of today's business, he is almost surely a troubled man. And yet—.[28]

But executives *must* afford a conscience; Mr. Miller is one who does—and sets all an example.

There is always the possibility of that "saving remnant," a minority at first, perhaps a single person, turning the tide. There are always others who have conflicts about the matter and are on the verge of joining the reform. There are "good sides" to even the most resolute Philistine. That one man has conviction and conscience

[28] Dan Miller, Chicago *Daily News*, July 20, 1970, basing his comments on an essay by Albert Z. Carr, former government official, in the *Harvard Business Review*, July–August, 1970.

and courage enough to declare himself and his position is some-times enough to help others to do so who have been hesitant and silent.

Recall again, if you are discouraged, how unpopular it was early in the nineteenth century to speak against slavery or in favor of abolition, or even to be suspected of such subversive "socialistic" leanings!

Environmental Sins

The worldwide threat to the survival of human life springing from uncontrolled technology, unregulated industry, unlimited popula-tion growth, and ruthless wastage and pollution, is a moral prob-lem.[29] It goes back to our basic beliefs regarding the world and ourselves. Religion today repudiates and even challenges such once-held beliefs as that the universe exists for man's exclusive and unconditional use, that production and consumption must increase endlessly, that the earth's resources are unlimited, and that a major purpose of government is to make it easy for individuals and cor-porations to exploit the environment for the amassing of wealth and power for a few.

There are so many examples of this type of sin, and they are being so frequently and fully reported in the press, that I shall mention only a few, citing one at greater length at the end of this chapter.

A study made by Alexander Polikoff ("The Interlake Affair," *The Washington Monthly*, March, 1971) is a particularly illuminating one relating to this type of group sin:

> Frank Jacklovich was a steelworker of 29, living with his wife and three children on the Chicago side of the Calumet River. Every morning Jacklovich walked to work about 8 minutes away, crossing the river on a railroad bridge, from which he could see, quite plainly, a large pipe, over two feet in diameter, extending from the Interlake Steel Company mill and overhanging the river. He could also see, quite plainly, the steady coal-black stream which poured from the pipe and fell to the river three feet below.

[29] Scott I. Paradise, "Old Now Is Earth," *Presbyterian Life*, September 15, 1970, p. 8.

The Interlake, Inc., a steel company, owns 350 million dollars worth of property, including two plants in Chicago. It also controls Belgian, French, and German subsidiaries. In 1969, its sales were $325 million and its operating income over $42 million. Its president, the chairman of the board of directors, the general manager, and certainly some of the stockholders were presumably well aware of the fact that it was illegally poisoning the waters of Lake Michigan. But it was a single, undistinguished, unimportant employee, a modest citizen but one with a social conscience who saw his duty and did it. Mr. Jacklovich made a telephone call, not one but several, to the U.S. Coast Guard. This was in June, 1968.

One of the Guard's duties is to check on violations of the venerable Refuse Act, a criminal law passed in 1899. It responded to Jacklovich's reports, and promptly took water samples from the pipe near the bridge and delivered them to the Chicago District Office of the U.S. Army Corps of Engineers. The samples analyzed showed oil and flaked-steel particles and, since these violated the Refuse Act, the Corps passed its information on to the local official responsible for legal enforcement. Not until six months later (December, 1968) did a U.S. Attorney charge Interlake with violating the Refuse Act. The case was assigned to the Federal District Court in Chicago.

Interlake (of course) pleaded not guilty, and its lawyer Henry Pitts, first vice president of the Illinois State Bar Association and a senior partner in a large and prestigious Chicago law firm, attacked the whole idea of prosecuting Interlake. . . .

Finally, Pitts said the U.S. Attorney shouldn't be allowed to proceed against a defendant who was "all the while in compliance with the modern, up-to-date standards for water pollution control set by another arm of the government." He was referring to standards set by an agency of the State of Illinois, the Sanitary Water Board, and his argument implied that Interlake was meeting those standards. The fact was that Interlake was not. Indeed, the next year the Water Board would ask the Illinois Attorney General to sue Interlake for *not* meeting its standards.

In March, 1969, Chief Judge Edwin Robson brushed Pitts' arguments aside and ordered Interlake to go on trial on May 26, 1969. Precisely on that date, with the trial ready to go on, Interlake changed its plea to *nolo contendore*, meaning it wouldn't fight the charges but neither would it plead guilty. Interlake also filed an affidavit by

Frank Armour, its vice president of engineering, saying, yes, Interlake had discharged mill scale into the Little Calumet River from Outfall No. 18 on June 3, 1968, but that it was all an accident.

Armour said that Interlake's system removed mill scale and oil before discharging water into the river but that a drain leading to Outfall No. 18 had broken open and the break had caused the accident. The affidavit also said that the drain problem had been corrected "by reblocking the drain with a heavy steel plate sealed into place and supported by the pouring of a concrete base and providing additional bulkheading." Armour added, "This installation has corrected the problem, as evidenced by the fact that there have been no further incidents."

The affidavit also advised the court that Interlake was in the midst of a $30 million pollution abatement program, that it was the co-developer of the "pickle liquor" treatment process for handling waste acids to which President MacDonald had referred, and that Interlake was "attempting to cooperate fully with all federal, state, and local pollution control agencies."

MacDonald's speech was included as an exhibit to the affidavit, along with an Izaak Walton League citation for "great progress" in water pollution abatement which called Interlake "an outstanding example of industry in action and forward motion." Also included was a letter Interlake had received from the Cook County Clean Streams Committee. The Committee's letter said it had been "very disturbed" to read of the charges against Interlake since Interlake was "the Chicago area leader" in progress against pollution.

Pages and pages of events followed the above brief prelude. Numerous state and federal agencies became involved. More suits were brought, fought, and settled. The pollution continued. The threatened ruin of Lake Michigan continued and public alarm grew. But the case was closed. The company was found guilty and fined $500, the minimum permitted.

And what of the man of conscience—Jacklovich? Well, he was fired—of course!

It is disturbing to *me* that Lake Michigan is being polluted by a corporation that denies the crime. It harms *me* that Lake Erie has been destroyed; it was partly *my* lake. It alarms *me* that our rivers, *my* rivers, are being dammed and dredged; the smog that covers our cities impairs *my* health. Those are *our* forests and *our* wild animals which are being ruthlessly destroyed by a greedy few for the "fun" of it. *I* have an interest in these coyotes and bears that my government is taxing me to have killed by hired poisoners. And *I* have a responsibility to fight against these evil practices. Once I know of them, I may not remain silent.

Why does it take a thousand earnest news stories by alerted reporters to awaken us to the realization that the house is on fire?

Who would not be shocked by these headlines?

"WORLD OXYGEN LEVEL THREATENED BY
PESTICIDES; AIR POLLUTION WILL REQUIRE
BREATHING HELMETS BY 1985"

"NEED CITED FOR INTERNATIONAL POLLUTION
SLEUTHS"

"MILLIONS FACE THREAT OF STARVATION"

"MAY BE TOO LATE TO CONTROL POPULATION,
SCIENTIST WARNS"

"LAST POCKET OF CLEAN AIR IN UNITED STATES
DISAPPEARS"

"WORLD LOSING WATER POLLUTION BATTLE DESPITE
STEPPED-UP CONTROL EFFORTS"

"CHEMICAL FERTILIZERS CALLED THREAT TO
WATER RESOURCES"

"NIXON STARTS POLLUTION WAR; SAYS IT'S
'NOW OR NEVER'"

"WORLD FOOD SUPPLIES SEEN RUNNING OUT BY
YEAR 2000; EXPERTS SAY HUMAN RACE MAY HAVE
ONLY 35 YEARS LEFT"[30]

All this, and nobody feels guilty? No one thinks any sin was involved?

[30] "The Alternative Is Extinction," Editorial Comments, *Outdoor America*, 36:4 (March, 1971). (Excerpted from a speech delivered by Dr. Ralph A. McMullan, director of the Michigan Department of Natural Resources.)

And this is not just an American dilemma. The crisis is world-wide.

> Only 14 percent of Italy's long coastline is relatively clean. The Baltic . . . has become a cesspool. All around it the countries of Germany, Denmark, Sweden, Poland, Finland and Russia dump industrial waste and sewage. . . .[31]

It is we who are at fault—we with our greediness and our ruthlessness and rapaciousness, ignorance and indifference. People can't really believe the ship is sinking. Our incredibly self-centered notion that "man is the measure of all things" blinds us to our impending self-ruin. Forgotten is Albert Schweitzer's noble proposal of reverence for all life, or the American Indian philosophy that the earth belongs to God for all men to use, care for, and preserve.[32]

Cruelty to nature is a new concept for many people. It is customary rather to speak of the conquest of nature, the victory over the forces of the elements, the conquering of the wilderness. This process of conquest has varied from sawing down in a few minutes trees which took years to grow to tearing up the sod with a plow, a sod centuries in development that ought never to have been broken.

Some feel that the greatest mistake man has committed in his efforts to utilize nature was the tearing up and destroying of native grass and forest coverings. Others think that the destruction of wildlife (less by hunting and trapping than by poisoning and starving) has been equally disastrous. The pollution of the rivers and lakes seems to others the most awful.

No one who has lived on a farm can forget how at times the farmer feels beleaguered by drought, weeds, winds, insects, heat, cold, dust, snow, hail, and wild animals large and small. It is as if he were in a fierce war with a many-headed hydra. But it was his friend he was battling, his friend in disguise, and in his determined campaign with enlisted technology he may have gone too far.

Automobiles are said to occupy more space in America than do people! As our cities sprawl out in all directions, they swallow up a

[31] Samuel Mines, *The Last Days of Mankind, Ecological Survival or Extinction* (New York: Simon & Schuster, 1971).

[32] See Ian G. Barbous, "An Ecological Ethics," *The Christian Century*, October 7, 1970, and Frank Waters, *Book of the Hopi* (New York: Viking, 1963).

tremendous number of tillable acres. Increasingly, we are
aware of the critical scarcity of places for the disposal
The average daily waste per household amounts to 4.8
For many states refuse disposal is a major problem. Califo
example, has nearly 20 million residents. Each person throv
about 20 pounds of solid wastes a day. In one year's time this
would build a wall 100 feet wide and 30 feet high stretching all
the way from Oregon to Mexico![33]

In *Dams and Other Disasters* (Boston: Porter Sargent, 1971)
Arthur E. Morgan describes the dreadful record of ruinous projects
forced on the American public by its U.S. Army Corps of Engineers.
Their ignorance, small-mindedness, arrogance, and presumption
have produced an almost inhuman disregard of powerless people,
and their careless destruction of natural beauty are akin to this state
of mind, acquired, Morgan believes, in their militancy training for
the emergencies and ruthlessness of war, and in the rigid psychological milieu of West Point Military Academy.

Other Group Sins

The handgun scandal is another contemporary issue. In a complex civilized society containing many unstable, erratic, unpredictable individuals, it is senseless to permit everyone and anyone to
buy and retain and carry about killing machines. Of course all guns
fall into this category, but handguns are rarely used to blast animals;
they are specifically human-being killers. And which human beings?
Guns almost never protect anybody from other people's guns. They
kill many people annually. Yet any attempt to prohibit or even to
regulate them stirs up waves of noisy protest from people who have
no intention of killing anyone but who do not want the means of
doing so removed.

A curious thing about this obsession is the self-destructiveness of
it. It is a common type of self-deception to take on a danger to
combat or diminish danger. Many people start taking drugs to
avoid a feared personality disorganization, which the drugs then
induce. Cruel imprisonment to correct criminals and promote safety
only increases their resentment and desperation. Obtaining and

[33] "Environmental Crimes," *Sierra Club Bulletin*, June, 1970, p. 9.

carrying a handgun "for protection" increases the danger of personal injury by at least 1,000 percent—as has been repeatedly demonstrated statistically.

Psychoanalysts relate the intensity of this feeling for possessing a handgun to an obvious symbolic meaning of the handgun and of its loss for some men. It relates to a great, common, unconscious (i.e., forgotten) fear—the threatened removal of masculinity. American men seem to be much more fearful on this score than British, European, and Oriental men, none of whom are legally permitted to carry guns, but the difference is that for several generations in this country it has been permitted and it is the process of taking away which revives the infantile fear.

The consistent suppression and exploitation of females is another piece of group wickedness for which few individuals want to take the blame, but for which many men and many groups of men and even some women are guiltily responsible. Similar prejudices and suppression of black people, brown people, red people, yellow people, and other minorities are sins of which individuals and groups are notoriously guilty.

Where Does the Responsibility Lie?

I have endeavored in this chapter to collect examples of wrong-doings by groups for which an individual would surely be charged were they his acts alone, but for which he seemingly has no responsibility because they are sponsored or committed by a group of which he may or may not be a member.

As people have become more numerous, groups of people have also become more numerous; group activities have multiplied and group competitions have increased. We have ceased to be so completely individualistic and have joined together with others in many ways to do and to share many things, including responsibility for crime and sin.

If a group is guilty of an act that would be a crime for an individual to do, just how much blame *should* the participant individuals take upon themselves personally? If four "thugs" cooperate in a robbery or murder, all are usually accounted guilty and punished.

But suppose 400 or 4,000 persons join in the robbery, e.g., the robbery of the Hopi Indians? What then *is* the moral responsibility of the individual?

This ancient question which Thoreau dramatized so vividly has never been satisfactorily answered. The Nüremberg trials (and the more recent Calley affair) clearly pointed up the inconsistencies and ambiguities of public expressions about this dilemma.

If the group activity were a constructive one, each individual would certainly receive—at least claim—a certain amount of the benefit and also the credit. In the case of destructive acts, are only the officers guilty?

At the 1971 meeting of the Synod of (Roman Catholic) Bishops and of the National Federation of (Roman) Priests' Councils it was emphasized by Father Robert Kennedy that "no evil intention is needed for sin to exist within an institution if that institution is so structured as to bring about injustice or oppression. But is it a sin of omission if we don't take personal action to fight that injustice?"

The *National Catholic Reporter* comments that we have been so used to taking such a personal view of sin it is easy to forget that sin—and virtue (as I said above)—involves other people.[34]

The individual cannot hide from himself what he knows to be illegal or immoral actions by the group. What he can do to purge himself of the guilt will depend upon many factors, but his obligation to do *something* is clear.

But what can the *group* do, granted that it admits the wrongdoing, repents it, and desires to atone for it? Occasionally it can make some amends, usually pitifully inadequate, as Germany is now doing in regard to wronged and robbed Jewish citizens. Usually the offending group "gets off" by some bribery or lying.

With various manipulations of "the rules" it was always possible for the state or the church to steal from an individual. The Jews, the Huguenots, the Waldensians and Albigensians, the Poles, the Lithuanians and Estonians, and the Mexicans know about this, to their sorrow. And we took the Great Smoky Mountains from the Cherokees; Minnesota and the Black Hills from the Sioux; Colorado

[34] *National Catholic Reporter*, January 31, 1972, p. 10. The editor continues, at this point, thus: "Many good people, in their own spiritual cycles, have moved beyond concern for 'institutional sin' and into the charismatic of Jesus movements which often lack a 'social passion.'"

from the Utes; New Mexico, Arizona, Texas, and California from the Mexicans, the Navajo, and the Apaches.

A thousand hilarious jokes have been told around bars about clever tricks played on stupid Indians—or maybe intoxicated (poisoned) ones. All's fair in love, war, and dealing with "ignorant savages" or helpless weaker nations. It looks far more reprehensible when Russia does it, or Germany, or the (ancient) Catholic Church, or the (ancient) British Empire, but it is the same great and wicked steal.

Acknowledgment of sin is a start, but it is not enough. We all realize and deplore the fact that the automobiles we drive contribute to the smog which we and others must breathe and which we agree must be eliminated. But we drive on. We confess our participation in many of the group activities which we now agree to have been— to still be—improper ones. Some of us can confess it to a relatively large public. We can point to our collective sins, sins that are being done in our name and with our support. But, having pointed, what more can we do about it?

We may join and slightly increase the size of the "penitent portion" of the society, but what can the penitent portion do? It is a small minority, unlikely at present to change the course of the group activity. But it is growing and may become noisy enough to attract the attention and gain the support of some of the previously indifferent.

Gradual reversals may be effected in some of the self-destructive trends. This usually involves old-fashioned hard work. If we can influence enough of our neighbors, friends, and readers, some change can be accomplished. Every newspaper editor wistfully hopes he is helping to do just this. Every magazine writer on critical topics has this goal in mind. Often it remains little more than a wistful hope.

But sooner or later some of these efforts take effect. Many of us have wrung our hands and shed our tears publicly for years regarding the U.S. Government's vicious program of wildlife poisoning. Then suddenly and happily in March, 1972, President Nixon announced its termination. (Nevertheless the orgy continues at the hands of private stockmen.[35]) This was a long-worked-for but little expected and serendipitous outcome.

[35] *Time*, 1972.

Advertising, public relations work, promotion programs, daily conversation—indeed almost every form of communication—is likely to contain an element of attempted persuasion. "Can I interest you in this?" "Can I persuade you to do that?" "Can I convince you that the whole community would profit by this change?" (And can I be objective in computing whether or not the welfare of the others matters enough to me in a particular instance for me to suppress my sorrow at the personal loss it means to me?)

There is a danger in the individualization of the sense of guilt regarding group sins. Stanley Elkins, in a book on slavery, insists that a great many fervent abolitionists actually retarded the achievement of abolition by their overindividualism and their failure to get organized into an institutional force.[36] Britain had long since established abolition by totally nonviolent means. Numerous excellent proposals had been made for utilizing existing social channels to end slavery in the U.S., but these were unacceptable to the overwrought and idealistic abolitionists.

G. Clarke Chapman, Jr., suggests that it seems as true today as then that America lacks accessible institutional channels for moral energies:

> . . . our informal social fabric and our romantic notion of the individual's sovereignty over his environment combined to permit awareness of evil to arouse in the public an enormous and unmanageable sense of guilt . . . thus the perception of injustice becomes a highly personal sense of guilt which, if unrelieved, can be intolerable . . . a burst of moral energy flares up, then dissipates because it fails to achieve structure or merely proliferates ineffectual ones.[37]

These ineffectual agencies are certainly numerous and our weakness seems to lie in an inability to get them subsumed or assumed by any one strong political party. An example was the end-the-war goal in the 1972 political campaign.

Population Dyscontrol

I must add to this chapter the mention of a kind of human behavior which seems to some people to be the fullest expression of the

[36] Stanley M. Elkins, *Slavery* (Chicago: University of Chicago Press, 1968).

[37] G. Clarke Chapman, Jr., "Peaceniks, Abolitionists and the Institutional Beast," *The Christian Century*, 89:424–426 (April 12, 1972).

will of God, and to others—myself definitely included—as almost the fullest expression of the sinful, selfish will of men.

I am referring to the reckless indulgence in reproduction, bringing more and more children into an already overpopulated world where they will either tend to starve or tend to make other children starve.

Population control used to be considered a seditious and unrighteous topic, even for discussion. It has gradually become respectable, even debatable. I am so partisan in regard to it, I feel so strongly that it is a world imperative, that I dare not trust my objectivity in presenting it. Ruthlessness, indifference, lack of restraint in reproduction, or ignorance and indifference regarding its world consequences seem to me the expression of a most heinous sin.

I have made this position statement a kind of postscript because I don't know where to properly put it in this book. It belongs everywhere. More children to go hungry, to compete, to consume, to require supplies and transportation and heat and pavement, to further crowd the schools and fill the welfare lists. "Oh, but you are assuming the worst, that mere numbers. . . ." No, I'm not assuming that. I know it. And you, too, dear reader; you know where the excess births occur, and the greatest poverty, and the greatest crowding, and the most crime and ill health. You know, and you know why.

The Plight of the Indians

Throughout the Southwest the desire for electricity has continued to grow many times faster than the population. This along with smog and water shortage and city expansion made for many problems. One solution to these problems was for someone to go after the resources of the American Indians most of whom were living at a subsistence level on dry farms with a family income of under $3,000 a year and much malnutrition and alcoholism.

The Southwestern Power Companies, joining with the United States Bureau of Reclamation, developed a far-reaching plan to do this. They would strip-mine coal on the Navajo and Hopi reservations to run giant generating plants cooled with Colorado River water, and carry the power to Los Angeles and other cities over long-distance transmission lines.

America's largest strip-miner, the Peabody Coal Company, was brought in to dig up Black Mesa in the heart of Navajo and Hopi country. Peter Barnes wrote most lucidly about this in 1971.[38] "Thus far two [power plants] are completed—the Mohave plant, operated by Southern California Edison, and the Four Corners plant, operated by Arizona Public Service. [This is the one that blackens the clear skies of Arizona for hundreds of miles.] Four more are scheduled for completion by 1977, and when all six are fully operational they will emit more ash and dust than New York City. . . .

"What do the Indians get . . . ? Well, for 65,000 acres of land on Black Mesa, Peabody is paying the Navajos and Hopis $1 an acre per year. For the coal itself, from what will be the largest strip-mine in the world, Peabody is giving the Indians 25 cents a ton. (By contrast, Peabody chips in 40 cents a ton to the United Mine Workers health, welfare and pension fund.) In addition to coal, Peabody is extracting nearly a billion gallons a year of pure fossil water from thousands of feet below the surface of Black Mesa. Peabody mixes this water with pulverized coal to form slurry, which is then carried to the Mohave generating plant 275 miles away by means of a giant pipeline. For this valuable water Peabody pays the Navajos and Hopis about $20,000.

"Most interesting of all is the highly complicated shuffle by which the Navajos were coaxed into surrendering their precious Colorado River water rights in exchange for the many 'benefits' that strip-mining and power-generating will bring. Because it is the only steady source of water in a region that is essentially a desert, the Colorado is probably the most contested river in the world. Navajo rights to the Colorado date back to 1868, and thus have priority—or rather *had* priority—over most recent claims. Navajo rights were also potentially very large—equal, according to U.S. Supreme Court rulings, to the amount of water necessary to irrigate all the practicably irrigable land on the reservation. Other claimants to the Colorado's waters—and there are more claims than there is water—were understandably fearful that someday the Navajos would exercise their rights. Arizona was particularly nervous, since its plan to pump billions of gallons of Colorado water to Phoenix and Tucson

[38] Peter Barnes, "Trinkets for the Navajos; Los Angeles vs. the Indians," *The New Republic*, July 3, 1971.

hinged upon nonuse by the Navajos of their entitlements. All fears were resolved in 1968 when the Navajos were persuaded to limit their claim to 50,000 acre-feet of upper basin water, and, what was more, to give two-thirds of that to the power companies—free of charge—for cooling one of their coal-burning plants. In return for this extraordinary concession the Navajos were given Peabody's meager payments, enumerated above, a grant of $125,000 for the Navajo Community College, plus a few hundred jobs in the mines and generating plants. It was like trading away Manhattan Island for $24 worth of trinkets.

"Sadly, the Navajo leaders who agreed to the contracts felt they were acting in the best interests of the tribe. They were told by Peabody, by the power companies and by the Interior Department that nuclear energy was the coming thing, that if they ever wanted to sell their coal, they had better do so right away. They were advised to keep prices low in order to be 'competitive,' though it was not clear whom they were competing against, or why the real competition should not have been in bidding between Peabody and other coal companies. Above all, they were desperate for jobs and revenue, and felt that any deal they could get was better than nothing. They had little knowledge of the adverse effects of strip-mining or air pollution, and the Interior Department's Bureau of Indian Affairs, which is supposed to protect the Indians' interests, did nothing to enlighten them. In fact, the BIA actively encouraged Navajo leaders to accept the contracts without quibbling, perhaps because another arm of the Interior Department, the Bureau of Reclamation, would be a prime user of Black Mesa power.

"Even if the Navajos had gotten better terms for their resources, it's doubtful that strip-mining would benefit them in the long run. Peabody promises to employ about 375 persons at Black Mesa, of whom 300 or so will be Indians. But these jobs will last only until the coal is depleted in about 35 years. Meanwhile, 50 Navajo families currently sheepherding on the north rim of Black Mesa will lose their livelihoods.

"There is also great concern about the Indians' water supply. Peabody firmly insists that its slurry wells are so deep they will have no effect upon subsurface water tables. But the U.S. Geological Survey has stated that the water table north of the strip-mine may drop 100 feet over the life of Peabody's lease. And, say the

Indians, the gouging of Black Mesa has already blocked off natural springs and washes, interrupting the surface flow of water to livestock and crops.

"And after 35 years? The jobs then will be gone, leaving only empty hulks of generating plants and mountains of overturned earth as monuments to America's hunger for electricity. 'We will be like the people of Appalachia,' says Robert Salabye, a Navajo Vietnam veteran, 'where coal mines have destroyed the health of the people who worked in them, left the land scarred and the people without hope.' True economic development, many Navajos are coming to believe, would be for the tribe to develop its own resources, not give them away; to promote clean industry that is permanent, not dirty industry that exploits and ruins; to use Navajo water for irrigation, not for slurry lines or for cooling power plants that benefit cities hundreds of miles away.

"So the Navajos are in a quandary. Many tribal council members, while admitting they entered into the contracts without full knowledge, are nevertheless reluctant to back out now; they fear the loss of tribal revenue and that other corporations will not build plants on the reservation if Peabody is kicked off. A lot of younger Navajos are not so cautious. They call for lawsuits, strict regulations and other pressures that would eventually force Peabody to stop mining. Some talk of sabotage.

"Peter MacDonald, the newly-elected tribal chairman, is caught in the crossfire. MacDonald is an electronics engineer (he worked on the Polaris missile guidance system), a Republican and a believer in private enterprise. He's also a shrewd politician who takes pride in standing up for his people. Lately he has called for renegotiation of the Peabody contract and a halt on new power plant construction until adequate pollution controls can be installed, and he could go further if his constituents demand it.

"Because they will spew forth an enormous amount of pollutants, smogging not only Indian land but vast expanses of the pristine Southwest, the power plants of the Colorado plateau are fast becoming one of the hottest ecological issues since the SST. At hearings in Albuquerque last month, Senate Interior Committee chairman Henry M. Jackson (D, Wash.), who fancies himself something of an environmentalist, defined the region's task as one of reconciling the 'urgent' need for increased electric power with the equally pressing need for protecting the environment. That's not the real issue. The root problem is to decrease America's appetite for neon glitter, artificial air and electricity-devouring conveniences such as aluminum beer cans—or, if that can't be done, to arrange that those who desire electricity bear the full costs of its production. 'Why should Indians be forced to suffer the consequences of America's power madness?' asks Peterson Zah, a young Navajo legal aide. 'If the cities must have power, let them put up with the filth that their power greed produces.'"

8

The Old Seven Deadly Sins
(and Some New Ones)

We come finally to sins which are clearly and simply personal derelictions. That there are still some of these, most of us would admit. If sin has actually disappeared completely, what is it that believers confess and pray to be forgiven for each Sunday morning, or once a year at Lent and Yom Kippur? What are the trespasses that we forgive others for and for which we ourselves beg pardon? (We'll skip the nonbelievers who don't pray, for the time being—but we'll return to them.)

How quaint and puritanical it is to feel guilty about working on Sunday or for having a sexual fantasy—or, if we are Catholics, eating meat on Good Friday and, if we are Jews, eating bacon and eggs for breakfast! But still, in our minds and even in our daily speech, we constantly acknowledge that there are some important shoulds and should nots, that some acts are wrong even though they are not called crimes and are certainly not regarded as symptoms. We suspect—indeed we *know*—that there are still some plain old-fashioned homemade sins lying around which go unmarked. And for most of us, believers and nonbelievers, there is always that still small voice of our conscience.

What *is* this "sinning" that seems real in private but which gets swiftly and successfully swept under the rug in public discussion? What are those mortal sins, the classical seven of olden times, that stood firm for so many people for so many centuries? Are they gone?

What about the famous Ten Commandments? They have been a basic guide for many more centuries. We learned them by heart once. Coveting (envy) and disrespect for God and parents cer-

133

tainly remain with us. Are these not properly called instances or attitudes of sinful nature?

Envy (covetousness) was, as a matter of fact, the *first* on the list of the famous seven cardinal sins later proclaimed by the early church fathers, two millenniums after the Decalogue. Disrespect for God, for parents, for seniority and authority is a frequent part of the antinomian revolution of the present younger generation. This has been noted in other times.

> Our youth today love luxury. They have bad manners, contempt for authority, disrespect for older people. Children nowadays are tyrants. They contradict their parents, gobble their food and tyrannize their teachers.[1]

The age of the observer affects his interpretation of this social phenomenon and I cannot present it with any degree of objectivity; I will let the reader decide if it is still a "sin," and if it still abounds and increases.

The forms of sin in the traditional list of seven were envy, anger, pride, sloth, avarice, gluttony, and lust. This list varied somewhat in later patristic literature. Johannes Cassianus (360–435) added *fornication, dejection (tristitia),* and *vainglory* (instead of pride) but dropped "envy"! Gregory the Great, Pope from 590 to 604, put *pride* (hubris) at the head of the list and considered it the source of all the others (*Moralia,* XXVI, 28). His list came to prevail, with *dejection* deleted and *acedia* reinstated. Curiously—to our thinking today—none of the lists included dishonesty, vindictiveness, cruelty, bigotry, or infidelity.[2]

If we translate the official names of the cardinal sins into their approximate equivalents in modern speech, they begin to sparkle with relevance.

Remember, as we run down each of these individual acts or attitudes, which for convenience we will refer to as sins, that each is not THE sin per se, but only a form or expression of it. Sin is not against rules, but against people—and it is the "against-ness" or aggression in the intent or motivation that constitutes the designa-

---

[1] Socrates, *circa* 425 B.C. Quoted in Joel Fort, *The Pleasure Seekers* (Indianapolis: Bobbs-Merrill, 1969).

[2] See Thomas Aquinas, *Summa Theologica,* II, 2.

tion sin. The form of it varies, and we may call these forms sin, but only with literary license to facilitate the description.

Let us begin, as Gregory did, with pride.

Sin Manifested as Pride

Pride, a virtue under certain circumstances, was—and still is—considered by theologians the basic form of sin. Sensuality was (in former times) a close second.[3] Synonyms for pride are vanity, egocentricity, hubris, arrogance, self-adoration, selfishness, self-love, and narcissism; all of these are subject to contemporary condemnation. They are not called crimes or diseases (yet!) but they are disliked. All of them have an unpleasant, offensive, unsocial, self-pleasing quality, which is in striking contrast to that meaning of pride which makes it a brave and admirable virtue. I leave to the reader the pleasure of defining the distinction.

Pride is divided, theologically, into the pride of power, the pride of knowledge, and the pride of virtue. It starts out, presumably, with the Adam-old ambition to be identified with—or to become—God Himself.

"Every man would like to be God," wrote Bertrand Russell, "if it were possible; some few find it difficult to admit the impossibility."[4] The sin of pride appears most conspicuously in group pride —tribalism, nationalism, jingoism, and racism—as well as in individual pride. Reinhold Niebuhr said:

> Collective pride is . . . man's last, and in some respects most pathetic, effort to deny the determinate and contingent character of his existence: The very essence of human sin is in it. This form of human sin is also most fruitful of human guilt, that is, of objective, social and historical evil.
>
> Prophetic religion had its very inception in a conflict with national self-deification. Beginning with Amos, all the great Hebrew prophets challenged the simple identification between God and the nation, or

[3] Augustine, Luther, Pascal, Aquinas, Calvin, and others are in general agreement about this. Niebuhr says the ways in which other sins are derived from pride is seen differently by different theologians.

[4] Bertrand Russell, *Power, A New Social Analysis* (New York: Norton, 1969), p. 11.

the naive confidence of the nation in its exclusive relation to God. . . .
Judgment would overtake not only Israel but every nation, including
the great nations who were used for the moment to execute divine
judgment upon Israel but were also equally guilty of exalting themselves beyond measure (Is. 47; Jer. 25:15; Ez. 24–39).[5]

The group as a nation may identify itself or its leader with God
("pretend to be God," Niebuhr puts it). The unconditional loyalty
of all citizens is demanded in the name of public safety and personal survival. Soon the individuals have identified themselves with
the group (and thus with God) and then it is one for all, all for
one. Anything the group leaders decide to do is right.

I refrain with the greatest difficulty from suggesting any modern-
day parallels.

Returning to the individual and his sins of pride, we must recognize that self-respect, self-approval, and self-confidence are favor-
able aspects of a normal self-concern. A marked imbalance of
self-concern and others-concern is what psychoanalysis calls excessive narcissism. Arrogance, narcissism, and egocentrism are usually
symptomatic residuals of early ego injury. They serve to salve
unhealed wounds of self-esteem or persistent diffidence and fears of
contact, but the remedy can be most obnoxious to one's fellows.

Self-love, narcissism, conflicts with reason and with love of
others. We borrow from our original supply of narcissism, Freud
believed, to invest love in others, and the more we borrow or take,
the better. Some just can't bring themselves to part with the hoarded
treasure. The goal of all the great historic religions can be summarized as being the overcoming of one's self-love. This is clearly
expressed in Buddhism, which teaches that man can save himself
from suffering only by relinquishing his illusions and becoming
aware of the realities of sickness, old age, and death. Becoming
aware of these things makes it imperative to replace one's narcissism with relatedness to the world.

Infatuations and love affairs are often determined by heavy
mutual exchanges or gratifications of narcissism, which explains why
they fail as marriages. Such people do not have much real interest

---

[5] Reinhold Niebuhr, *The Nature and Destiny of Man* (New York: Scribner's, 1949).

in each other, nor in anyone else. They are apt to be touchy, suspicious, and susceptible to distraction by new objects which gratify their narcissism.[6]

To describe narcissism as a character deformity or as emotional underdevelopment is to put it in a category of clinical disability, presumably for medical mending. And if, indeed, excessive narcissism can be shown to be amenable to therapeutic effort, it may be properly denoted symptomatic, although even some psychiatrists vigorously reject the label of disease for this type of "characterological defect." But this does not prevent its being considered also a moral dereliction, a form of sin. It could be both. Seen as sin, this type of behavior and characterology can be altered by a corrective process other than clinical, one *not* called therapeutic. Character revision is not the private domain of any single professional discipline.

Personal self-deification is common enough all around us. Various motivations are ascribed to ubiquitous forms of this sin, which a thousand kings and presidents and board chairmen and business executives have emulated, consciously or unconsciously. The lure of the God role would seem to stem chiefly from power lust, but there is often a conscious narcissistic element in it.

I have a friend who has a friend whom he describes as being on the way to becoming God. He was always energetic. He excelled in almost every sport in college. He strove most vigorously to win every game he played at all costs to himself.

He learned to pilot his own plane. Although he is a lawyer by training, he built or acquired several businesses. He has a large apartment in the city and a regal office from which he is constantly striving to control everything and everybody. For summer diversion, he has a thirty-room mansion in the country.

I should say, he is *going to have* a thirty-room house, because it is not yet completed. He is building it himself! He is an expert on gadgetry and electronics and hi-fi; the electrical gimmicks strung through the house number in the hundreds. He has installed elaborate safety devices throughout. There are many extra closets because he cannot bring himself to give away any of his possessions.

[6] See Erich Fromm, "Individual and Social Narcissism," in William A. Sadler, Jr., ed., *Personality and Religion* (New York: Harper & Row, 1970), pp. 129–130.

All his clothes must be kept, stored, inventoried. He keeps in telephone communication with all of his associates so that he can feel that everything is strictly controlled at all times. This extends to his wife and children.

Such a lust for power and possession and production need not condemn a man; indeed, many might regard this chap as a model of successful achievement. Many of my colleagues would suspect him of dangerously intense feelings of insecurity. Whatever his psychological structure may be, his behavior is that of a "little tin god"—a man who conceives of himself as properly ruling and possessing—if not the earth, a definite portion of it. This God-identification is not unfamiliar; it is just rarely ever this successful.

> The little front wave ran up on the sand
> And frothed there, wildly elated.
> "I am the tide," said the little front wave
> "And the waves before me are dated!"[7]

The Sins of Sensuality—
Lust, Fornication, Adultery, and Pornography

In a discussion of the sin of *lust*[8] we have to allow for a considerable shift in the social code during the past century. It has been called a revolution, and perhaps it is. Many forms of sexual activity which for centuries were considered reprehensible, immoral, and sinful *anywhere,* and their public exhibition simply *anathema,* are now talked and written about and exhibited on the stage and screen. Many of these acts were considered intrinsically criminal, even apart from their visibility. The word "lust" in English implies a kind of ruthless, evil, and sinful indulgence of the sexual drive. But this is allied to the general notion of the sixteenth and nineteenth centuries that except for procreation, all sexual pleasure was *ipso facto* sinful.

For centuries a distinction was made between sacred and profane love, between the carnal and the spiritual, between sexual

[7] Simeon Stylites, *Christian Century*, January 22, 1958.

[8] Aquinas, Luther, and others regard concupiscence as a consequence and derivative of self-love, i.e., "pride" in the theological sense.

purity and impurity. For centuries "being good" meant to millions of people something about restraining, suppressing, or denying sexual feelings and actions.

I shall not tediously review the schisms and battles within the church over this—both before and since Augustine—they are well known. And it is this exaggerated and distorted emphasis on the danger of sexual *sin* that, in our own century, brought the severest attacks from psychoanalysis. Psychoanalysts attacked especially the hypocrisy involved in the denunciation as sinful of just those activities in which the denouncers themselves were indulging. This was done not only by the powerful and "pious" authorities but by well-meaning parents.

The great "sin" of lust, as it existed in Western civilization until the twentieth-century enlightenment, was exemplified primarily by "adultery" for adults, and by masturbation for adolescents. Because it is so tremendous and yet so personal and private an experience, masturbation is one of the great concerns of the child's life, the more so if it is represented by the adults as a wicked and dangerous sin. How this disapproval was expressed in theories of punishment by disease, disfigurement, or "insanity" I have detailed in an earlier chapter. The resulting psychological conflict between control and indulgence in this lustful but dreadful joy evokes in the child fear, guilt, shame, and perplexity.

Numerous books, including the contemporary novel *Portnoy's Complaint*, depict some of this turmoil and the extent to which it absorbs and tortures the waking thoughts of the adolescent boy. It was formerly assumed that no comparable degree of conflict and anxiety occurred in girls, partly because for millions it was axiomatic that any sexual awareness in a young female was *a priori* evidence of unchastity and evil propensities. Nor should this be ascribed exclusively to Jewish or Christian taboos. Up to the present moment little girls in Arabia and Egypt are reported to be mutilated regularly (clitorectomy) by their parents in order to prevent them from being lustful, sensuous, and tempted to passionate indulgence.

The fictional Portnoy stresses his defiant reactive excesses more than his shame or guilt; his Gargantuan effort to escape the clutches of his masturbation habit lead to equally lustful and narcissistic exploitations of females. Many marriages occur as an escape from the masturbation conflict because intravaginal masturbation (which characterizes unloving coitus) is believed by many to be a more "normal" act, free from the subtle physical consequences of manually induced orgasms.

The anguished struggle of religious devotees as pictured in the life of St. Anthony and others, and as experienced by millions of priests and nuns since Augustine, centers largely about masturbation. An incalculable amount of pain could have been spared them, and spared millions of young boys and girls if, in some way, it could have been made common knowledge long before 1900 that there is no harm in masturbation, no evil in it, and no sinfulness in it, the former religious stipulations notwithstanding.

No healthy child is going to masturbate excessively any more than he is going to urinate or defecate excessively, and the comparative pleasurableness of the functions will not vitiate this principle. It is more "fun" to eat food than to breathe oxygen, but we are not likely to cease or overdo one in favor of the other. Excess of any function at any time is symptomatic and deserves help. The Pope has been repeatedly petitioned to permit priests to marry in order to have a more complete sexual and social life. I have not heard of any petition that masturbation cease to be listed as a carnal sin.

In the modern trend to deny the intrinsic sinfulness of anything connected with sex, there is frequently a scotomatization of the fact that the sexual instinct is often exploited by aggressive, hurtful, and destructive intentions. Certainly not all sex is bad, but there is such a thing as bad sexual behavior, nonetheless. Such behavior is not "bad" because it is "indecent," "orgiastic," "perverted," "bestial," "unnatural," and so on, but because it corrupts or destroys the personality of the participants. Rape, for example, is characteristically less a sexual act than a form of assault and mayhem—a form of hurting, debasing, and destroying another person for power-drive satisfaction. That's sin!

Adultery, likewise, is less "sinful" for its sexual content than for its violation of trust and integrity. Indeed, the sin of infidelity, of personal disloyalty to a spouse, to a family, to a friend, to trusting friends, to students—this we should surely record as a major sin. In many connections it is an official and actionable crime, but I would emphasize the kind of infidelity and broken trust which may not break the law but does break the heart. It is no misrepresentation of true life that in *Pilgrim's Progress* the hero, Christian, is accompanied to the end by one *Faithful*. Steadfast loyalty is surely a rare and precious jewel, and disloyalty a sin which few can avoid committing.

The Sin of Gluttony—Foods, Drinks, and Drugs

One hears a great deal these days about the evils of self-administered drugs. On March 19, 1972, this was officially called "America's No. 1 problem." The reference was to the use of heroin and marihuana, ignoring alcohol and nicotine, which do far more harm to far more people. Indeed, if these latter two are included, it *is* a serious national problem.

Self-administered substances other than water and food have been used to alter mood, sensation, and consciousness for thousands of years. The underlying physiological fact is that in varying degrees many substances can temporarily affect the way in which the world is perceived and the way in which we feel about what is perceived, internally and externally.

From pleasure and choice, from habit and custom, or from physiological addiction one may become habituated to the use of one or several of these chemicals, and sometimes to harmful excess. Coffee, tea, alcohol, morphine, tobacco, cocaine, heroin, hashish, barbituric acid salts, lysergic acid, and marihuana are currently prevalent. A great many more new drugs will undoubtedly be added to this list in the coming years, and changed values will be assigned to those we already know and use. Marihuana, like peyote, will very likely be cleared of the charges of dangerousness, while the harm and threat of using tobacco will be more and more recognized.

Exactly what is the sin involved in this self-medicating, self-stimulating, self-sedating procedure? Why are parents alarmed? Is it the fact that an individual can so artificially change his mood by taking a pill? Is it the absorbing excitement it seems to induce? Yet we are not alarmed if a lonely English spinster has her cup of tea with friends. Only the strictest parents would be distressed today by their children having a Coca-Cola in the afternoon, and even non-smokers would probably condone an old gentleman having a quiet pipe by the fire. Most people would *not* regard this as sinful, although millions of other people *would* and *do* consider the taking of coffee and tea and tobacco harmful and hence sinful (Moslems, Seventh-Day Adventists, Latter-Day Saints, and members of some other groups). To ingest an unnecessary and unprescribed drug merely for the pleasurable effect it affords is, they believe, wrong. Arbitrary, yes, but clear and consistent.

Many of us are neither. "Well," we say, "it is perhaps the gluttony, the taking of these things to excess which is bad. Then the body is injured and the mind is confused. But in small amounts—"

It is not a matter of quantity, say others. There is a qualitative difference between drugs. Coffee, nicotine, and Scotch are "all right," in moderation, but heroin and lysergic acid are not! There are good drugs and bad.

Neither the quality nor the quantity determines the evilness, say still others. It lies in the seemingly inescapable tendency to want not only a repetition of the experience but with a larger dose of the chemical, so that slavish dependence upon the drug is established and almost any sacrifice made to obtain it.

We can't pass over the sin of gluttony as a purely quantitative imbalance. "Nothing to excess," as the Greeks counseled, was never more applicable. The taking of far more food and drink than one needs, despite the threat of complications such as obesity, diabetes, nephritis, is often seen in people who declare themselves helpless in the throes of the craving. This can be a symptom of disease as well as a sin. I once had a young woman patient who would eat six or seven steaks a day if not prevented from doing so physically, an intervention for which she thanked us! However, she knew that this was not only a symptom but a sin.[9]

Gluttony in all its forms is sinful in that it represents a degree of self-love which is self-destructive, and is a kind of escapist effort, to abandon the prison of self "by seeking a god in a process or a prison outside the self" or a "subconscious existence."[10]

---

[9] *"The Importance of Being Greedy"* was a headline in *Time* recently. "In Downey, Calif., a man in his early 20s went through the prime-ribs line seven times at Marmac's, a restaurant that provides an unlimited amount of roast beef for only $3.50. . . . He wound up in a hospital, having his stomach pumped out. But less than a week later, he was back in the beef line at the same restaurant. The Downey episode is just one of many similar instances of gluttony that occur daily across the U.S. in an ever-increasing number of 'all-you-can-eat' restaurants. . . ." (*Time*, October 23, 1972).

[10] Reinhold Niebuhr, op. cit., pp. 239–240.

The Sins of Anger, Violence, and Aggression

The words "anger," "aggression," and "violence" have come to be used—very incorrectly—as almost synonymous with "wrongdoing." I suppose if an opinion poll were to be taken as to the most serious and prevalent sin in the country *today*, "violence" would win. This is, of course, absurd—not only because violence has so many faces and forms, most of them not harmful, but because destructive violence in social and individual behavior has been steadily diminishing for several thousand years![11]

Unfortunately, counterviolence—especially the official kind—is not disappearing so rapidly; it gets revived upon the slightest pretext for the combating of someone else's violence. The outcome is nearly always disappointing to everyone. The Attica Prison riot is such a superb illustration of the fallacy and futility of counterviolence as a remedy that it scarcely needs any comment. Almost *any* other maneuver would have been a better solution than just gunning down everyone in sight—friend and foe—without further parley.

Civilization consists, in large part, in finding and using alternatives to the physical violence which was once—except for flight—man's chief defensive resource. With each succeeding generation the public awareness of violence grows and with the awareness disapproval also grows. Each new form or fad of demonstrating rage and resentment seems at first to be the worst ever.

Anger, leading to hurtful words or acts, can be a personal, individual transgression which has to be controlled in its outward expression before it dictates destructive behavior.

Control is not synonymous with suppression, nor is expression necessarily synonymous with murder, mayhem, and other forms of violent rage. Curiously, none of our conventional "crimes" were included in any of the ancient lists of mortal sins. But ill humor, sharp words, denunciation or destructive criticism, glares, curses, and even blows, reflect unpleasant and injurious relationships which characterize all of us occasionally and some of us frequently. As an honest expression of resentment or disapproval, anger has a

---

[11] That crime is, overall, diminishing in frequency and extent is hard for the average person to believe, until he reconstructs in his mind the social world of 100, 500, or 1,000 years ago and compares it with the present times. Troublesome.

place, perhaps; better out than in. But there is always a temptation to use it as a whip, and what begins as a device for relief continues as a weapon for aggression.[12]

A lesser but still important form of violence, which I'd like to propose as a form of sin, is sheer *rudeness*—ill-mannered and discourteous disregard of amenities and the sensitivities of other people. In its extreme form, I suppose, it is represented by vandalism, and it is certainly one of the most difficult forms of "protest" behavior to understand or forgive.

In a lesser degree violence appears in the hurling of epithets and coarse speech; and in still lesser dimensions by all sorts of inconsiderate, hostile, hurtful discourtesies. To be shouted at, cursed, called "fool," "pig," or "nigger," told to shut up, jostled and pushed—these are injurious, provocative forms of behavior which some people rarely experience and from which some other people seldom escape.

As one considers the subway train, the department store bargain counter, the police station, the county jail, the college campus gathering, the football game, the city street, the turbulent home—a thousand forms of discourtesy and ill-mannerliness come to mind. Some groups and some crowds are quite free from it, which only emphasizes how unnecessary it is. The very poor and the well-to-do are both likely to escape it; they deal gently and considerately with one another, i.e., within the group. But outside the group, and in the great mass of middle-level people, there are many who are customarily rough and rude to one another and especially to people they consider beneath them.

The importance of good manners and the sinfulness of bad man-

---

[12] Aggression, which by definition and by proper usage means hurtful attack on someone or something, is often perverted in use to mean energetic forwardness. Usually it is used ambiguously, and left undefined. E. B. White pointed this out (*The New Yorker*, December 15, 1956) in connection with the Charter of the United Nations: "The word 'aggression' pops up right at the very beginning of the Charter: Chapter I, Article 1, Paragraph 1. Aggression is the keystone of the Charter. It is what every member is pledged to suppress. It is also what nobody has been able to define. In 1945, the founding fathers agreed among themselves that it would be unwise to include a definition of aggression in the Charter, on the score that somebody would surely find a loophole in it. But in 1954 a special U.N. committee was appointed to see if it could arrive at a definition of aggression. The committee was called the United Nations Special Committee on the Question of Defining Aggression. It huffed and it puffed, but it did not come up with a definition, and around the first of last month it adjourned."

ners could be the subject matter of a book far larger than this one. Senator George McGovern declared that in his opinion rudeness was "almost a cardinal sin."[13] I select arbitrarily two prevalent forms that particularly aggrieve me. Most of us, I suppose, have memories of being told to "always say 'Thank you.'" Not as a mere customary nicety, which any well-bred person observes almost automatically, nor as a mere ejaculation like "Thanks!" or (in Britain) "K'you!" but as a symbolic acknowledgment and repayment for a service. I have the impression that gratitude has gone out of style. Do the young people who are so peer-conscious permit one another to renounce all such amenities?

A psychoanalytic colleague, Dr. Gert Heilbrunn, recently made a study of "Thank You":

> The expression of gratitude maintains a dynamic equilibrium between donor and receiver. Through word or action the primary donor offers a quantity of love . . . its acknowledgment provides satisfaction of his dependent needs. . . . Delay or omission of grateful acknowledgment is equated with rejection. . . .[14]

Should we regard the ubiquitous inability or neglect to express gratitude as a constitutional lack, like mental retardation or color blindness? People can be, of course, too overwhelmed with emotion or too distracted with other matters to make the appropriate verbal return. But does the sin (or "symptom") of ingratitude lie in not *acknowledging* the gratefulness or in not having the feeling? Does this characterize the *majority* of people? Is there no inborn human trait which would be the opposite of vengefulness?

This sin of omission, as I would hold it to be, is only one form of rudeness and inconsiderateness. But it is an offensive one, sharper than a serpent's tooth and responsible for much suffering and emptiness in life, especially for parents, retiring employees, and many other older people. There are many unsung, unmourned, uncomforted, unattended King Lears. And *Queen* Lears, too!

Worse even than ingratitude are those searing and abrasive political and administrative moves that disregard and traumatize the sentiment, the self-respect, the pride and the hopes of little people,

---

[13] *Life*, July 7, 1972, p. 34.
[14] Dr. Gert Heilbrunn, "Thank You," *Journal American Psa. Assn.*, 20:513 (1972).

underlings, and faithful workers in a system. Often it is the brashness and inconsiderateness of the action even more than the act itself. I have in mind all sorts of structural moves in government and industrial organizations—transfers, replacements, dismissals, cancellations, urban renewals and removals, and other reorganizations that interrupt old patterns and satisfactions small and great. To injure someone's self-respect, his pride, his status among friends and equals may be to quietly kill him. No crime. But sin, I say.

The Sin of Sloth ("Acedia")

One of the good old long-lost Anglo-Saxon words that carried a real punch is "sloth."[15] Inactivity and unresponsiveness in those upon whose cooperative efforts we depend always *feels* to us like sinful negligence. The persistence of this taboo over the centuries of social cooperation testifies to the universality of the temptation to shirk or "goof off." It is described as "laziness," avoidance of exertion, idling, a propensity for "taking it easy." It was the privilege of the master, not of the slave, of the wealthy, not of the proletariat. But inactivity and idleness may (also) be an expression of fear, self-distrust, or self-misunderstanding.

One can never be sure whether indifference is an aspect of sloth (acedia) or a perceptual intellectual deficiency—"a certain blindness in human beings," as William James called it. In some individuals it can be an egocentricity—already mentioned—born of fearfulness and uncertainty, or of a lack of imagination. It appears as a "don't care" attitude which no amount of sentimentalizing as "contentedness," "minding one's own business," and "living and letting live" can cover up. A common excuse for inaction, indifference, or lukewarm response is the "fear of becoming involved." Exactly, yet all life is a matter of involvement somewhere with something, many somethings, and this chronic fear and consequent withdrawal is surely a common sin. It is a kind of "being scared to death"—at least to nonlife.

---

[15] Actually "sloth" is probably a poor translation for acedia, which apparently described an (internal) inhibition to do some duty or task which the pious monks, for example, wanted earnestly to do but couldn't.

That there are "reasons" behind sin does not correct its offensiveness, its destructiveness, its essential wrongness. If "ignorance of the law excuses no one," ignorance of the truth surely cannot absolve one from all sins of omission. Call it sloth, acedia, apathy, indifference, laziness, callousness, or whatever—if refusal to learn permits the continuance of destructive evil, such willful ignorance is surely wrong.

Some of us can remember in the late thirties how some of our intelligent friends refused to believe what was reported about Hitler's horrible acts and systematic genocide. Granted, the crime was so huge and awful that it staggered the imagination, let alone the credulity of the civilized world. But there were plenty of burning fragments from the great fire thrown into the air for everyone to see and shudder and weep. But many averted their eyes—and ears—striving for a selfish safety which no one could entirely achieve.

It is an unpleasant line of thought to reflect how little we understand about human motivation—so little, indeed, that despite the steady flow of books on the subject, it is almost axiomatic that any book with the word "motivation" in the title is likely to be disregarded by sophisticated and scientific readers. What these books all say is that there are carrots in front and sticks behind the donkey and both help. Sweeten the carrots, sharpen the stick, and use them differently. Hundreds of "courses" are given on techniques of motivating by such devices or ploys as encouragement, reward, inspiration, persuasive induction. Self-improvement is constantly offered to school teachers, salesmen, and promoters—people who are engaged in urging others to do something. Antidotes are spelled out for timidity, self-distrust, and the like.

But for sheer laziness and the yen to make oneself as comfortable as possible with as little exertion as possible, no remedies are offered. In fact, the whole world seems to be seeking this very goal. Labor saving is the objective of much technological "improvement." We are, we say, eliminating drudgery (since we no longer have slaves to do it). So we are proud of our dishwashing machines, electric can openers, shoe shiners, and a thousand other gadgets. To enjoy work, we are told, is morbid. And, similarly, to exert oneself in an unnecessary direction is only to get tired, and invite trouble. Why concern yourself? Let James do it. *Someone* will pick it up. What we don't know about won't hurt us.

All the sins of omission couldn't possibly be listed here. And all the vectors which determine inactivity, indifference, unconcern, and all the other synonyms could not be listed, either. We are not attempting to supply a checklist, only a few suggestions. But let it stand that there is a sin of not doing, of not knowing, of not finding out what one must do—in short, of not caring. This is the literal meaning of acedia, recognized as a sin for so many centuries and plaguing us still. We shall return to it in a later chapter.

The Sins of Envy, Greed, Avarice, and Affluence

Among the seven cardinal sins esteemed as such by the moralists of the Middle Ages, four had been listed thirty centuries earlier in the Sinaitic decalogue. "Thou shalt not covet" was spelled out with considerable specification and it seems that always the coveter and not the one coveted was considered the sinner.

In the course of time, coveting became better known as envy— the yearning to possess, to possess as one's "own" what belongs to someone else. As we repeat these words "possess," "own," "belongs," we must be aware of the silent assumptions we are making in using them, assumptions which people in other cultures and countries would dispute or reject. How is it, they might say, that you can claim as your own what really belongs to all of you? No wonder some people resent it, and "covet" or envy.

Most of us assume this right of possession today and take it for granted that someone else may own something we want, something we covet or envy. Perhaps we can buy it—or buy something like it or perhaps even finer or more valuable than the other fellow has. Let *him* suffer the gnawing pains of envy as he compares his petty "possessions" with ours!

Envy is thus a sister of greed, and a half sister of stealing. One can, it is true, work hard and gain the money to buy one's heart's desire, but it is commendably shrewd to use one's wits, and even one's clever fingers, and thus save time and shoe leather. Grasping, seizing, taking, stuffing away—this rodent propensity in which some human beings excel—has its psychological explanation. The competitive preoccupation of sibling sucklings with the pleasant task of filling their little bellies can be called cute, amusing, or even beautiful when seen in almost any species of mammal. But persistence of the same techniques and the same single-mindedness in the behavior of adults is not beautiful; it is not amusing; it is no longer cute.

Greediness in an adult arouses disgust in observers, but this reaction is usually not deterrent. The vulgarity of this residual infantile behavior is precisely what education in self-control and social concern is supposed to avert. Severe frustration or threatened frustration at some point in the development of the child, with bungling of the delivery of the usually successive substitutes for the original nectar, may leave a residue of infantile bestiality. And when the underlying explanations are invisible—as they usually are —what is left is the stark ugliness of the most primitive propensity of predacious mammals.

I suppose we should expect greed to appear in the emotional spectrum of nearly every human being reared in a capitalistic society. So long as its expression can be controlled and blanketed as profit, earnings, winnings, and the like, it seems legitimate, even praiseworthy. When does the sinful aspect of this phenomenon appear? Indeed, what's wrong with it?

What's wrong with it is precisely the crucial issue which has split off various economic systems such as socialism and communism which purported to correct it. These movements sought to eliminate the evil of aggressive overacquisition. They tried. But, as Freud patiently explained to his communist friends many years ago, communists are still human beings with the same instincts as capitalists, the same lust for power, the same greed and yen for acquisition, and the same impulses to fight and to be self-destructive. And in the present context, we may add "with the same propensity to envy."

What then is wrong with inequity, with unfairness, with disparity of advantage or fortune? Is it not God's will? Am I my brother's keeper? Hundreds of wise voices have spoken to this problem but who listens?

The Sin of Affluence

"It is preoccupation with possession," said Bertrand Russell "more than anything else that prevents men from living freely and nobly."

This was a profound conclusion by a very wise man; does it receive any serious consideration?

"The rich Christian—an anomalous man" is the caption on an editiorial by Father William Toohey in the forthright *National Catholic Reporter*. The Biblical text on the sinfulness of riches is clear enough, he said. In His advice to the rich young ruler, Jesus was not simply warning against great possessions as though it were all right to be rich if you keep spending it. Anyone who has tried to preach this highly unpopular aspect of the gospel can tell you about the cold reception it gets from the congregation. Christians talk about rich men trying in vain to get into the Kingdom of Heaven, but they don't pay much attention to the implication.[16]

We read these sentiments almost incredulously. Does anyone really believe that? Why, the rich are so fortunate and they are so smart (else why aren't they poor?) and so lucky. But wicked? Sinful? Only misers are meant, surely. Not just ordinary people of means, comfortably well off or a little better. Few will go along with calling that sin. Except the communists of course!

Neither Bertrand Russell nor Father Toohey were communists.

St. Ambrose was moved to exclaim: "How far, O rich, do you extend your senseless avarice? Do you intend to be the sole inhabitants of the earth? Why do you drive out the fellow sharers of nature, and claim it all for yourselves? The earth was made for all, rich and poor, in common. Why do you rich claim it as your exclusive right?"

And Andrew Carnegie: "It's a disgrace to die rich." Carnegie worked very hard to avoid this disgrace (sin), although he had fewer compunctions about some dubious business practices used to acquire the wealth he gave away.[17]

And John Ruskin, who wrote: "The art of making yourself rich in the ordinary mercantile economic sense, is therefore equally and necessarily the art of keeping your neighbor poor."

Even as far back as 1810 when counting in this country had just started, 1 percent of the families in America owned 21 percent of the wealth. And today 2 percent own 35 percent of the wealth. These are "The Rich." "Middle Class" people own another 35 percent. The very rich, the top 1 percent, own 25 percent of all per-

---

[16] *National Catholic Reporter*, February 4, 1972.
[17] See Joseph F. Wall, *Andrew Carnegie* (New York: Oxford, 1970).

sonal financial assets, about eight times that owned by the bottom 50 percent of people (100,000,000).[18]

Is the deplored dedication to the acquisition of possessions in itself sinful? Is *having* huge possessions in some way or other a continuing sin? Or is it the *getting*? Or the *keeping*? Poverty has been for centuries in many cultures one of the prime requirements of a priest. There was perhaps an institutional reason for the requirement, in addition to the moral reason. It was one way for the institutions to keep control over the individuals, who received "spiritual blessings" galore, while the bishops, lords of the manor, and other rulers dwelt in palaces. But don't cast reproachful eyes at the Church. Doesn't our industrial system manage somewhat similarly despite the variable success of labor unions?

The old "Protestant ethic," as Max Weber labeled it, is what many of us grew up in: to be thrifty, hardworking, and frugal, and then to accept fortune or riches as "grace." Something similar was certainly the Jewish ethic, and no doubt the ethic of many other peoples; seeking great possessions is not a national or a religious monopoly. The prophets railed at the consequences, over and over.

But the "pile-up-wealth ethic" prospered and has come to be associated today with a doctrine of imperative and accelerated consumption. We are urged and tempted and exhorted to buy even during a presentation of the days news happenings. We must buy, spend, waste, want, and borrow lest we retard the engines of production.

And "how are we to avoid the moral dangers of high pressure consumerism?" asks Kenneth Mauldin. "Many are beginning to wonder if we really do need three cars cluttering up every driveway. The garage, of course, is already filled with a boat and various and sundry other pieces of equipment."[19]

Robert Maynard Hutchins put the matter poignantly: "Our real problems are concealed from us by our current remarkable prosperity which results in part from our production of arms, which we do not expect to use, and in part from our new way of getting rich, which is to buy things from one another that we do not want, at

[18] Robert Gallman, James D. Smith, and others, cited in Peter Barnes, "The GNP Machine," *The New Republic*, September 30, 1972.

[19] Sermon delivered October 31, 1971, First Presbyterian Church, Topeka, Kansas.

prices we cannot pay, on terms we cannot meet, because of advertising we do not believe."[20]

What we can't avoid seeing is the obvious disparity in living between one man even *having* a billion dollars and a billion people having scarcely one dollar. This disparity, it seems to me, is irreconcilable with an ethic which assumes that human beings are brothers, living together on the same borrowed earth, and trying to love one another for the mutual benefit of doing so. I will be reminded that the discrepancy is not as great as my hyperbolic illustration. But the few rich do grow richer, and the many poor grow poorer; that we know. The fact is that while many have more to eat than they should have, others have far less to eat than they should have—in the very same country.

Affluence rests upon the subtle, widely held illusion of possession. We think we can own something! If by proper and sufficient effort —or even otherwise—one comes into the nominal and recognized "possession" of something formerly "possessed" by someone else (or its legal tender equivalent), one gains a measure of prestige and power. He may increase this. One becomes a "have" rather than a "have not," a little "have" or a big "have." This status makes possible a little more motility, a little more security, and some greater luxury in daily living. But here the distinction from others is minimal. In the main what it does is to make the individual feel safer from danger and excused from more labor and worry. (Of course it sometimes fails to do these things.)

Acquisition becomes more important than possession. Feverish motivation spurs on people who cannot believe that "Small is beautiful," and could never understand the "theology of 'Enough'" proposed by E. F. Schumacher, who declares that the idolatry of possession has molded a system which now molds us and shapes our thinking.[21] "The bigger—the more—the better." For years R. Buckminster Fuller, a very much traveled man of great means *and* wisdom, has not owned an automobile but rents (and returns) many rental cars at airports. He has consistently decried accumulation and the owning of things.

[20] T. K. Thompson, ed., *Stewardship in Contemporary Theology* (New York: Association Press, 1960), p. 242.

[21] E. F. Schumacher, "Small Is Beautiful: Toward a Theology of 'Enough,'" *The Christian Century*, July 28, 1971.

The way in which the sin of greed grows into something in the realm of the symptom is apparent to all of us in certain of our friends less eccentric than Silas Marner. Yet rarely is greed itself, or even affluence, treated as a psychiatric peculiarity.

But greed, with other symptoms, is frequently seen—not treated! The sense of helplessness which this propensity in a patient choked by his great possessions can arouse in a therapist is great. Two of my former patients come to mind. One, whose annual income was over a million dollars, was brought by relatives for treatment after he had made an attempt at suicide. Life, he said, no longer held anything of interest for him. "And I haven't the slightest idea," he said, "what to do with all my money. I don't need it, but I can't bear to give any away."

"So you decide to kill yourself," I asked, "in order to get away from it?"

"Well, what else can I do?" he replied weakly.

"Could you establish a memorial to your beloved father, endowing certain art forms in the smaller cities over the country, all named for him?"

"Oh," he said, brightening, "that would be wonderful! He would have loved that. Sure, I could do it, easily. I would enjoy it. It would honor him, well, both of us, forever. Let me think about it. I might just do that."

But he didn't. He didn't do anything. He existed for a few more years, then died, prematurely, to the satisfaction of his heirs and business associates who were not yet in his predicament, although they suffered from the same "disease."

I remember another patient who would become very angry when approached by anyone for a contribution to a cause.

"Why should I give what I have to others?" he demanded. "It's mine. I'm no socialist. I earned this—some of it—and I'm keeping it, not sharing it. It is mine, I tell you."

"But," I reminded him, "you are very unhappy with it. And you are very lonely. You have no heirs. You could make many people happier, including yourself, by disbursing some of it. Why be Mr. Scrooge?"

But he, too, went away sorrowing, for he, too, had great possessions. That was twenty years ago. He is still an unhappy Scrooge, still "in treatment" with one of my colleagues for the relief of all sorts of symptoms other than greed.

It is reassuring to remember that even Jesus didn't always cure this affliction. I have wondered whether theologians are impressed by the contrast of this failure in dealing with "a certain rich man" and the many successes in healing that are reported.

In real life greed and affluence rarely look as bad as these words and examples sound. The rich are generally "such nice people"—a few of them "beautiful people"—and very generous. There are some in every big city. They live decently, even graciously, and associate together in groups. Many of them have their pet charity. They are flattered by poor relations and wistful friends. They are admired and envied by the public. There is a kind of excitement in the thought of their power and the great things which they could and just *might* do with their wealth. They often have expensive but interesting hobbies. They are a romantic element in our social structure.

Clergymen bear a cross in connection with them. Being themselves mostly underpaid and innocent of the sin of affluence, clergymen see it all about them, and throughout their congregations. Hence, if they denounce it from the pulpit, they sound envious and personal. If all the rich young rulers in the congregations were to face up to the judgment, there might be an embarrassing exodus, including old ones. Some would seek a church where righteousness is equated with success and success with accumulation. Others would settle for materialism without benefit of clergy. Still others would seek a church which denies all realities except affluence. These escapes all occur frequently, I am told. It is disappointing to learn how few people conscientiously tithe in regard to their benevolences. Even the internal revenue department encourages it.

Now the reader may have begun to wonder if I am infected with a masochistic identification with the poor of the earth and am disparaging wealth from sheer envy. Do you mean, I hear him ask, that envy is a sin provoked by affluence, and hence (envy) should be forgiven and the affluence be punished?

Well, it does sound like that. I'm afraid there is some circular reasoning in what I have said. I don't pretend to know which is the greater sin. Perhaps some envy is necesary to stimulate work and some affluence is necessary to stimulate envy. So some affluence and some envy are "all right"; i.e., they are not the products of a sinful heart.

I can't solve all that. I'm a doctor, a day laborer, not a theologian. A clergyman friend commented to me on this frankly and pointedly. "You are, of course, yourself a member of a professional group gravely tempted to deal with envy by engaging in a practice so lucrative as to make covetousness superfluous. [I had to read this sentence over several times before I could grasp it. Why?] Further, very few of you ever define your own economic base as affluence; it's those 'rich guys.' The clergy largely suppress their envy, but let them—or you doctors—get into difficulties and obtain counsel and the gnawing enviousness comes out clearly."

Well, let me make one thing clear (meaning that I'm not sure I can). By affluence, in this discussion, I do not refer exclusively to what we vaguely designate as millionaires. I really have in mind the upper-class bourgeois citizens of our society—many of them my friends—*and I include myself.* I am far from being rich but I have more than I need. Many of us do, I think.

Certainly many of us possess too much. The high esteem placed on acquiring, accumulating, saving, and storing away can be attributed in part to the habits and virtues necessary in an earlier age when thrift and saving determined survival. My grandparents' hardships were not experienced by me, but they were remembered in our home. Today the abundance of goods, the surfeit of desirable, pleasure-giving things, and the urge for increased consumerism all make for a curious dilemma of choice.

"There is a high degree of psychological conflict as between incompatible or alternative options . . . which may provoke coping strategies to reduce the intensity of ensuing unpleasant feelings and frustration. The psychosocial effects of both the stimulus surfeit per se, and the resulting conflicts from failure of their successful resolution are serious and widespread. . . ."[22] This is quaint scientific jargon for saying that we are disastrously overwhelmed with opportunities.

[22] Z. J. Lipowski, "The Conflict of Buridan's Ass or Some Dilemmas of Affluence: The Theory of Attractive Stimulus Overload," *Amer. J. Psychiat.*, 127:3 (September, 1970), pp. 273–279. See also his "Critique and Comment. Surfeit of Attractive Information Inputs: A Hallmark of Our Environment," *Behavioral Science*, 16:5 (September–October, 1971), pp. 467–471.

We can't decide *which* of several television programs to watch;
we can't get nearly all the new journals read, and new books seem
about to engulf us. The housewife must choose from a plethora of
things at the supermarket. There are a thousand cities to which we
could make a visit that could be completed in twenty-four hours. We
can be in London for dinner tonight. Instead of these luxuries being
a blessing, they have become a vexatious burden. The overload of
possessions, things, gadgets, opportunities, and money requires us to
make innumerable choices. The "simple life" with its privations has
been replaced with a complex life, with many frustrations—and, let
us add, with many guilt feelings! We know we are throwing away
many opportunities! We know we may be making the "wrong"—at
least the less desirable—choice. And we know we are contributing
to the sin of waste.

The Sin of Waste

It is largely the great affluence of our American people which
determines the present ecological threat of extinction to this planet.
It encourages the overconsumption of luxuries, and hence of all
natural resources of which we have had luxurious amounts—water,
oil, soil, wildlife. It contributes to the pollution of our air, with all
the evil complications thereof, through transportation and manufacturing, through comfort and convenience. Worst of all, it contributes to perhaps our greatest national sin—*waste!*

All this is common knowledge. But how many of us in this country
are considering a voluntary reduction of our standard of living?
How many of us are planning to renounce the use of our automobiles, our air conditioning, our daily bath, and other luxuries
which depend essentially on having gotten there first and grabbing
successfully? We used to call it rugged individualism and private
initiative; we used to praise the very values we now realize to be a
threat to our existence as a people. How many of us are really
concerned about our national waste?

Many of us are dissipating great quantities of energy, water,
resources, and money. Oh, we say, we can afford it. Simpler to
throw it away than to take pains to preserve it. The horrible piles
of debris left along strip-mining devastations are typical. Waste.

Wasted beauty, lumber, water, soil, and people's health. Why worry? There's plenty more and there's big money in this strip-mining, and we need energy, we need electricity for keeping people's homes cooler and for raising garage doors. Meantime, we also waste human lives recklessly in ghettos and slums and in the great iron cages of idleness—the latter at public expense!

Cheating and Stealing

The American Indians did not believe in the "owning" of land by anyone. They regarded land and air and water as a common bounty given to them all in trust by the Great Father, to be used, guarded, shared, and enjoyed but not claimed or staked off, owned or exploited. They were—and are—horrified at the great land grabs and steals that have made some of us Americans famous, and more of us rich.

Such grotesque performances as the appropriation of the land and the treasures beneath its surface (in Arizona and northern Alaska, for example) is seen by them as a sacrilege and an outrage against God and His world. On the other hand, until they learned of our hypocritical, ostensible taboo on it, they did not regard taking little possessions from others as a very serious offense. Is our civilization merely one in which it is all right to steal if the theft is big enough?

It might seem curious that so human a propensity as violation of the sixth commandment should have been omitted from the list of cardinal sins. For is anything more typical of man or beast than to try to *get* some of his brother's envied portion, despite the rules against it? But if just to envy or covet it is already the sin, then the attitude or readiness, the act of taking it, is a continuation of the sin.

Jacob's contrivances to rob Esau are described in almost paradigmatic form as a shrewdly successful program for getting on and getting ahead. Swindling and cleverness of this sort was admired by our moral ancestors. The name of the game was—get ahead if you can but avoid theft. Match thy wits against fellow creatures and gain such advantage over them as thou canst, but don't get caught breaking the rules, for that is stealing.

Big-league stealing isn't aspired to by the average individual.

Better to imitate Jacob and use one's "wits." Failure to do so implies stupidity. "If you're so smart, why aren't you rich?"

Your employer, bless his heart, can afford to be relieved of a little of his surplus. What are you doing that *he* isn't? Just a minor rule fracture or two, amounting to 4 billion dollars in the United States in 1969.[23]

"Some employees call it fringe benefits," said the Chicago *Sun-Times*, June 19, 1970, "but most employers call it thievery. . . . Lie detector samplings . . . showed 72 per cent of the tested department store employees [were involved] . . . 86 per cent of the sampled truck drivers and 82 per cent of the bank employees"!

This cheating, which is reflected in behavior in school classrooms, school locker rooms, stores, stock rooms, banks, docks, broom factories, and jewelry stores is obviously not a symptom of illness. No one would faintly suggest that 72 percent of store employees or 83 percent of bank employees are "sick" because they pilfer. Almost no one is charged; no one is convicted. Obviously these are not "criminals." What is this, then, I would ask, other than clear, typical unadulterated SIN? What else can you call it?

I don't mean to imply by this rhetorical question that there is *nothing* else one can "call" stealing. One can call it crime, of course, but there is an increasing trend away from doing even this. It will surely be urged upon us that stealing is often "symptomatic," which is only to say that the psychodynamics behind it are fairly visible and "sick."

For example, it could be said of a certain shoplifter that her home life deprives her of all self-assertion and complementary interpersonal exchange. Her husband is a brute. In such a state of imbalance, she yearns—not for a box of crackers, which is what she takes—but for an opportunity to assert her own power over a piece of the environment, using not her husband's money but her own skill, courage, and daring. Thus she sacrifices her standards to enhance her internal security.

But to call this situation-reaction a sickness and her stealing a symptom in every instance in which it occurs distorts the commonly understood meaning of illness.

The housewives and youth of this country are not *ill* in any such

---

[23] *Wall Street Journal*, February 5, 1970.

peculiar way or in such astounding numbers; the thieving employees in the stockrooms are not sick as we ordinarily think of sickness. In old-fashioned nursery language, they are just plain "naughty," i.e., willfully, if trivially, disobedient. They flout—in a small and secret way—the old code regarding property ownership and exchange. They are doing something they know to be unfair and dishonest; they are cheating. They are fully aware it is illegal, that it injures someone. But it's so easy to do, so easy to escape detection. It brings a slight material reward, a slight tingle of excitement, to relieve the boredom of routine shopping. And then there is that sense of winning in a game! If "everybody is doing it," the ordinarily corresponding guilt feelings can be stifled. Can everyone be wrong about what's right? It's a new deal. How can it be a sin? Need anyone feel guilty?[24]

Pressures upon individual integrity in the face of group attitudes of this kind are particularly burdensome for children. Studies of the family by Urie Bronfenbrenner at Cornell University have tended to show that the average child of ten in the United States has already developed a noncondemning attitude toward cheating. He is, in fact, taught by his surroundings that it is unrealistic to maintain standards of honesty that are ridiculed by his friends and ignored by his elders. Exemplary characters, which are the most powerful influence in education, are too weak to offset the evidence of his daily experience of how other people "get by."[25]

[24] Headlines:
"A Way Out. MANY EMPLOYEES, HURT BY SLUMP, COMPENSATE BY STEALING FROM FIRMS. Fraud, Embezzlement, Theft Rise Alarmingly; Losses Put at $400 Million a Year. Mrs. Robin Hood at the Till." (*Wall Street Journal*, February 9, 1971, p. 1)
"An Inside Job. MORE WORKERS STEAL FROM THEIR EMPLOYERS AND GET AWAY WITH IT. Most Thieves Lack Cunning. But So Do Company Spies; Selling the Loot is Easy. Many Firings, Few Arrests." (*Wall Street Journal*, February 5, 1971)
"CHEATERS IN BUSINESS. Forty-eight men and 29 electrical manufacturing companies have been fined and seven of the men have received 30-day jail sentences for violating the antitrust laws. In this largest of all criminal antitrust cases, brought by the U.S. Department of Justice in Philadelphia, these excerpts from news reports are illuminating: . . . From Judge J. Cullen Ganey's presentencing statement: '. . . This is a shocking indictment of a vast section of our economy, for what is really at stake here is the survival of the kind of economy under which America has grown to greatness, the free enterprise system.' " (*Presbyterian Outlook*, February 20, 1961)
[25] Urie Bronfenbrenner, *Two Worlds of Children: US and USSR* (New York: Russell Sage Foundation, 1970).

The Sin of Lying

So vast and varied is the territory of intentional deception that I introduce the topic with trepidation. Shall I not be challenged with reminders of all the camouflages of nature and polite society, the very devices whereby species and individuals survive? The hiding of wild animals, the stealth of predators, the artistry of cosmetics on our ladies, the design and cut of our clothes?

But most of these distortions or concealment of the "truth" (or the fact) occur with no verbal or written assertion that it is indeed otherwise. Only man with his capacity to anticipate the future and to check the record of the past can really *tell* a lie. And man has become very adept at passing counterfeit information—in social intercourse, in business, in political maneuvering, in international affairs, and in person-to-person relationships as intimate as that of marriage.

The rules of the lying game become stereotyped in its various forms of usage. Poker players may lie in word and action about the content of their hands of cards, and the best "liar" often wins, to the admiration, if also envy, of all his fellow players. But about certain things he may not, under any circumstances, lie or deceive —for example, whether or not he has been dealt too many cards, whether or not he has "looked" at his hole card. The penalty has often been death, more commonly elimination and ostracism. One may lie boldly in fashioning excuses for declining an invitation or in expressing appreciation of a hospitality. But he may not lie about other features of a social affair—his acquaintanceship with certain guests, for example.

Perhaps most of us learned early to think of lying as one of the most likely of sins, the one any of us could and all of us did commit frequently. The veniality of the sin depended on the content of the lie. Peter's denial of his association with Jesus was a self-protective negative alibi that has been used by millions of others before and since. But had Peter gone further and declared that he knew the accused to be a villain, a rebel, a conspirator, an anarchist—such lies would surely rate as more serious offenses because by their nature they would have been more damaging and hurtful to Jesus.

Actually, little more about the sin of lying would need to be said, first because everyone knows about it from firsthand experience both in himself and in others, and secondly, because it is so complicated a subject, were it not for the fact that lying has lately seemed to be gaining respectability. It is even practiced without apology by persons and agencies in high places.

Lies, Lies, Lies

I well remember the afternoon of Friday, May 7, 1915. A half-dozen medical students at the University of Wisconsin were leaving the laboratory to go home for the day. A newcomer arrived with an exciting message. "They have done it!" he cried. "The Germans have torpedoed the *Lusitania*. And now the fat's in the fire. There was no ammunition on that ship."

The argument as to whether Britain or Germany was most at fault continued for months and years afterward. Sentiment turned increasingly against the Germans, and war began to be mentioned. Finally, two years later, we were persuaded. Over fifty years later, shortly before its own tragic demise, *Life* (October 13, 1972) published an excerpt from *Lusitania*, by Colin Simpson, a British journalist who had carefully examined all the old and much new information about the *Lusitania*. And what does he say?

That the *Lusitania* was indeed heavily armed, that her manifests had been falsified to hide a large cargo of munitions and other contraband, that the English admiralty was strangely negligent in protecting the ship against attack, and that for some thirty years the United States Government purposely withheld the truth about the sinking from the public; it denied the facts and falsely accused Germany of an atrocity to arouse American sentiment against Germany.

In other words, while one cannot say that the event was staged, it was very largely maneuvered and greatly misrepresented and exploited by the British *and* American governments to induce hatred in the American people toward the German people. In short, we were lied to by our leaders to maneuver our country into a war for political reasons and *not* to "save democracy." By order of President Wilson, the truth about the *Lusitania* was buried until the time of President Franklin Roosevelt.

One hero stood out in all this shameful business. On September

20, 1917, Senator Robert La Follette of Wisconsin stated in a public speech that it was true that the *Lusitania* had been carrying munitions and the President was aware of it. *The Senate promptly attempted to expel him for this treachery!* La Follette demanded exhibition of the true manifest of the *Lusitania*. This was refused. Dudley Field Malone, the Collector of Customs in New York, quietly offered to testify on La Follette's behalf, and the Senate dropped the shameful charges. La Follette was one of the few public leaders who would not join in that great political lie which led to the death and maiming of millions of human beings.

I lived through these days and these conflicts of opinion and contradictory news dispatches, and the tragic years that followed. For me, lying is a sin in large letters, and lying by leaders is unforgivable.

Cruelty as a Form of Sin

Whipping, beating, burning, cutting, or otherwise causing pain to a helpless animal, child, wife, slave, or prisoner sounds irredeemably evil. It is so unpleasant that we prefer to think of it as a near extinct, uncivilized practice. But the enjoyment of the indulgence and of the spectacle and sounds of inflicted pain are still widely prevalent in all cultures. Even among the most miserable, this special misery is sometimes added and conventionalized, for example, in the reputedly almost universal wife-beating among Mexican peasants. In this respect civilization creeps forward at a snail's pace.

Cruelties of many kinds are daily fare in many prisons, even yet. This is especially true, I am ashamed to record, in detention centers and other semipenal institutions for children.

It is not my purpose to contribute a lengthy essay on the infliction, endurance, and avoidance of pain. But we have been speaking of sin, of the performance of acts which injure others, and surely the intentional unnecessary infliction of pain falls in that category. Inflicted pain *can* institute or accompany recovery from illness, or from other danger—for example, in reviving a cold-stupefied person, or in the lancing of an abscess. Mild inflicted pain can, no doubt, be used to teach something crucial—for example, the avoidance of a dangerous step or contact. But this is not the great sin of cruelty of which I am speaking.

If we go through pages of history reading the tortures joyfully or solemnly inflicted upon victims—often before great crowds of sightseers—if we review the books of martyrs, slavers, inquisitors, jailers, conquistadors, Indian hunters, soldiers, and other brave, fierce men, if we recall the reasons leading to the founding of the Society for the Prevention of Cruelty to Children and of the humane societies for animals, we are made keenly aware of the apparently ineradicable streak of cruelty in all human beings, as well as the strong reactions against its indulgence. Sometimes it is rationalized as serving this purpose or that, but, usually, what emerges is the plain ugly fact of sadism.

Cruelty to Animals

Since slaves, prisoners of war, and convicted criminals are unavailable to most people, animals and children are the commonest objects for indulging this secret—or not so secret—sinful yearning. The manifested suffering of the helpless victim adds to the pleasure of the torture, as the Marquis de Sade declared and illustrated. The fun of choking and gouging and teasing and biting and finally shooting a bear or wolf cub to death was greatly enhanced by having its paws roped together.

The spectacles of bear- and bull-baiting in England and Europe 150 years ago sound most gruesome today. In bull-baiting, the crowd is said to have become most excited when the tenacious jaws of the mauled dog tore off the entire lips of the harassed bull as it thrashed its tormentor to and fro. Cockfighting, bull-baiting, and bear-baiting are less common today but heartless, useless "big game shooting," the slaughter of beautiful and harmless creatures by expensive technological machinery—machinery for transportation, visualization, and evisceration—seems equally grim to me. Especially evil, I think, is wolf and bear shooting from helicopters and airplanes.

Sometimes the frightened wild thing is "given a chance." A game is played, with the rules established by and known only to the winner. This is known as "sport." All states and nations provide it for their kings and rich men. The privilege is sometimes extended in diluted forms to the common herd. The physical exertions and perils endured in this vandalism are always stressed; photographs and portions of the slaughtered quarry are proudly exhibited or distributed to friends. The frightened agonies and death struggles of the quarry are occasionally noted, even piously deplored, but they are really not considered important. Actually they are an essential element, thrilling but better not discussed.

In recent years there have been loud public outcries regarding many forms of cruelty to animals for which—at first—no apology was forthcoming. The clubbing of baby seals, the running to death of mustangs with airplanes, the shooting of Alaskan and polar bears and mountain sheep with rifles fitted with telescopic sights, the poisoning of prairie dogs and of their enemy (but our friend) the coyote, the horrible whale slaughter—these have preempted some of the attention formerly concentrated on campaigns against vivisection of dogs and cats in scientific laboratories or against the mangling and torture of wild animals in steel traps.

The slow death of birds and animals in the crates and bins of so-called "road-side zoos" is a common form of commercialized torture. But even the scientifically run zoos, which do a great service in teaching children that wild animals are beautiful and deserve respect and protection, have their troubles with the cruel propensities of their human visitors. A typical example was recently recorded in a news magazine:

> The director of the Detroit zoo hired four new security guards last week, not to contain the wildness within the cages, but to protect the animals from the inhumanity of man. In the past two years, the zoo population has been victimized by deliberate acts of brutality.
>
> A baby Australian wallaby left the protection of its mother's pouch and was stoned to death; a duck died with a steel-tipped hunting arrow in its breast. A pregnant reindeer miscarried after firecracker-hurling youths bombed the frantic animal into convulsions. Visitors have been observed dropping lighted cigar butts on the backs of alligators, watching the ashes burn through the reptiles' skin, then breaking into laughter when the alligators reacted to the severe burn.
>
> Finally, the zoo's male hippopotamus choked to death last week

after someone responded to the hippo's open-mouth begging for peanuts by rolling a tennis ball down its throat.[26]

If one tries to define the psychological devices whereby some individuals can permit themselves to enjoy these hideous acts, it soon becomes clear that there is a complete *discontinuity* in their minds between pain as *they* know it and feel it, and pain as it is experienced by others, including animals. Horace Greeley of the New York *Tribune*, while on a trip to Kansas in 1859, traveling across the state to Colorado, made this observation:

> I noticed with sorrow that the oxen which draw these great supply wagons are often treated cruelly, not merely in respect to the beating and whaling which every human brute delights in bestowing on every live thing over which he domineers, but with regard to food and drink. Here were cattle that had stood in the yoke all that hot, dry day with nothing to eat or drink; and, when they came down to the river mad with thirst, they were all but knocked down for trying to drink. I was assured that oxen are sometimes kept in the yoke, without food or drink, for two days, while making one of these river crossings.[27]

A hundred years later these same poor beasts were still being ritualistically tortured in weekly spectacles in scores of cities— rodeos in our Southwest and in bloodier teasing south of the border (bull fights). If it is any consolation to us, the bull dies bravely. It

> is the only animal—or, surely, the only mammal—that dies without a protest against death. It dies like a heroic human being, ashamed of the ugliness of anguish and agony.
>
> Many times I have watched an awkward *torero*, unable to kill with that famous stroke of mercy which cuts life off instantly. Such a *torero* hacks the bull's throat, veins, aorta with his sword, and the animal is immobilized. It stands awhile, as if it knew its inevitable

[26] *Time*, June 28, 1971.
[27] *Kansas Historical Quarterly*, May, 1940, p. 127. Greeley also protested the heartlessness of providing no winter protection—"even but cutting a stick of prairie hay" for the shivering, freezing cattle and horses.

destiny; though blood is streaming in torrents from its nostrils, it does not try to escape its doom. Then, slowly, beautifully, it collapses on already powerless forelegs.

And—most pathetic and moving—the bull dies *silently*. Every animal with enough power to scream, cry, ululate, thrash about, snuffle, rampage, does it; only the bull ends with no sound. He fought, he lost, he accepts his fate with dignity. The contrast between the violent vitality of the mass of muscles a few minutes ago and the sudden, quiet resignation is appeasing. It erases our feelings of guilt, of harm done. If the bull tried to crawl away, if it moaned, jerked, howled like a wolf, we would be overcome by pity and terror. But the bull cares for attitude, pride, immaculate honor, and heroism, and this makes its death *spectacular* and thus *bearable*, evoking no compassion. We human beings eagerly witness the end of grandeur, but we are rarely very emotional about it. The bull's silence in death was discovered ages ago by the Spaniards; they have used it to create a national pastime.[28]

Pastime! Sport? Joy!

Cruelty to Children

How about cruelty to children, of which we hear so much these days? Children and fellow humans are treated by some people as shamefully and brutally as animals are treated by others. The frequency of fearful and revolting abuse of children by burning, beating, and choking is shocking to all of us.

Our child discipline standards in Puritan days were very harsh, both at home and in the courts. But the fierce abuse of children which has become so abundant was presumably hidden in humble homes and denied as much as possible. I remember as a boy, however, that all of us in my aunt's home knew about the abuse meted out to the children in the home of one of our neighbors and I remember discussions concerning what we might do to interrupt it.

To see an infant or a child of one or two years with blackened eyes, broken bones, burns and bruises over its body, scalded areas on its legs, and evidences of the blatant cruelty of its parents is a

[28] *The New Yorker*, December 21, 1968.

shocking experience. To realize that perhaps most infant deaths occur from such mistreatment is even more shocking.[29] "It is simply impossible to believe the kinds of things people do to their children," said Dr. Lowene Brown, pediatrician at Cook County (Illinois) Hospital (*American Medical Writers Association Newsletter*, December, 1972).

In any event, it makes you believe in the persistence of sin!

Many child-rearing practices highly regarded *less* than a century ago would be condemned if advocated or openly practiced now. But child battery goes far beyond being a device for training, although just that reason is offered in justification for much of it. The high level of child-beating has been attributed to a widespread acceptance among Americans of the use of physical force and corporal punishment as legitimate procedure in child rearing. Dr. David G. Gil of Brandeis analyzed 13,000 child-beating reports from all fifty states. "American culture," said he, "encourages in subtle, and at times not so subtle, ways the use of 'a certain measure' of physical force in rearing children in order to modify their inherently nonsocial inclinations."[30]

This is not just something a few frenzied or heartless parents do secretly in the seclusion of the home where no one is likely to see or interfere with the process. In the public schools of Dallas, Texas—a proud and thriving metropolis—there were officially reported in 1971 a total of 24,305 instances of whippings by teachers of pupils in the public school system. Protests and legal challenges have thus far been rejected by the courts in that state, and by the U.S. Supreme Court in November, 1972. (It is, by the way, illegal in New Jersey and Massachusetts.)[31]

However, the "battered child syndrome" is a more severe form of abuse. Reliable statistics are hard to obtain, but Dr. Gil's estimate is that 2½ million children are abused every year.

Dr. Gil's belief that child abuse stems from society's sanctioning

[29] Vincent J. Fontana, *The Maltreated Child* (Springfield, Ill.: Thomas, 1964). See also: R. E. Helfer and C. H. Kempe, *The Battered Child* (Chicago: University of Chicago Press, 1968); David G. Gil, *Violence Against Children* (Cambridge, Mass.: Harvard University Press, 1970); David Bakan, *Slaughter of the Innocents* (San Francisco: Jossey-Bass, 1971).

[30] Gil, *op. cit.*

[31] See Gene Maeroff, *New York Times*, May 8, 1972, and *Dallas Morning News*, May 20, 1972.

of corporal punishment is based upon the very low incidence of abuse in cultures that have strong taboos against striking children, such as the American Indian. The Indians disciplined their young mainly through example and shame. The Aztecs might have set us an example. (The American Indians eschewed all child torture.)

According to the Codex Mendoza the pre-Mexicans permitted the parents to threaten their children in case of disobedience at the age of eight with maguey spikes "so that they weep for fear . . . at the age of 9, when a son is disobedient, the father ties him hand and foot and thrusts *maguey* spikes into his shoulders and body; the mother pricks her daughter's wrist . . . at the age of ten, children who are disobedient and will not work are beaten with a stick . . . at the age of eleven, compelled to inhale *axì* . . . at the age of twelve, . . . took his son and laid him, naked and bound, on damp ground keeping him there a whole day. . . ."[32]

Psychological Cruelty

Cruelty is generally thought of in terms of physical pain. But there is a kind of personal injury, given and taken, which is not physically but psychologically painful, and which may also be economically and socially damaging. I refer to the use of words as weapons. Perhaps this could be regarded as a partial sublimation, a lessening of the force of an aggression through conversion of a physical into a symbolic missile.

[32] The Codex Mendoza (1548) was made by native scribes *tlacuilos* at the request of the Viceroy of Mexico, Antonio de Mendoza (1491–1552) in order to offer the Spanish Emperor Charles V a description of the life of Mexican Indians before their conquest. It is written on 72 leaves of European paper with illustrations in colour after the pre-Columbian pictographic technique and explanatory text in Spanish. It was sent to Spain in 1549, but the ship carrying the Codex fell into the hands of French corsairs and thus the codex passed in 1553 to the ownership of A. Thevet, the French royal cosmographer. . . . Richard Hakluyt bought it in 1584 while he was chaplain to the English ambassador in Paris and it finally ended up at the Bodleian Library, Oxford. . . . The first 18 plates . . . depict the founding and progress of Tenochtitlán or Mexico City, showing the expanding influence of the Aztecs year by year. There follow 39 plates of taxation records . . . and finally a description of the life of the Mexicans, their education, artisans, wars, laws, marriage and many interesting aspects of their customs and behaviour.

Cited by Francisco Guerra, *The Pre-Columbian Mind* (London and New York: Seminar Press, 1971), p. 81.

For all the consolation of the nursery rhyme that "sticks and stones may break my bones but words can never hurt me," words, ridiculing, and name-calling can and do *hurt*. Name-calling has a magic quality—we may think of it at first as a puerile weapon of weaker children. Hurled from the hoarse throat of a more powerful figure, accompanied by threats of injury, reinforced by angry facial contortions and physical gestures, "name-calling" and cursing can become cruelly painful.

That vituperation can incite even well-trained, adult police officers to lose their self-control and violate the law they are hired and trained to enforce has been exemplified in many recent public outbreaks. Even in calmer moments, the use of "nigger," "pig," and various synonyms for sexual deviate can arouse fierce physical reaction. Applied to children, or to prisoners and "convicts" who cannot react physically, they are merely additional flagellations.

Such vulgar name-calling, while common enough, is no temptation for the average citizen. Most of us have long since abandoned the use of profanity and obscenity to injure our neighbors and friends. There is always quiet, inferential slander, disseminated by discreet gossip. Defamation of character is hard to prove; lies are hard to locate and refute. Banks can protect their reputations by prompt legal injunctions; individuals, for the most part, cannot.

One form of name-calling which has troubled me in recent years is the name-calling in which my professional colleagues and I indulge. Scientific medicine early laid down principles of identification and diagnosis to be established by comparing symptoms, signs, etiologies, and the history of the evolution of the illness with similar cases recorded by other physicians.

In time, some of these syndromes acquired very bad names. Occasionally, the horror inspired by the name was justified—as in the case of syphilis (although euphemisms and code words were often substituted for it). But often the *public* notion of the condition connoted by a label was incorrect; thousands of persons infected with Hansen's bacilli have been forcibly removed from friends and society to the isolation and imprisonment of leper colonies.

The very word "tuberculosis" (or "consumption") used to inspire a fear that often prevented any real therapeutic benefit. I can remember my father's dismay when, in an effort to secure appropriate treatment for one of his patients, he explained to the members of her family the relatively good prognosis of "tuberculosis" if promptly and correctly treated, only to have them eject him from the case and from the house, assuring him that no such dread affliction had ever involved a member of their family or ever would. (The daughter died of tuberculosis two years later under my care.)

It is apparently a human propensity to identify others by a single, perhaps conspicuous attribute, as did the American Indians, John Bunyan in *Pilgrim's Progress*, and all children. It is easily overlooked that Chief Lone Wolf, Mr. Pliable, and Shorty Jones have other more important and truly characteristic qualities than the ones indicated by their names, which may no longer be representative, but still painful to the bearer.

Something similar to this developed in psychiatry. At first our patients were just "insane." They had one disease as far as the public was concerned—"What is it to be mad but to be simply mad?"

To be mad was a serious taboo. Gradually some acquired special designations such as "melancholia," "dementia," and "kleptomania" (also a few more esoteric labels). As psychiatry emerged from its medieval forms and aspired to achieve a scientific structure, it began to take more and more seriously the correct labeling of the different pictures of psychiatric illness.

This proved to be a far more difficult task than was the case in general medicine. The microscope, so useful to the latter discipline, was of little help to the psychiatrist. Urinalysis, blood chemistry, and X-rays likewise yielded only negative or puzzling data. There were no organs to be investigated. The behavior picture, on the other hand, was capable of such highly variable interpretations that not hundreds but *thousands* of "diseases" were identified and named by eager clinicians in various countries.[33]

American psychiatrists dealt quite pragmatically with this confusion and in 1917 reduced the many hundreds of current designations of mental illnesses to a dozen (Southard) or a few more (APA-1917). But the tide turned after a few years and the official list has now burgeoned with loud computer chattering to a grand parade of more than 200 species!

Species of what? Lists of what? Lists of names to call patients! Lists from which psychiatrists may (must) choose a word to

[33] See the Appendix of *The Vital Balance* (New York: Viking, 1963).

describe the configuration of symptoms exhibited by each of his patients! These are names he may use to identify his patients' afflictions, and they become the names by which he must label his patients, and even by which the patients are designated.

A patient becomes a "schizophrenic," and that he may also be a Caucasian, a Methodist, a carpenter, a Democrat, a vegetarian, a Pennsylvanian, a chess player, and a widower diminishes in importance. We once thought such labeling would help us better understand the nature of peculiar behavior. Perhaps it did. But it led to a kind of treatment by pigeonholing and social stratification which hurt many of our patients irrevocably. It often destroys all hope in the patient and loved ones.[34]

The use of diagnostic labels in a pejorative way is a sin of which I have myself been guilty. I began to see how much harm it caused and consequently I have discontinued it. Dr. Thomas Szasz of New York State goes further than I; he will not even concede the existence of *any* "mental illness." He believes this to be a mythical, political, and damaging designation. I have myself proposed that we speak rather of "Personality Dysorganization" of various degrees rather than "mental disease," psychosis, neurosis, and the like. At any rate, to apply a term, for ease of verbal reference, to a medical condition which has become pejorative seems to me to be a professional "sin" we doctors should abjure.

Other Common Sins

I have said nothing in this chapter about some familiar saddening sins such as breaking faith or promises, betrayal, conspiracy to harm, and others that will come to the reader's mind. Nor have I perhaps dealt adequately with the emotion of hate which is at the root of so much sin.

Hate usually seems to the hater to be so logical, so appropriate, so justified, that it is difficult for any healing power of love to interpose its neutralizing effect before some aggressive expression has occurred. The instincts have, as Freud called it, become defused, and the hate that had been controlled becomes unleashed

---

[34] See Karl A. Menninger, "Psychiatrists Use Dangerous Words," *Saturday Evening Post*, 237:12 (April 25, 1964).

and directed first (Freud thought) inwardly and, because this is so painful, it is redirected outwardly as aggression against someone or something. But this entails guilt feelings, and a need for self-punishment, a secondary self-attack. We observe it in many patients and occasionally in friends. In its less vigorous forms we recognize it in most of the sins I have listed.

Here I wish to say something in loud tones; if this were a speech I would raise my voice. THESE OFFENSES I HAVE ENUMERATED DO NOT CONSTITUTE AN OFFICIAL LIST OF SINS, not even of wrongdoings. At best (or worst) they are forms of behavior resulting from sinful intent or neglect. They are samples of the behavior dictated by a *mens rea*, a wrong attitude, a hard heart, a cold heart, an evil heart.

I do not believe anyone would seriously classify them as either crime or disease. I'm aware that psychological jargon can be employed which relates many of them to peculiarities of conditioning, special inhibitions, interactional incompatibilities, and a dozen other technical constructs. I wouldn't dispute these; I just don't think they lead to the proper steps for correction.

If one wanted to find a germinal word to link all sins, perhaps *hate* would do it. In terms of action, however, the long-term consequences of hate are self-destruction. Thus the wages of sin really are death.

9

Sin, So What?

After the dreary recital of human error and sinful deed in the preceding chapters, the reader may turn to the author in irritation and take him sternly to task.

"Sad it may or may not be, but boring it certainly is," he may wish to exclaim. "You have catalogued some prevalent vices which we all deplore, and you want to call them sins. Go on and do so; most people—as you admit—don't and won't. They aren't going to worry much about them, either. They're concerned about other matters.

"Oh, we can agree about the prevalence of evil in the world and about the threats from the population explosion and the technology boom and the ecological dilemmas. Something ought to be done by someone about a lot of things. You are right about all that.

"Greed and graft, cheating and lying, mugging and murdering —sure it all goes on, and criminals are handled abominably. But they *are* kept out of circulation for a while if and when they are apprehended.

"Yes, evidences of human meanness and cruelty and violence are all over the place. But is that new? And isn't it getting better? You admit it is gradually diminishing, that civilization is edging up, little by little, and the mass of us is getting more pacific. Would you want to go back to the horrors and privations of life one hundred years ago? No decent lights or roads or telephones or heating or transportation or shower baths or air conditioning.

"And their old-fashioned, outworn morals and ethics all seem irrelevant to us. We live in the here and now, and we want to live it up! Expedience and effectiveness—they are the watchwords today, not morality.

"Those unfortunate ones you mention—*les misérables*—the proletariat, the underprivileged? Well, we've always had them—mil-

173

lions of them. They are hurting; they are pinched, they're crowded, to be sure. But they're mostly happy in their way, at least reconciled. And some of them climb out. Ultimately some of them can be like 'us'—us fortunate ones.

"So it's really a wonderful world, in spite of all that, and it's constantly improving. You used to be an optimist, but now suddenly you find a hair in the butter, a few spots on the linen. Come, come, now; we're only human. Let's not apologize for being human. Yes, we do err; we evidence 'sin,' as you want to call it. We hurt ourselves and often others, too.

"But not all the time! We're improving. We're getting further and further away from Plato's dark cave of shadowy knowledge, imperfect communication, residual superstition, primitive aggressiveness.

"So don't be impatient or reproachful. Give the old world another thousand years or so! It moves, as Galileo said. You want it all to happen in your lifetime.

"As to sin, we have transferred that old-fashioned breast-beating and guilt-seeking from the churches to the psychiatric clinic. And trouble enough it was to do, too. There were, and there still are, reactionaries who threaten hell on earth and then worse hell after death. You yourself have denounced punishment for crime as being simply another crime, and we were with you, then. So what are you trying to do now? Encourage the tough boys—the "law-and-order" chanters? Go back to the puritanical and Jesuitical [he meant to say Dominican, no doubt[1]] inflexibility of judgment and punitive counterviolence?

"So where, indeed, do you think you *are* going? Instead of rejoicing in the weakening of the sin-people's dour influence as being a victory of intelligence and civilization, you seem to deplore it! In fact, you deny such a victory. Sin *hasn't* disappeared, you say —it has merely been called something else or swept under the rug. It is still with us. In us. And all about us. We can't do without sin— apparently—or without the notion of it, so you seem to say. With all that guilt and penance and accountability stuff.

"But some of us *are through* with it. Old-fashioned sin *is* out. You

---

[1] A Baptist theologian who read the manuscript of this book commented, "How about both Jesuitical *and* Dominican plus Baptist, Methodist, Presbyterian, and a few dozen other adjectival modifiers?"

had to scrape the barrel to dig up that rogue's gallery of stuff in the preceding chapter. Who is going to take seriously your idea that lifting a pack of cigarettes from the store shelf is a sin? Not the stores; they get it back. Not the insurance companies; they can raise their rates (and will). Not the customers; it helps make shopping a little more fun for the housewife. Or who is going to beat his breast if a little injustice is done, or a little cheating? It might save a life. It may even lead to a little prosperity! And affluence! Sensible people don't feel guilty for sinfulness or 'sins' anymore, and thank God they don't. What sort of morbid, morose, artificial, synthetic gloom was that moral smog in which our ancestors lived? Do you want to continue it?

"And you—a psychoanalyst! Do psychoanalysts tend to lose that magic insight and clear vision which they were at so much pains to acquire, and begin to revert to the irrational thinking patterns of their childhood—like sinning and guilt feelings and worry over the fate of the world?

"You admit that your sense of right and wrong was derived from your mother's teachings. You concede that your moral schedule was formed on parental patterns. Seventy years ago! Some of them were all right, too, in their day. But were hundreds of painful psychoanalytic hours insufficient to purge you of your infantile irrationalities of 1910?

"You say you have modified your original superego code somewhat since your psychoanalytic 'experiences.' But though the code may have altered slightly, is the pattern not about the same? You 'believe in' a sense of guilt (and actually you also believe in punishment, although you repudiate that word; you want to call it 'penalty'). You say a penalty—unlike punishment—doesn't add injustice to repayment, or operate chiefly to gratify the irrational yen for revenge. And you shake your finger at us sternly like an old Calvin and say that there is still much sin to be repented and atoned for in a wicked, worried world.

"You say—and we agree—that the source of some of our troubles is group irresponsibility, group arrogance, tribalism, nationalism, racism—all those terrible things of which we, your generation, used to be so proud; even the once-prized patriotism. But these are not individual transgressions, so why should the individual feel guilty? What can *he* do, except in an occasional instance? For the clergy to reproach him does no good nor does berating and denouncing the organization. The average individual is already discouraged and troubled enough; if the clergymen would just 'comfort my people' and spread a little sweetness and light and impart a little hope and encouragement, the average pewholder would be grateful and the rest of us wouldn't be bothered. And the same applies to you! Why not dispense a little hope and cheer for a change?"

The Author Attempts a Rebuttal

Well, this is a challenging charge. It is true that in our great world some things *are* improving. This is part of the paradox—that so many "things" are so much better, while the totality is so much worse. There are fewer murders per million people, but some of these millions are more fearful than formerly of personal violence happening to them or their friends. There are fewer wars in progress than ever in history, but never so costly, destructive, and senseless a conflict as that just concluded in Vietnam. More people than ever before are interested in preserving the beauties of our planet, yet never has so widespread and ruthless a destruction of them been in process and carried on by so many people.

At the same time there is no longer any "safe" place for anyone. The entire world is threatened and, we are told, could be destroyed in seconds. Any place on the globe can be reached by the long arm of aggression. Cain is everywhere, no longer exiled; he lives with us and daily confronts us.

We humans were created equipped with a single weapon—the sword (or the club or the arrow or the poison) of aggression. It can be used crudely and grossly, as it usually was at first. Over thousands of years and after millions of deaths it has been refined into many forms—the plowshare, the sculptor's tool, the writer's pen, and the atomic bomb. Reversions to primitive forms and uses constantly occur; each time it is a tragedy; each time a destructive lurch; each time a partial suicide. (Each time it is a "sin"!) And suddenly the cumulative effect of these is felt and the destruction is complete.[2] *"There are no internal affairs left on our crowded*

[2] Cf. William Golding, *Lord of the Flies* (New York, Putnam, 1959).

earth!" wrote the modern prophet Solzhenitsyn.[3] Mankind—*our* kind—is constantly engaged in self-destruction. Waste, exploitation, and pollution go on concurrently with social and civil wars in many lands. Direct aggressions continue to be poorly controlled at all levels—from myriad Cain-and-Abel affairs to huge, organized mass orgies of murder and destructiveness, with the incessant stockpiling of more weapons to insure the continuance of this insanity.

Yet, as my interrupter says, it isn't all bad. Civilized people have become more sensitive to injustice and cruelty than in olden days and more aware of the devastation of their world both in war and in peacetime. This is all to the good. I hope this book will increase that sensitivity and arouse more opposition to "sin." If there is more awareness, more sense of responsibility in the world today, there will be less self-destruction. Recognizing our apathy and our denial is a step toward abandoning both. There is "sin" among us, in us, called by various names.

How Can Man Control Man?

What can we do about it? What is to be done by those of us moved to attempt to stay the self-destruction of the world? Behavior regarded as "crime" is dealt with officially, with great clumsiness and ineffectiveness, to be sure. As "illness," some aggressive behavior is capably but expensively corrected without moral stigmatization. But beyond these the great bulk of human aggression proceeds with only symbolic restraint, and in some areas not even that. Meanwhile, the population grows greater, but not correspondingly wiser, and that in itself is an aspect of self-destruction.

Notions of guilt and sin which formerly served as some restraint on aggression have become eroded by the presumption that the individual has less to do with his actions than we had assumed, and hence any sense of personal responsibility (or guilt) is inappropriate. This philosophy comes as a comforting relief for many, an alarming threat of powerlessness for others, and an inflammatory challenge for others.

[3] Alexander Solzhenitsyn, *The New Yorker*, September 9, 1972, p. 29.

Constantly operative, of course, and presumably with great and increasing effectiveness, are the constructive devices developed by civilization for the absorption of (sublimated) aggressive energy. Athletic contests, both participant and exhibitionist types, are increasingly popular. Cultural developments increase in quality and in quantity, as well as in popularity and participation. The control of disease and disability advances swiftly, albeit expensively. Group discussions, conventions, and other meetings become ever more numerous and more comprehensive. There *is* a United Nations; there *is* a peace movement. There are still many sizable religious groups with ideals and programs of action as well as opportunities for formal worship.

But, as I have elaborated in the preceding chapters, there is still an abundance of uncontrolled aggression in the world, some of it even defended. And there are more individuals and more groups to generate and express the aggression, and to assist in the exploration of resources. But an anxious, discouraged, depressed mood prevails among these increasing peoples. One thinks of the famous one-line explanation of the child's suicide in Hardy's *Jude the Obscure:* "Because we are too menny."

My proposal is for the revival or reassertion of personal responsibility in all human acts, good and bad. Not total responsibility, but not zero either. I believe that all evildoing in which we become involved to any degree tends to evoke guilt feelings and depression. These may or may not be clearly perceived, but they affect us. They may be reacted to and covered up by all kinds of escapism, rationalization, and reaction or symptom formation. To revive the half-submerged idea of personal responsibility and to seek appropriate measures of reparation might turn the tide of our aggressions and of the moral struggle in which much of the world population is engaged.

We will see our world dilemmas more and more as expressing *internal* personal moral problems instead of seeing them only as *external*, social, legal, or environmental complexities.

Someone may exclaim here that this is just what the criminal law seems to assume. It is never the environment in which the offender has grown up and in which he lives that is to blame; it is not his poverty, his misfortunes, his mistreatment, or his provocation. It is he who acted, he who committed the crime, and is "responsible" for it, and it is he who must be given punishment.

I am not concurring with this old formula. There is always some environmental determination and always some individual determination, and it is improper to exclude either. In the courtroom, everyone is responsible; elsewhere, almost no one seems to be.

And lest we still seem to be too deterministic, let us remember the factor of adventitious circumstance—pure "luck," if you like. The great physicist Max Born flatly disputed the metaphysical principle that everything must have a cause. It is inevitable, he said, that a monistic concept of experience has to be abandoned. "If quantum theory has any philosophical importance at all, it lies in the fact that it demonstrates . . . the necessity of dual aspects and complementary considerations. . . . Nature is ruled by laws of cause and laws of chance *in a certain mixture*."[4] (Italics mine) Some "behaviorists" forget this.

If a dozen people are in a lifeboat and one of them discovers a leak near where he is sitting, is there any doubt as to his responsibility? Not for having *made* the hole, or for finding it, but for attempting to repair it! To ignore it or to keep silent about it is almost equivalent to having made it!

Thus even in group situations and group actions, there is a degree of personal responsibility, either for doing or for not doing—or for declaring a position about it. The word "sin" involves these considerations, and upon this I base the usefulness of a revival of the concept, if not the word, sin.

My father, who was a thoroughgoing naturalist and botanist, used to object to our referring to any growing plants as weeds, even when we were removing them—at his instigation—from his peony or rose beds. "Nearly every plant is called a weed by people somewhere, and what we here call weeds may be prize specimens in some lands." Scientifically true, of course, but calling certain plants in our garden "weeds" did enable us to have better peonies and roses. As an operative term *sin* has this value: it identifies something to be eliminated or avoided.

[4] Max Born, *Natural Philosophy of Cause and Chance* (London: Oxford University, 1949).

The Designation Sin Implies Further Action

"Sin is a 'weary word,'" said Bernard Murchland, "but the reality it signifies is energetic and destructive. . . . Our age is as haunted by the presence of sin as any other—perhaps more so. . . . The problem of sin is the axial problem of human thought and no effort of man's mind has any lasting importance that is not concerned with that problem."[5]

The word "sin" does carry an implication of cost, of penalty, of answerability. The wages of *some* sins are death, without doubt; and the wages of lesser sins, while less than death, are substantial, including reparation, restitution, and atonement. Sinning is never with impunity, but the assessment and the penalization are not our business. They are not a judge's business as in the case of crime. They are between the sinner, his conscience, his God, and his victim. Sin must be dealt with in the private courts of the individual heart, sometimes with self-indulgence, sometimes with self-reproach but without penalty, sometimes with symbolic cancellations, sometimes with stern self-punishment.

Self-punishment always involves severe conflict. The mounting internal stress of unrelieved conscience disturbs the equilibrium and organization of the personality. The organism protests the painful and threatening treatment it is receiving (from a part of itself), and attempts to escape. Various devices—projection, denial, symptom formation, or ritualistic undoing—are available. The threat of total disequilibration is held in check; if it becomes greater, the organism is pushed to greater salvaging efforts.

The logical, reasonable, effective solution for tension reduction in such a circumstance is to make atonement, as theology calls it, or amends, as we say, by restitution, acknowledgment, and revised tactics. But sometimes this is hard to do. Some of the sins for which punishment or the threat of punishment brings great anxiety and symptomatology to the individual may be at the moment unknown to him. They have been forgotten, repressed into unconsciousness. The clinical process of psychoanalytic "treatment" aims at penetrating and recovering this material, bringing to mind previously repressed,

---

[5] Mark Oraison et al., *Sin*, trans. by Bernard Murchland and Raymond Meyerpeter with an Introduction by Bernard Murchland (New York: Macmillan, 1962).

nearly forgotten offenses. Once these reminiscences which entailed so much distress are made conscious and the guilt feeling attached to them realized, both the offenses and the guilt can be more rationally dealt with.

Psychoanalysis has been much admired for its demonstrated successes in accomplishing this result in many people. But it has also received much criticism, not alone for its frequent failures to achieve the relief sought, but also for constituting what seemed to many to be a punitively expensive process for rationalizing and intellectualizing aggressive behavior. The individual himself may feel more relieved than is his environment—and perhaps for the wrong reason! This is bowdlerized in Anna Russell's sardonic jab:

> At three I had a feeling of
> Ambivalence toward my brothers,
> And so it follows naturally
> I poisoned all my lovers.
> But now I'm happy; I have learned
> The lesson this has taught;
> That everything I do that's wrong
> Is someone else's fault.[6]

Some individuals, like some other animals, proceed and appear as if their aggressions (like all their other behavior) were the right and proper and "natural" thing to do, involving no internal consequences, regardless of the external consequences. Toward such individuals, judges and psychiatrists, both, often take a paradoxical attitude. The man "has no conscience," he kills ruthlessly and demonstrates a total lack of concern, remorse, regret, or self-reproach. In the judge's view this is the most heinous, inhuman, and unpardonable wickedness, "deserving" the harshest punishment; on the other hand, in the eyes of the psychiatrists, it is also a demonstration of serious mental illness, a state of "moral imbecility," an indication of "psychopathic personality," "borderline character," or other denigrating terms meaning a dire sickness.

But in most human beings a sense of guilt is aroused by the awareness of participation in events regarded as forbidden, dis-

---

[6] Anna Russell, "Psychiatric Folksong," in O. Hobart Mowrer, *The Crisis in Psychiatry and Religion* (Princeton, N.J.: Van Nostrand, 1961), p. 49.

approved, incompatible with the accepted ideals, whether or not the designation "sin" is involved. Guilt feelings give rise to a need for self-justification in further attack, or for atonement by means of punishment (moral, physical, verbal, painful, or merely symbolic). Since the conscience—while more or less vigilant—is demonstrably corruptible, it may be palliated with bribes (excuses, compensations) or counterfeit tokens easily forthcoming.

In a way, pain is one of those counterfeits; to "kick oneself" does not really undo a *faux pas*; to cut off one's own right hand does not really repair the damage the offending member had caused. But the pain and other cost of such acts assuage the guilt feelings and pass for appropriate penance.

But there *are* penalties which tend toward mending the harm done. Restitution, for example, is both a penalty and a constructive move toward reparation. It is a civilized or educated type of penalty, one not common to human nature or to criminal law. The law would rather, it seems, spend $100,000 maintaining a robber in prison idleness for stealing a car than permit him to restore the car three times over by honest and properly compensated labor. And this insult to common sense nevertheless expresses a common *popular* (i.e., as well as legal) attitude.

Dr. O. Hobart Mowrer's position on this is that many functional "neuroses" are indications of a *hidden* (but not *forgotten*) history of serious misconduct—which had not been adequately acknowledged, atoned for, propitiated, or otherwise "canceled out." "And if this be so, then confession, expiation, and 'a new life in Christ' (or some equivalent type of conversion) have a practical pertinence which far exceeds the boundaries behind which some theologians have attempted to hold them."[7]

Francisco Guerra in his recent book about the cultures and mores of early Indians on the North American continent speaks succinctly of the use of confession by the Occidental and Yucatec Indians:

> There also existed among the Occidental Indians their kind of oral confession of sins, I mean of those sins that were considered such by those peoples, such as homicide, theft, and adultery, etc. although it was not uniform nor of the same kind in all regions. The Yucatecan

[7] Mowrer, op. cit., p. 57.

Indians had the custom of confessing themselves once in their lives, and this when they felt they were so near death that they could not escape, and they made this confession of theirs in public and before anyone who wished to hear it, telling the whole course of their lives and telling there their public and private guilts, and sometimes many troubles and dissensions arose from this, especially from the confessions of the women with regard to their husbands, if it happened that they escaped and survived their illness, so that in all ways that infernal spirit, either all at once or by degrees, always managed to make trouble among those poor people. . . .

[On the other hand] The Yucatecs knew by nature when they did evil, and in the belief that because of evil and sin came deaths, diseases and suffering, they have the custom of confession when they felt proper, in this manner: when by illness or something else they were in danger of death, they confessed their sin, and if they neglected it, their closest relations or friends reminded them of it, and then they publicly said their sins, if the priest was there to him, if not to the fathers and the mothers, and wives to husbands and husbands to wives.

The sins of which they usually accused themselves were theft, homicide, of the flesh, false testimony, and with this they thought they were safe and many times if they escaped there were quarrels between husband and wife, on account of the unhappy events, or with those who motivated them.[8]

The Pleasure of Sin

In an earlier chapter (on symptoms) we outlined the complex multiple motivation, purpose, function, and meaning of symptoms. I think one could do much the same for behavior that is designated as sinful. It is aggressive, it is pleasure-giving, it is attention-getting, it is problem-solving, it is self-injuring and destroying. The pleasure-giving in sin is more apt to be conscious than unconscious.

There is some "fun" in most sinning. Perhaps in a way we assume this to be the motive for it. The anticipated pleasure makes for the greater temptation of it. Not all acts of sin have the same meaning or

[8] Francisco Guerra, *The Pre-Columbian Mind* (London and New York: Seminar Press, 1971).

degree of pleasure-giving function. Few people would feel tempted to indulge in child-beating or horse-whipping or slaughtering wildlife or car-stealing or defrauding the ignorant, yet for some individuals each of these things affords great pleasure.

In other words, just as the *symptom* has numerous functions, so the *sin* not only serves the sinner as a means of aggression with which he can repay aggression that he feels was directed against him, but it affords him a certain amount of pleasure. We can stand off and decry that kind of pleasure, but the fact remains that there is no accounting for tastes. Our forms of sinful enjoyment may be just as abhorrent to other people as theirs are to us. (I am using "we" and "us" and "they" in a highly indefinite and categorical manner.)

And there is a popular corollary assumption that reverses the formula; e.g., "all fun is fattening or sinful." The stern prohibitions of the Puritans regarding behavior on the Sabbath, or of the early Methodists regarding games and dancing, are examples of this reversal morality. That such exaggerations have at times become current only confirms an essential if elusive truth.

Some sinners deny any pleasure whatsoever in the commission of their sins. I am not prepared to say that this stems from repression or untruthfulness or some other psychological mechanism. The fact that guilt and fear hang over the sinner may also detract from the pleasure. But some individuals seem to hate their sins rather than enjoy them, even at the moment of commission. Their motivation is quite other than the pleasure derived from the sin. And some pleasure in sinning derives from the sinful satisfaction of revenge, i.e., rationalized aggression.

But the satisfactions obtained from sin are often seemingly greater (at the time) than those which accrue from conformity and nonviolation; the self-assertion of the one is easier than the self-control of the other. To the sinner his choice must seem sensible or expedient because of this gain, a gain which must far exceed its cost in alienation, guilt feelings, and possible penalization. To outside observers this behavior appears too costly, and offensive and destructive. And although symptoms are apt to arouse sympathy and pity in outsiders, sins often provoke disapproval if perceived, and even sharp condemnation. (Of course, some observers identify themselves with the sinner, and do their "sinning" secretly and vicariously; other join in wholeheartedly.)

Scientific literature by the ton—research reports, didactic treatises, philosophical debates, theorems and countertheorems—has been contributed to the theme of motivation of behavior. Are we spontaneously impelled from within or only tempted or threatened from without? Have we some cognitive control over some acts, over all acts, over no acts? Notwithstanding the evidence of the new behaviorism, most of us favor the "common sense" view that by taking thought we can control, modify, restrain *some* of our behavior *some* of the time.

Neither the pleasurableness nor the usefulness of a sin can be regarded as the motive. Many other meanings reside in it unseen, concealed from both the observers and the sinner himself. Rarely does a thief steal a watch for the fun of stealing, or for the sake of telling the time, nor yet (as many would assume) for the sheer money value of the watch. Motivation is far more complex and subtle.

Certainly Lee Harvey Oswald shot President Kennedy for reasons other than to depose a leader. Whether this makes any crime less criminal, or the sin less sinful, it dispels the simplistic explanation usually given for lesser crimes, and it answers the question so often asked in the case of bizarre crimes, "Why on earth would anyone want to do that?"

What can a sin possibly accomplish for the good of the soul or the integrity of the organism or the welfare of society? Do the principles of organismic or system theory apply here? Might a lesser sin serve to prevent a greater sin being committed? (The Roman Catholic Church thinks and says so.) Does all that has been said about symptoms also apply, in some measure, to sins? Does sin— through the pain of guilt—serve to lead the sinner to some effort at restitution and atonement which in the end may leave him a better man than before?

This phenomenon of becoming "weller than well" after an illness is one with which all doctors are familiar. But illness is so unwelcome and its disappearance so much a cause of rejoicing that the added, unexpected blessing of further growth or improvement is often overlooked. Not so the "reformed" sinner. The Prodigal Son's sinful experiences led to a state of existence far better, we are led to believe, than his original one. Mary Magdalene, Peter, Saul, Paul, and St. Augustine were all prodigal sons—"sinners" indeed—who became "weller than well."

We have to keep reminding ourselves—because it goes against our common sense and beliefs—that the voluntary element is never as voluntary as it seems. As stated earlier, every visible act of every human· being is *partially* voluntary and *partially* involuntary; its motivation is partially conscious, partially unconscious. What we are doing every minute of every hour is determined in part by "reasons" from the residue of previous experiences which we have forgotten—if we ever knew—and in part by immediate obvious indications. Thus there is little sense in asking anyone why he did something except to stimulate reflection and discussion.

Why Did You Do It?

A subject so interrogated is always impeded in his reply by at least four factors: (1) he may *know* a (not necessarily *the*) reason and be unwilling to reveal it; (2) he may be aware of reasons and be unable to explain them; (3) he may not know any reasonable reason; (4) there may be no reason. A man who slips on a wet sidewalk can't give any motive for it. Any explanation a person offers for an act is therefore almost certain to be partly if not totally incorrect, even if it is extorted by threat or torture.

Specious as it is, the attempt to distinguish between symptom and sin by the degree of conscious voluntariness and the satisfaction achieved (the fun) is almost universal. It just will not be given up. Judges, parents, and teachers will continue to ask, "Why did you do it?" and expect the culprit to justify it, i.e., rationalize his act—or admit he enjoyed it and therefore "willed" to do it. Reporters will continue to search for and write about "the motive" or "the cause," which has or "hasn't been found." What on earth do they mean? What are they seeking?

"The combination of causes of phenomena is beyond the grasp of the human intellect. But the impulse to seek causes is innate in the soul of man. And the human intellect, with no inkling of the immense variety and complexity of circumstances conditioning a phenomenon, any one of which may be separately conceived of as the cause of it, snatches at the first and most easily understood approximation, and says here is the cause."[9]

Back of their inquiries—and ours—is a wistful, fearful existential terror lest the bulwarks of the good life be swept away by unmitigated, unneutralized, uncontrolled EVIL. It seems to be coming from outside, from others, from another being similar to ourselves but more alienated (sinful). This is the perennial motivation for the "why" whip. "Why did you rock the boat?" we cry. "Why do you strike at our society? If you are so death-seeking and death-dealing, why should we not rid ourselves of you quickly in self-defense? How can we make you feel sorry?"

"Please!" begs the sinner. "I confess my guilt and I concede my defenselessness. I cannot adequately answer your 'why.' My hand was forced. Your 'society' has attacked me. I confess my resentment, my aggressiveness but also my misery, my terror. Call it my sin; sentence me; punish me. Avenge yourselves on me but ultimately shrive me. Forgive me and take me back. Might it not have been you?"

The contemporary hubbub over Professor Skinner's contention that there is no personal decision involved in behavior, and hence no guilt, no responsibility, recalls the ancient contest over "free will." Skinner's position essentially restates Augustine's. St. Augustine resolved the paradox of inevitability and responsibility at the expense of the latter and glorified grace by belittling nature and free will.[10]

Is grace, then, the only hope? If sin be recognized, if it be confessed, if it be repented, if restitution be made and atonement achieved, is this the end of it? The circle closed, do we just go on—and sin again, confess again, repent again? Have we no hope to offer?

Yes, a conscious sense of guilt, and implicit or explicit repentance, would be consequences of the revival of an acknowledgment of error, transgression, offense, and responsibility—in short, of sin. This is the answer to the reader's question—"So what?" This is one difference it would make.

[9] Count Leo Tolstoy, *War and Peace* (New York: Random House), part III, p. 928, opening sentence.

[10] Fraust Rei. Grat. 1.13 (CSEL 21:44); Jaroslav Pelikan, *The Emergence of the Catholic* (Chicago: University of Chicago, 1971).

And what would be the good of that? someone asks. Do we need more breast-beaters? Shall we add depression to the already mentioned gloom and world uneasiness? Why not a "no-fault" theology, equivalent to no-fault casualty insurance: no one to blame? Things just happen, alas? The assumption that there is sin in it somewhere implies both a possibility and an obligation for intervention. Presumably something is possible which can be reparative, corrective, meliorative, and that something involves me and mercy—we want them, too. But we want to think we can help ourselves and our fellows if only a modicum.

Hence sin is the only hopeful view. The present world miasma and depression are partly the result of our self-induced conviction that since sin has ceased to be, only the neurotics need to be treated and the criminals punished. The rest may stand around and read the newspapers. Or look at television. Do your thing and keep your eye on the road leading to the main chance.

As it is, vague, amorphous evil appears all about us, and when this or that awful thing is happening and this terrible thing goes on and that wretched circumstance has developed, and yet, withal, when no one is responsible, no one is guilty, no moral questions are asked, when there is, in short, just nothing to do, we sink to despairing helplessness. We wait from day to day for improvement, expectantly but not hopefully.

Therefore I say that the consequence of my proposal would not be more depression, but less. If the concept of personal responsibility and answerability for ourselves and for others were to return to common acceptance, hope would return to the world with it!

10

The Bluebird on the Dung Heap

O nly a few pages remain in which to spell out the promise of the closing paragraphs of the preceding chapter. We must relate the morality for which we have opted in this book to the mental health and hygiene goals which we have long proclaimed.

Forty years ago I wrote a modest description of the scope of medical psychology entitled *The Human Mind.* It dealt with the diagnosis and treatment of mental illness. The present book, now drawing to its conclusion, could be viewed as a modest testament of mental hygiene. It proposes that mental hygiene is a reality, not a metaphor, that people can be happier, healthier, kinder, and more secure in the integrity of their being by a few intentionally preventive measures. Self-destructiveness can be lessened, painful coping efforts assisted, anxiety attenuated, not by mere reassurance or comforting words or minimization or distraction, but by a deliberate renunciation of apathy and a courageous facing of the responsibility for evil.

The reader must surely know that I would not claim his attention for these many pages of commiseration on our common discomforts and misfortunes only to propose the amendment of our vocabulary by the one word "sin." What then is the message?

The message is simple. It is that concern is the touchstone. Caring. Relinquishing the sin of indifference. This recognizes acedia as the Great Sin; the heart of all sin. Some call it selfishness. Some call it alienation. Some call it schizophrenia. Some call it egocentricity. Some call it separation.

"Have the men of our time lost a feeling of the meaning of sin?" asked Paul Tillich. "Do they realize that sin does not mean an immoral act, that 'sin' should never be used in the plural, and that not our sins, but rather our *sin* is the great, all-pervading problem of our life? To be in the state of sin is to be in the state of separation." "Separation," he continued, "may be from one's fellowmen, from one's own true self and/or from his God."[1] (Tillich used "Ground of Being"; the reader can choose his own word.)

Separation is another word not only for sin, but for mental illness, for crime, for nonfunctioning, for aggression, for alienation, for death. Some prefer one or the other, but all these words describe the same thing.

I am influenced in all my thinking, of course, by my life work as a physician, as a psychiatrist. If a person I knew was observed *to be* acting as self-destructively as *mankind* has been doing, if this person alternately exhibited depression and a show of cheery *sangfroid* and pseudo-optimism, if he busied himself with furious activity one week and slumped in despairing gloom the next—such a person would arouse our concern. We would fear that his disturbed emotional state, his personality disorganization, his failing self-control, might soon bring him into inextricable difficulties and lead to acts of very bad judgment, great unpleasantness, or serious self-injury.

If this were a friend or a patient of mine, I would feel a responsibility to act immediately, to intervene in the process in an effort to prevent tragedy and to guide his return to a healthy progression. The incubus of his depression can be lifted, not pooh-poohed, or exorcised or swept under the rug or concealed by euphemisms and myths or by Greek neologisms—but examined, recognized, acknowledged, and then corrected in an intelligent and adequate way. From this he will become a transformed man. He will have "recovered." Someone must recognize his need and help him to meet it. (Or so I believe; some would say let him do as he likes. Let him save—or destroy—himself.)

Our world situation may not be analogous, but perhaps it is in some respects comparable. And who feels responsible for the world's suffering? Illness only partially conquered, crime miserably controlled, individual and collective depredations abundant. A sense of personal moral responsibility is faint and apparently growing fainter. Depression, discouragement, acedia, and likewise megalomania and power-flaunting are widespread. We each do our part in a total process of wasting, spending, polluting, defiling, stealing,

[1] Paul Tillich, "You Are Accepted," *A.D.*, 1:36–40 (September, 1972).

hoarding, exhausting, and destroying. We pause occasionally to gaze about in alarm and apprehensiveness; we acknowledge a general pall of depression. But no corrective peccavi or *mea culpa* escape our lips.

Some ascribe our griefs to the human condition, to repetitious, irremediable loss. Centuries ago states of mental anguish were ascribed to demonic possession, and their victims were regarded as wicked creatures. With the coming of scientific insights the contribution of toxins and infections and constitutional disorders were recognized. Later, the effects of social pressures and personal experiences became even more important, but demon possession was not. The new scientific explanations, for good historical reasons, skirted consideration of anything that would look like the old notion of sin. But now that the idea of sin has been reconsidered theologically and ethically, the time has come for *scientists* to reconsider it also and to give it an appropriate place in their work.

We know something about the effect of sorrows and disappointments and defective genes and disturbed body chemistry and derangements of fantasy and reactions to trauma. We can better recognize, now, the subtler factors of "bad" character identifications, habitual error, sloth, meanness, and disguised aggression with elaborate rationalizations. For some, the aggressiveness, selfishness, greediness, destructiveness, ruthlessness, and pride of our fellow travelers are but expressions of our "humanity." "And why apologize for it? Need we be ashamed of being human?" they ask. "That's the way we are, and let there be no reproaches, no regret, guilt, depression, repentance, responsibility. Begone such words as 'sin'!"

But do these feelings go away?

Do these imprecations bring back the peace and beauty and health and happiness that have been destroyed?

Do such people become our paragons of mental health or our moral leaders?

"Suppose," asks Toynbee, "that in the next generation the ablest minds and the most perceptive spirits were to come to Socrates' conclusion that the most urgent business on mankind's agenda was to close the morality gap."

Well, just suppose it. Shut your eyes and wish fervently. Pray for it!

Imagine leaders striving—not to heal the sick, not to comfort the anguished, not to feed the starving, not to terminate the waste and pollution of our resources but—"to close the morality gap"! To establish more firmly in national, international, and personal affairs the supreme importance of distinguishing right from wrong. To end the concealment of sin under various euphemistic disguises, but to confess it and atone for it and desist from it. If the word "sin" is unacceptable to you, I challenge you to suggest a better one.

Toynbee's proposal for action was directed toward the leaders, the ablest minds and spirits. But who and where are they? Where are those leaders who can choose for us the least encumbered paths and warn us against the unseen dangers and correct our erring steps? Like sheep, all of us have gone astray or followed false shepherds after pausing to kill our emergent prophets. Political leaders we have in abundance, as well as military leaders, business leaders, social leaders, intellectual leaders. But moral leadership languishes, and upon moral leadership we still rely for salvation.

The President, surely; the leading political figures; our statesmen. It would certainly mean the leading educators—university presidents and professors—and no doubt many lesser figures in that same great professional fraternity, committed as it is to intellectual attainment and leadership. And the press, of course—our editors, writers, and poets. And some of us doctors and other professional men. It would surely include the clergy of all faiths. Toynbee's prescription is, in principle, already their program. They might want to say— "That's what we have been advocating, week after week, year after year to our diminishing audiences. Why is there not more perceptible effect? Why does no one listen? Why does the morality gap constantly widen? Why do the people steal and the big enterprises cheat and the statesmen lie? And why is the notion of sin—never mind the word—discarded as obsolete, even by us, the clergy?"

The Role of the Clergy

If the moribund term "sin" with its full implications is ever revived, we will all have to have a voice in it. But the clergy will have reasserted an authority for leadership in the moral field which they have let slip from their hands. It is their special prerogative to study sin—or whatever they call it—to identify it, to define it, to warn us about it, and to spur measures for combating and rectifying it. Have they been diverted or discouraged from their task? Have they succumbed to the feeling that law and science and technology have proved morality and moral leadership irrelevant? Did they, too, fall for the illusion that sin had really vanished?

We laymen have a responsibility for supporting the clergymen; we are reminded of the priesthood of all believers. Week in and week out believers listen to their shepherds, men whom they regard as expert in the knowledge of right and wrong in daily life. They are listened to with (more or less) open ears and hearts. What do their listeners hear?

Millions of words have been set down regarding what the parishioners *should* hear: reassurance about the existence of God, His mercifulness, His grace, His goodness, His expectations of mankind to forgive and to love, His sure forgiveness of repented sin, the assurance of life everlasting. These worthy themes support the faith. But they will not reach to the heart of *some* listeners for whom the roar and rumble of guilt drown out the reassurances. If, occasionally, a congregation is gently scolded, is it for absenteeism, violation of the Sabbath, or niggardly support of the church budget?

How often does a modern sermon deal with sin? Sin in general or in particular? The civil rights struggle in our country certainly had its brave clergymen spokesmen, and leaders—perhaps more often in action than in preaching—but they were a pitiful minority of the profession. Many were threatened and deterred by reactionary congregations.

Actions speak louder than words, of course. But has the reader ever heard a sermon, for example, in which cigarette smoking or wildlife destruction or political lying or business dishonesty were dealt with as sins? Some members of the congregation would no doubt rebuke such a pastor for his lack of spirituality. *"One should not preach of such things,"* they told Micah when he became specific (Mic. 2:6).

They still try to give our contemporary Micahs that same admonition. They have been reproaching and rebuking and intimidating clergymen for being specific ever since. Small wonder that some preachers have become conformist, banal, and dull. When some statement or action by the minister offends a group of the sinners, they cry out that morality is none of the church's business. They subtract funds from its support as punishment.

"Should the church stick its neck out?" asks J. Irwin Miller, a distinguished layman and industrialist. He was answering the attack which the *Reader's Digest* launched at the World Council of Churches for its upright stand. "The church must speak," said Miller, "with words *and* deeds. . . . In times past this has meant leading the fight against child labor, slavery . . . and for prison reform, for the right of the working man to form unions . . . for complete racial equality, for the elimination of poverty and hunger. . . . Sometimes the church is wrong . . . but there is no way [it] can play it safe and be true to the Gospel. . . . Whose job *is* it to cause society to 'repent' if not the church's? . . . The role of prophet [minister] is active, often disruptive and always painful. . . . I know this, because, if the church today were to do its full duty, I would be among those called to repent."[2]

Most of us in the congregation sit in our pews quietly and smugly. Does the minister remember that if, indeed, we are but dust, we are very guilty dust? Does he remember that we are all "worried"? Every member of this, and every other, congregation is worried about something, little or big—health, finances, family relations, impending decisions, threats, rumors, bad news from afar, and especially guilt feelings. Things he ought to do—or not to do.

Mrs. A in the front pew is thinking about her sister who is better off than she but has cancer. There has been a queer twist in her envy. Mrs. B nearby has three children, two of whom have to be taken to the dentist this week, a great expense which is going to anger her husband and disarrange their summer plans. Besides which she is worried about some deceptions. Miss C has no children to worry about and no husband to be angered, but why doesn't she have them? She wonders what is wrong with her that she doesn't have a husband and children. Perhaps, she reasons, it is because of something she can't bear to recall. Mr. D is dreading tomorrow when the bank examiners come again; will they notice? Mr. E should go to see his employer; but how he dreads it! Can he postpone the confrontation? Mr. F is not worried, just bored.

"What can I say that will reach these worriers?" broods the poor clergyman. He knows about many of the anxieties in the pews, but how about his own? He, too, is worried and troubled. His salary is

[2] J. Irwin Miller, Chief Executive Officer of the Cummins Engine Company, "Should Churches 'Play It Safe'?" *Reader's Digest*, April, 1972, pp.207–212.

small, his younger daughter is unhappy, the clerk of the session is disagreeable, the "ministry of music" is presumptuous, and there are dissident factions in the education department. Each Sunday morning there are more empty seats. Is he at fault or is it the times? Nevertheless, he must go on and preach and really say something.

What shall he say to these pople? Scold them? Warn them? Tell them that he is worried, too? Bless them and urge them to pray? Promise them peace? Should he, like Moses, cover his face so as not to look too holy? God is good, he could remind them; God means well for all of us; He has promised us His grace; He has forgiven us already. It is darkest just before dawn. So the Lord bless you and keep you . . . make His face to shine . . . and please, will you all come back again next week?

Inadequate? He realizes that. He knows it is only partly relevant; he knows it is only slightly reassuring; he knows it goes unheard by most of the congregation.

Perhaps he asks us, what do *we* think should be said, and heard.

He asks us, now, what he should say. And what do we reply?

On the basis of psychiatric experience, can we offer him any guidelines? We could assure him, I think, that whatever his parishioners are worrying about is very likely not the whole shape of their anxiety; people generally focus on the "wrong" things. He might tell them that. He might remind them that all of us feel guilty. He might raise the "why?" question, as well as pointing to the "what." The church is indeed a place to come for the assurance of forgiveness; but there is a step before that. Confession must include a recognition of the aggression of the sins committed. "So long as a person lives under the shadow of real, unacknowledged, and unexpiated guilt," says Professor Hobart Mowrer, "he . . . will continue to hate himself and to suffer the inevitable consequences of self-hatred. But the moment he . . . begins to accept his guilt and his sinfulness, the possibility of radical reformation opens up; and . . . a new freedom of self-respect and peace."[3]

Mowrer is neither a psychiatrist nor a minister, but an experienced psychologist. Yet few clergymen nowadays venture to call for repentance, as did the prophets and John the Baptist and Jonathan Edwards and Professor Mowrer. They fear the public reproach of

[3] O. Hobart Mowrer, *The Crisis in Psychiatry and Religion* (Princeton, N.J.: Van Nostrand, 1961), pp. 54–55.

having reverted (as some extremists have) to threats of fire-and-brimstone damnation. They dread this accusation so much that they don't speak out even what they believe should be heard and heeded by the man in the pew. (Of course, many laymen are not in the pews, and are not exposed to any sort of moral suasion by the clergy. To this problem of the wandering sheep I shall return after a few more words to the clergy.)

"But can I really reach them from the pulpit?" asks the diffident pastor. "Can I start a train of thought that will lead to some self-disclosure by my parishioners? Should I direct their attention to their consciences, as my Catholic colleagues do in the confessional? I might try. I might ask: 'What have you done this week to hurt your neighbor, your sister, your wife? What have you done to hurt yourself? What have you done to hurt this church or the ideals for which it stands? What have you done to hurt this city, this land on which we live? What have you done this week against the interests of the next generation? What have you left undone for the suffering, damaged, polluted, exploited earth and its hungry, miserable, exploited population?' "

Yes, you might—and your congregation might like it very much and be helped by it. I have occasionally heard such sermons. They take courage—and they give it.

One such that I heard recently began this way:

> As one who previously took pleasure in believing that he was "liberal" and "progressive," it is not enjoyable now to be in the role of a "conservative" or a "puritan." Puritanism is so disdained today, and so jibed at, that one recoils from the very word itself as though it were some sort of disease. Yet, I doubt that the cure for puritanism is impuritanism, and I have genuine difficulty adjusting to the blatant unrestraint of today. *And a preacher must be true to himself, and proclaim what he believes to be true, whether it be popular or not.* [Italics mine]
>
> We live in an undisciplined age. It concerns me that apparently our clamor is for right without responsibility, for privilege without painful striving, for cultural and intellectual short-cuts that should be described as self-deceiving.
>
> The Greeks had a saying that the fair things in life are hard; that strength—be it physical, mental, or moral—was gained only by

effort and self-discipline. Is this truth outdated? Must we not admit that, as a people, we are morally and religiously undisciplined? In the name of freedom and liberation we have fled every yoke and every restriction as though work, art, study, and religion are disciplines we can do without.

The very concept of self-discipline has come under attack, and my personal conviction is that this is one reason that for many people life has lost its dimensions. The heights and depths are gone, and life has become flat and dull and cheap and frivolous. The pleasures sought are the pleasures of a smoking heart and a pulsating nerve— and when the thrill is gone, the refuge is drink and drugs.

It may very well be that as adults we have been so captured by the cult of comfort ourselves that we are incapable of challenging our own young people with the great needs of a world that is bewildered, uprooted, beaten down, and more than half-starved.[4]

St. Paul (or another early Christian) once preached a sermon by mail in which he advised renewing our minds and hearts, discontinuing our lying and adhering to the truth. And if any of us is angry about something, he said, let him avoid aggressive revenge and make peace, before the sun sets. Cease stealing, he said (it was going on then, you see), discard envy and greed, and direct our energies into constructive and benevolent activities. Renounce all our bitterness and hate and anger and noise and foul talk and malice. Yes, and be kind to one another, kind and gentle and forgiving, so that we ourselves can be forgiven. "And walk in love," he said, "as dear children of God."[5]

That was specific, and it was direct.

The widespread need for open avowal and acknowledgment and confession occasionally comes to light in the blooming of some new cult in which communication and disclosure are made a part of self-realization. Such cults are often evanescent because they depend too much on superficial solutions, but they are popular because unconfessed guilt feelings are hard to bear. They must be confessed to someone!

[4] "Discipleship and Discipline," sermon by Dr. Kenneth L. Mauldin, First Presbyterian Church, Topeka, Kansas, January 9, 1972.

[5] Eph. 4:23–32 and 5:13.

And the clergyman is a very special "someone." He stands in a special place; he has special authority. Not just because he has had education in theology and perhaps in psychology, but because he is "a man of God." He is dedicated. He is unselfish. He has no wish to hurt but only to help people—and this is rare.

If the minister says, "This is clearly sin," we usually accept that decision. Criminal or not, symptomatic or not, sinful he says it is, and the wages of sin are death. But there is a solution: penitence, confession, restitution, atonement. Relief from a sense of guilt then begins automatically.

The human conscience is like the police; it may be eluded, stifled, drugged, or bribed. But not without cost. We know some of these costs.

Some clergymen evade responsibility with the advice, "Sin is an old-fashioned notion. No need to feel guilty and repent to me, old fellow. You are no sinner but either sick or criminal, so I need only direct you to the left or to the right, to the doctor or to the police."

The clergyman cannot minimize sin and maintain his proper role in our culture. If he, or we ourselves, "say we have no sin, we deceive ourselves, and the truth is not in us" (John 1:8). We need him as our umpire to direct us, to accuse us, to reproach us, to exhort us, to intercede for us, to shrive us. Failure to do so is *his* sin.

I say "us," meaning me and my fellow parishioners. (They, of course, sin much more than I do but it would be presumptuous and unseemly for *me* to reproach them, and besides it would make me very unpopular.) No, it's the preacher's job! Am I my brother's keeper?

Alexander Solzhenitsyn, Russia's winner of the 1970 Nobel Prize for Literature, has a quick affirmative answer to that question: ". . . mankind's sole salvation lies in everyone making everything his business."[6]

Yes! The preacher can declaim; he can deplore; he can denounce; he can reprove and exhort and inspire. He can point out the responsibility of us all for the failure of us all. He can remind us of the priestly function of every member and he can recall to us the reality of sin and the validity of social morality.

But until I recognize and acknowledge that *I am* my brother's

---

[6] "The Talk of the Town," *The New Yorker*, September 9, 1972.

keeper, the tide of human self-destructiveness will not be stemmed. We will not have achieved either moral or mental health, and it is the minister's task to keep telling us that.

Buddha, Confucius, Lao-tze, Socrates, Zeno, and all the Hebrew prophets from Amos to Jesus taught that sin, hate, alienation, aggression—call it what you will—could be conquered by love. What we have been calling sin, Toynbee calls human egocentricity —making the universe a desirable place for oneself with plenty of free time, relaxation, comfort, security, and good health, and with no hunger or poverty. To transcend one's own self-centeredness is not a virtue; it is a saving necessity.

As you see, I am elevating the image of the minister. I want to stimulate an increase in his appreciation and self-esteem. He is far more influential than he realizes and his responsibility is great. He is right to be concerned about his sermons.

The technical word "transference" was used by Freud originally to describe the way in which a patient in the course of psycho-analytic treatment begins to feel and speak and act toward her relatively unknown therapist as if he were an incarnation of her father or mother or some other personage of her childhood toward whom she had strong feelings, some of them now forgotten. But the phenomenon was discovered to occur in many life situations other than psychotherapeutic treatment and the word was quickly picked up and used in general parlance, although not always quite correctly.

When I say that the clergyman (also the teacher, often, and the lawyer, occasionally) inevitably evokes transference effects (and affects!) from his parishioners (or clients), I mean that he will be both adored and detested *irrationally* by some people *for reasons not known to him or to them.* Young psychoanalysts are sometimes highly flattered by the esteem in which they find themselves held by patients, for a time, not fully realizing how completely undeserved and unintentional such feelings are. This becomes more evident when *negative* emotions and attitudes develop, which they always do if the analysis really progresses.

Clergyman—and others in helping professions—need to know this. And like the young doctor, the clergyman needs to be warned neither to take it at face value nor to ignore it. Such misidentifications with other persons are occurring by and to all of us constantly. Indeed, social life consists of all sorts of attachments and estrangements determined in part by this unconscious transposition and misidentification.

These irrational factors in the influence and power of the clergy-men are not the sole determinants. There are good rational and conscious reasons for his influence, also, and these are the more substantial bases of his power. But they are greatly enhanced by the transference effect, coupled with the religious taboo or awe which attaches to him as a "man of God."

This is why I think Toynbee's fantasy of moral leaders closing the morality gap, as he calls it, must indeed depend heavily upon the clergy. I am not proposing that clergymen should turn to the vivid threatening of an angry God, as did Jonathan Edwards, who seemed to feel that the devil was his enemy and an enemy of every clergyman, to be denounced and fought against and feared by every individual.[7] This position is too unsophisticated for the modern age, although there is apparently a considerable contemporary revival of satanism, astrology, demonology, and black magic.[8]

But Jonathan Edwards had a prodigious influence upon America, primarily a *constructive* influence. So also did William Lloyd Garrison, John Timothy Stone, John Cotton, Charles Finney, Harry Emerson Fosdick; so do Eugene Carson Blake, Carlyle Marney, Howard Thurman, and numerous others. Not even the most discouraged clergyman could doubt the efficacy of preaching in its influence upon the people of America, now and ever since colonial times.[9]

The minister standing before his flock week after week, speaking to them for half an hour under esthetic and hallowed auspices, has an unparalleled opportunity to lighten burdens, interrupt and redirect circular thinking, relieve the pressure of guilt feelings and

[7] For an interesting comment of this see Christopher R. Reaske, "The Devil and Jonathan Edwards," *The Journal of the History of Ideas*, vol. 33 (January–March, 1972), p. 123.

[8] The resurgence of the occult may be evidence of the wish to recognize evil as a mystery, even by accepting it as a ruling principle of life. But the silly rituals of propitiation, worship, and exorcism plus the attempted projection of evil into demons and witches, the attempted return to paganism and superstition do seem to announce a perception of sin as an entity in life. See *Time*, 99(25):62–68 (June 19, 1972).

[9] DeWitte T. Holland, ed., *Sermons in American History: Selected Issues in the American Pulpit 1630–1967* (Nashville, Tenn.: Abingdon, 1971).

their self-punishment, and inspire individual and social improvement. No psychiatrists or psychotherapists, even those with many patients, have the quantitative opportunity to cure souls and mend minds which the preacher enjoys. And the preacher also has a superb opportunity to do what few psychiatrists can, to prevent the development of chronic anxiety, depression, and other mental ills.

And yet, watching his comfortable, well-dressed congregation assemble, many a preacher must have had the bitter thoughts so well expressed by Elmer F. Suderman:

> Here they come,
> my nonchalants,
> my lazy daisies,
> their dainty perfume
> disturbing the room
> the succulent smell
> seductive as hell.
>
> Here they are
> my pampered flamboyants,
> status spoiled, who bring
> with exquisite zing
> their souls spick and span
> protected by Ban,
> their hearts young and gay
> decked in handsome cliché,
> exchanging at my call
> with no effort at all
> worship for whispering
> God for gossiping,
> theology for television.
>
> Baptized in the smell
> of classic Chanel
> I promote their nod
> to a jaunty God
> Who, they are sure,
> is a sparkling gem
> superbly right for them.

> There they go
> my in-crowd
> my soft-skinned crowd,
> my suntanned, so-so
> elegant, swellegant,
> natty, delectable,
> suave, cool, adorable
> DAMNED![10]

Yes, damned. Saved by grace perhaps. Certainly not helped by my cowardly silence. A word of reproof? A suggestion of sin? A confrontation? The parable of the rich young ruler? Something to disturb the Country Club coziness and complacency of my perfumed assembly? Dare I?

I am tempted to leave the matter right there. If sin is increasing and the feeling of guilt accumulating, if the nation's leaders are going to strive to close the morality gap, is it not the minister's prime concern? Are not the clergy the men of God? Do they not ascend Mount Sinai and confer with Jehovah and come back to us with the Tables of Stone under their arms? They will be there again next Sunday and we shall come to listen to them (some of us), weary from our work-filled week and facing another one ahead of us. We will bring regrets, anxieties, uneasiness, bad consciences— we are only poor weak human beings after all.

So temper the wind to the shorn lamb, we entreat. The music is very nice, especially since the new pipes have been added to the organ. And we will pray quickly for the forgiveness of our sins and sweepingly forgive those who have sinned against us. So let us go home now. Better? Bettered?

It was *after* his great discoveries regarding love patterns, sexuality, repression, transference, and other psychological mechanisms that Freud made the discovery and the admission that he had underestimated the importance of the destructive (read "sinful") element in man's psychological constitution—his hate, his envy, his aggressive drive turned outward and inward.

But the theologians had not overlooked it. They had just soft-pedaled it. Not the poets.

[10] Elmer F. Suderman, "The Smell of Perfumed Assemblies," *Theology Today*, 28:59 (1971).

Now am I veined by an eroding doubt,
Insidious as decay, with poison rife.
Is love indeed the end and law of life,
When lush, grimacing hates so quickly sprout?
I thought in ignorance I had cast out
The sneaking devils of continuing strife,
But as the cancer thwarts the surgeon's knife,
So does revenge my sword of reason flout.
But though hate rises in enfolding flame
At each renewed oppression, soon it dies;
It sinks as quickly as we saw it rise,
While love's small constant light burns still the same.
Know this: though love is weak and hate is strong,
Yet hate is short, and love is very long.[11]

The message that love can conquer hate can come from study and reflection, from counseling, from psychoanalysis, or from the pulpit. The clergyman, like the psychoanalyst, must point out the truth, temporarily painful though it may be to his listener(s). As in the analysis of a patient, the preacher's words may hurt, but they hurt for a purpose, for an enlightenment, for a freeing of bound energies. The moral leader risks being misunderstood or being understood too well. It is for these reasons that his popularity, his acceptance, his very life may be threatened. The clergyman's great opportunity is also a great hazard. Little wonder that many of those who see the opportunity lack the courage to seize it. (Ezekial 34)

This is the minister's message. It is the essence of all religions. But it would be cowardly, indeed, to put all the responsibility for our moral health and mental hygiene upon the clergy. Leaders they are and must be. But they cannot do it alone. We all have a role to play—all of us who are in the caring and ministering and counseling professions.

Other Moral Leaders

One would naturally think next of the lawyers who, in some cultures, were once identical with the priests. Lawyers and judges and

[11] "Nor to Avenge Any Wrong," reprinted by express permission of Kenneth Boulding, from There Is a Spirit: The Nayler Sonnets (New York: Fellowship Publications, 1945).

policemen are the official guardians or umpires of our behavior. Perhaps we should add those former dungeon keepers who have risen to the rank of jailers, wardens, correctional program officers; yes, and parole and probation officers. In the hands of these men we have placed the responsibility for dealing with the erring whose mistakes and transgressions are discovered.

For the inadequacy and expensiveness of our antique, inefficient machinery, we cannot lay the blame at any one level of the system. The wardens didn't design the prisons; the judges didn't write the statutes; the police don't counsel the wardens or the lawyers. It was some progressive young lawyers who first made me aware of our crime-producing system of "controlling" crime, and it is they who are now earnestly concerned with improving the ineffective, traditional methods. I have confidence that they and the concerned judges will succeed in effecting this transformation. The young lawyers group, at the present time, is especially effective in updating the old processes and procedures in one of the heartwarming reform movements of our times.

Lawyers (and judges, of course) can guide the restructuring of larger groups and the regulations that control them so that some of the injustices (sins) of group action will be diminished. The great United Nations organization was an effort in this direction. The new model penal code which has a national model and has been adopted in several states is another great effort (and succeeding). The lawyers have taken an increasing interest in the activities of political functioning in the direction of social control. They have supplied the majority of those who have taken on the responsibility of government.[12]

Judges, whom one would surely expect to be leaders in moral restitution and maintenance, cannot be appraised as a group in this

[12] Because I believe in lawyers and in the rule of law, it makes me sad indeed to learn of a reactionary swing in the American Bar Association represented, for example, by a proposal offered by an ABA committee for an examination for law students "to identify those significant elements of character that may predictably give rise to misconduct in violation of professional responsibilities." And the committee also urged bench and bar to intensify their efforts "to root out the known . . . character risks already engaged in the practice of law." This may sound innocent enough, but similar attempts to purge the bar of "undesirables" have frequently been made, all sharing a common objective, says Jerold Auerbach (p. 784, *The Nation,* 6/19/72) to exclude or anathematize those whose ethnic origins or religious backgrounds are politically distasteful to establishment lawyers.

regard. Some are, indeed, all that one could hope for—idealistic, humane, patient, wise, and far-seeing.[13]

Some judges are, unfortunately, petty, petulant, ignorant, and sadistic. Where one judge exerts every effort to discover the most helpful, the most remedial, and the most constructive ways to deal with a case, another brusquely and cruelly invokes sentences of 20, 50, 100, or even 1,000 years to indicate his implacability and vindictive harshness.

"My son is a judge," one wise, experienced lawyer told me sadly. "He has no interest in our efforts to reform the stupid penal practices; no time, he says, for such sentimentalism. He makes it a rule to assess in every case he hears which is found guilty the maximum penalty allowed by law. 'Just get them out of the way.'"

Whose way?

But this only illustrates the absurdities to which the process of sentencing has gone, an important and crucial responsibility of the judge in which few of them have had any training. Thus prisoners convicted of the same crime may be sentenced by different courts to terms of imprisonment as disparate as one year and ten years. All of the sentences tend to be far too long; much longer than in other civilized countries. The sentencing seminars and other "post-graduate" training experiences which have been organized in many states are tending to correct some of the abuses and mistakes of sentencing, but the whole business is in need of radical reform.

The Police as Moral Leaders

Police as "moral leaders" will startle some readers who think of the policeman as a remote, silently menacing figure—a threat to evildoers, but unrelated to ordinary life activities. This indicates to what a low level of prestige we have demoted our "peace officers" and in what direction their training and philosophy have led them. Once they were our sentinels, watchmen, guardians, friends of all good citizens. They were the calm, helpful reminders to us all of our civic rights and duties. But they became soldiers, armed and vehicled and sequestered, presumably instructed to look and act

[13] I had made a list of some of my friends belonging to this category; the list grew too long to print.

fierce. Their purpose is now less to help the "good" citizen than to intimidate and capture the "bad" citizen. Instead of reassurance and respect, they often inspire chiefly fear. The English people profess love for their kindly, unarmed police officers; Americans mostly make no concealment of their distrust, dislike, and even hate.

The police know all this; it grieves and angers and puzzles them. They don't quite understand how they can be so misjudged by the very people they are trying to protect. Their assigned task is increasingly one of "warring on criminal elements" which has already gotten far beyond the possibility of adequate police control of the present type. The "criminal element" joins "some of the best people" in every way in finding it expedient to prevent "difficulties" by financial arrangements with the police. But the poor, the black, the shabby, the ignorant, the dim-witted, the drunken, and the eccentric, all of whom can be made to *look* like bad and wicked and dangerous men and who have no recourse or defense against abuse and mistreatment—these supply the daily work with citizens.

Meanwhile, some police leaders and police schools are trying to return the police function to its once proud, brave status.[14] Next to clergymen, the people most directly responsible for watching over public morality are the police. Despite their reputation for abusing prisoners, shooting down unarmed people, or discriminating against blacks, Puerto Ricans, and Indians, and taking payoff money from some businesses, there are some very good policemen. Most police officers are humble, earnest, well-meaning men. But they have long been enmeshed in a corrupt and corrupting system which must first be corrected at the top. It was Renault Robinson and other good policemen in Chicago who in March, 1972, helped to expose some of the abuses going on in the department and strove valiantly to arrange to permit the police officers to go on duty unarmed. It was a policeman and a member of the New York Police Force since 1963, David Durk, a graduate of Amherst, who made these eloquent statements before the Knapp Commission investigating police corruption in New York City, February and March, 1972:

---

[14] As civilization progresses, more police will be moral leaders. The late O. W. Wilson, who inspired and taught me much; Patrick Murphy, former police commissioner of New York City—truly a gentleman and a scholar—and Edward M. Davis, police commissioner of Los Angeles, are among those I would class as leaders.

. . . We knew these things because we were involved in law enforcement in New York City, and anyone else who says he didn't know had to be blind, either by choice or by incompetence.

. . . We wanted to believe in the rule of law. We wanted to believe in a system of responsibility. But those in high places everywhere, in the department, in the DA's office, in City Hall, were determined not to enforce the law. They turned their heads away when law and justice were being sold on every street corner.

I saw that happening to men all around me; men who could have been good officers, men of decent impulse, men of ideas, but men who were without decent leadership, men who were told in a hundred ways every day, go along, forget about the law, don't make waves and shut up.

Like it or not, the policeman is convinced that he lives and works in the middle of a corrupt society, that everybody is getting theirs and why shouldn't he, and that if somebody cared about corruption, something would have been done about it a long time ago.

So your report has to tell us about the district attorneys and the courts and the bar, and the mayor and the governor and what they have done, and what they have failed to do, and how great a measure of responsibility they also bear. Otherwise, if you suggest or allow others to suggest that the responsibility belongs only to the police, then for the patrolmen on the beat and in the radio cars, this commission will be just another part of the swindle.[15]

In a few jurisdictions an entirely new police attitude and function has been introduced as the result of the work of Dr. Morton Bard of City College, City University of New York. Selected officers, at first ridiculed by their associates who now envy them, are trained to handle family crisis calls—wife-beating and similar misconduct cases—by quiet clinical investigation instead of with threats, blows, and arrests. Injuries to police officers in handling such cases have greatly diminished in the trial areas, the self-image of the police has been raised, their fear diminished, and law-induced violence has greatly decreased. This is perhaps twenty-first-century police functioning, but it has begun thanks to former Police Commissioner Patrick Murphy and Dr. Morton Bard.

[15] David Durk, Chicago *Sun-Times*, April 3, 1972.

Teachers as Moral Leaders

My relation to the profession of teaching is long and close. My grandfather, my father and mother, my brothers, my wife, and my daughter were or are teachers. Teachers have long carried the responsibility of instructing the youth, not only in how things are, but in how things ought to be. The only moral instruction which many children ever receive comes from school teachers. Teachers need commendation and encouragement and evidences of parental appreciation but, for the most part, they get neglect and reproach. Their dedication and idealism carry them through but sometimes they get very discouraged. They feel very much alone in trying to stem tides and divert currents. Occasionally the sense of isolation and the conviction of failure become overwhelming.

Teachers are essential in the faculty of morality-gap closers. What was said about the transference phenomenon in relation to clergy-men applies again here. The teacher becomes the ideal, the model person, for many a child whose parents fail to inspire him or cancel their positive influence by inattention, harshness, or outright neglect and rejection. And beyond the unconscious identifications with and emulations of the teacher, there is the simple didactic instruction and information she supplies as conscious mind improvement and tools of living, including moral values.

Teachers have told me that they are well aware of the powerful determinants of character and ideals which they supply for their pupils in the primary grades, the most formative years of the child's life. Some of them appreciate more than others to what extent they hold *Heaven in My Hand*, as Alice Lee Humphreys phrased it in the title of her book of eloquently recorded experiences.[16] But with each year and grade, the influence of the teacher diminishes as more experience, more acquaintances, more self-confidence, and more peer awareness develop.[17]

[16] Alice Lee Humphreys, *Heaven in My Hand* (Richmond, Va.: John Knox Press, 1950).

[17] I honestly doubt, my daughter Julia Gottesman, an experienced teacher told me, if the great majority of our high school students are much if at all influenced in the formation of their moral standards by anything we teachers do or say or are. Sometimes we give them food for thought. In our long discussion of this theme in *Love Against Hate* Jean and I concluded that what the teacher is, is more important for the formation of the pupils' minds and characters than the content of what she teaches. I may have been wrong about this, but I hate to think so.

Earlier we spoke of the controversial methods of discipline used by some teachers, including the infliction of pain, whipping, caning, and spanking. Humiliation, sarcasm, rebuke, and other verbal blows can be equally painful. This leads into a subject too big and complex for inclusion in this book—the learning process and teaching method. It is enough here to remind the reader that teaching is an increasingly complex professional discipline, and it does include moral leadership.

The Media and Moral Leadership

Fluctuations in the authority and popularity of the church have tended to let the brightest torch of moral leadership pass to the press and television. Many of us take our moral stance and guidance from articles, reports, and editorials rather than from sermons.

Such journals as *Harper's, The Nation, New Republic, New Yorker, Christian Century, Saturday Evening Post*, and the late lamented *Look, I. F. Stone's Weekly*, and *Saturday Review of Literature*—all these and others have been consistently outspoken against political, community, and business sin.

"The Corrupt Society" was the subject of an entire issue of *The Nation* over ten years ago (June, 1963) pointing up the continuing sins of big organizations, courts, manufacturers, police, government agencies, and other groups. *The New Yorker* has many times pointed the finger sternly and unambiguously at the sins of war, particularly ours in Southeast Asia. On February 19, 1972, in an editorial on our army's persistent use of poisonous defoliants, it said of our program of herbicidal warfare in Vietnam:

> In the last ten years, the American Military has sprayed or dumped upon the Vietnamese countryside and the Vietnamese people approximately fifty thousand tons of herbicides. In order to hurt the Vietcong and to turn inhabitants of Vietcong-controlled areas into refugees, it has carried on a huge campaign of crop destruction, but that is not all. In the course of the herbicidal warfare in Vietnam, the Americans have defoliated a seventh of the land, ruined a large part of the timber resources that in the postwar period would have to be considered South Vietnam's principal potential export, and

caused other grave ecological damages, some of which—like the infestation of certain defoliated areas by ineradicable bamboo—cannot be reversed for many generations. All this has been carried out to the accompaniment of repeated claims by the American military, and by the State Department as well, that the herbicides used are "not dangerous to man or animal life."

I cite this for its content, its courage, and its forthrightness in declaring a *mea culpa* for us all. Did you hear the *minister* say this? Why not?

That great American hero, editor, school teacher, and Presbyterian clergyman Elijah Lovejoy left the pulpit and returned to the press in order to be sure his words reached more people. The Civil War might have been averted and a peaceful emancipation of slaves achieved had there been more like him.

After observing one lynching, Lovejoy was committed forever to fighting uncompromisingly the awful sin of slavery. Mob action was brought against him time after time; neither this nor many threats and attempts on his life deterred him. Repeated destruction of his presses did not stop him. "If by compromise is meant that I should cease from my duty, I cannot make it. I fear God more than I fear man. Crush me if you will, but I shall die at my post. . . ."

And he did, four days later, at the hands of another mob. No one of the ruffians was prosecuted or indicted or punished in any way for this murder. (Some of Lovejoy's defenders were prosecuted! One of the mob assassins was later elected mayor of Alton!)

However, note this: One young man was around who was deeply moved by the Lovejoy martyrdom. He had just been elected to the Illinois legislature. His name was Abraham Lincoln.[18]

In recent times there have been some misgivings about the media's proud heritage. It has been challenged, attacked, and threatened. To a considerable extent the press has become institutionalized and impersonalized. The lure of profit exceeds the prestige of prophet. Editors grow weary and wary. One can read their discouragement in the lines and between the lines. It becomes easier to make a living by being funny or superficial and platitudinous, or

---

[18] Paul Simon, "Elijah Lovejoy," *Presbyterian Life*, 18:13 (November 1, 1965). See also M. M. Sheibley and J. W. Hoffman, "He Could Not Desert," *Presbyterian Life*, 6:15 (May 30, 1953).

wiseacre and cynical. But there are still many earnest, upright editors with conviction who speak their minds, speak them bravely, and speak them often and well. A few great American newspapers persist, led by *The New York Times*, the Washington *Post*, the Los Angeles *Times*, the Des Moines *Register and Tribune*, the Atlanta *Constitution*, the San Francisco *Chronicle*, and the *Christian Science Monitor*. These certainly are moral leaders, along with the clergy. But most clergymen read editorials and some editors listen to clergymen.

The television screen has rapidly become the most powerful and widespread dispenser of broadside communication. All I have said about the responsibility of the press is therefore applicable to radio and television, perhaps the more so because of the much larger audience of children. Perhaps children are more influenced in their opinions and attitudes by television than by any other agency—school, church, even home. We don't like to think so, but we must consider the possibility.

Statesmen and Politicians as Moral Leaders

Some people who have dispensed with ministers think we should expect the President of the United States to take over the role of moral leadership. " 'The President is expected to personify our betterness in an inspiring way,' says Yale professor David Barber, '. . . he ought to inspire our higher selves with an example of principled goodness.'

"Franklin Roosevelt said the Presidency was 'preeminently a place of moral leadership.' Nixon . . . invoked God five times in his [first] inaugural address and talked of the 'crisis of the spirit' in America and the need to 'build a great cathedral of the spirit.' " Later he reassigned this task to "parents, teachers, college administrators, local police, city councilmen and governors.

"The young White House aides who went to the campuses to search out the causes of dissatisfaction came back feeling that many of the youths who escaped the firm grip of Sunday school and became contemptuous of all organized religion consciously or unconsciously looked to the White House for a moral anchor. Then, disappointed by the human limitations and falterings so clearly discernible in the floodlighted Oval Office, they unfairly rejected the President. . . ."[19]

Two cartoons in *The New Yorker* (September 30, 1972) expressed a popular feeling about this. In both of them, two nondescript characters are chatting at the bar. In one cartoon the speaker says: "Look, Nixon's no dope. If the people really *wanted* moral leadership, he'd give them moral leadership." In the other cartoon, the speaker volunteers these sympathetic remarks: "I can understand his feelings. I, too, would hate to be the first President in history to call off a war for moral reasons."

An editorial in a later issue of *The New Yorker* had some cogent comments to make with respect to the relationship between the President, the Supreme Court, government in general, and the moral tone of our contemporary world and the issue of personal responsibility:

> The President speaks of putting an end to "the whole era of permissiveness." The idea seems to be that the government, besides cutting down our allowance ("goodies" is the President's word), is going to stiffen our punishments. But how can a President, who has enough trouble putting an end to particular social ailments, put an end to a "whole era"?
>
> President Nixon looks to the Supreme Court to do the job, and promises more "conservative" appointments. But if morality cannot be legislated, it cannot be appointed, either. The Supreme Court which is not, after all, a junta, will be powerless, even with a new "conservative" cast, to curb a wave of crime, just as the "liberal" Court that preceded it was powerless to cause one.
>
> Indeed, if the Court is truly conservative, and so is especially respectful of judicial precedent, its power to effect large social changes will be all the less, whatever those changes might be. The federal government cannot order up a new era as easily as that. For the average American is not a child—not a soft, spoiled child, not a chastened, obedient child. Nor is the government his parent or the guardian of his character and morals. The average American is a grown man or a grown woman. It is *he* who is the guardian—the

[19] Hugh Sidey, "The Presidency: Demand for 'Moral Leadership,'" *Life*, 69:2 (October 23, 1970).

guardian of his own morals, and the guardian, too, of the government he elects to serve him.[20]

Doctors as Moral Leaders

I come finally to my colleagues—doctors in general and psychiatrists in particular. What is *our* responsibility in the closure of the
morality gap? Counselors to individuals and to whole families doctors have always been; even more they have served as models of a
way of life. The restorative work in which doctors are constantly
engaged has an effect sooner or later on their own life philosophy
and on their character structure. As soldiers in the continuous war
against corporal disintegration, they are professional conservation
specialists. Self-destruction and ruthless destruction of any kind are
anathema to them.

The impression prevails that moral counsel is something about
which even doctors no longer concern themselves. Some of them
encourage this public image. There is a tradition definitely of tending the enemy wounded as well as one's own comrades, and making
no judgments on moral aspects of the patient's affliction. We remember the example of Dr. Samuel Mudd who, staunch patriot though
he was, rendered first aid to the wounded assassin of the beloved
Abraham Lincoln, for which he was afterward shamefully punished by the "law." But the tradition of impartiality does not mean
that doctors have not always "taken sides" and espoused causes
and moral positions.

What side the doctor is on is seldom an enigma to the patient. It
may be rationalized as the "healthy" thing to do or the "safe" course
of action or the "preferred" procedure. When the peril of smoking
cigarettes was discovered and publicized, most doctors quit smoking; many of us advised all people to do the same. We did not call
it "wrong" but "self-destructive." It is not for us to administer punishment (although, as I recorded above, punishment was and is
implicit in much medical treatment), but warnings we can give,
and do give. That our advice is ignored should not discomfit us—or
upset our equanimity, as our great teacher Osler counseled.

Therapeutic abortion is another case in point. Some doctors feel

[20] *The New Yorker*, November 25, 1972.

that however much an abortion might be indicated from a medical standpoint, it is contraindicated from a moral standpoint. Others feel that however undesirable abortion may be from a moral standpoint, it is sometimes the imperative course of action from a medical standpoint. They feel just as strongly that abortion under certain circumstances is ethical as do the other doctors that it is unethical under all circumstances. This is a matter of divergent opinion dependent on many factors and not limited to physicians. The doctor must express his opinion based on his convictions, but his specific *advice* will take into consideration his patient's convictions as well.

It may seem a little surprising that many psychiatrists are so cautious about offering advice to their patients, even when it is asked for. They say the patient must decide things for himself. Of course, but he can be counseled and the psychiatrist can and many times should give the needed counsel. The strictures of psychoanalytic treatment technique, whereby it is considered improper for the *psychoanalyst* to offer advice, do not apply to most psychiatric counseling, although some nonpsychoanalysts, influenced by this role, shun the role of counselor altogether and remain passive listeners. This, in my opinion, derives from a misunderstanding of the reason for the psychoanalyst's silence. He wants the patient to look further, even at the cost of painful suspense and anxiety, to continue with his introspections, knowing that, in time, forgotten factors and considerations will come to light making the question unnecessary. But in most psychotherapy, the doctor is not seeking deep unconscious explanations. If such exploration is essential, the patient had better be in psychoanalysis. The average person need not seek or expect to find the unconscious factors determining his every act or symptom.

The psychoanalyst, to be most effective, must avoid giving help in the form the patient seeks it (and has, perhaps, always sought it, vainly). The psychoanalyst assumes that the process in which he and the patient are engaged will turn out to be helpful, and it, rather than he, himself, is the "curer."[21] The psychotherapist, on the other hand, seeks to be helpful directly, and though it is easy for him to talk too much and to express some opinions better suppressed, the psychotherapist will and should offer counsel, advice,

[21] See Karl Menninger and Philip Holzman, *Theory of Psychoanalytic Technique* (New York: Basic Books, 1973).

warnings, and even prohibitions where a need for these is indicated. Even if he did not ask us, would we not inform a traveler which of several roads was the right one to his announced destination, if we had better reason to know than he? Or, to use Freud's illustration, would we refrain from warning ignorant travelers bound for the Arctic wearing summer clothes that frigid temperatures await them there? To let people commit suicide by withholding such information is surely little less than to assist in manslaughter.

But whether or not the psychotherapist or psychoanalyst declares his position on a moral issue, his life style will usually show it. In general, the voluntary patient knows what the psychiatrist stands for before he begins treatment; or he should. The assumption that all psychiatrists are alike and believe the same things and treat people the same way is surely too naïve to have any currency today.

Since one can rarely know *a priori* the moral position of a new, "strange" doctor, patients are, to be sure, somewhat at the mercy of chance in the initial choice of a psychotherapist aside from general reputation. Every psychotherapist does hold certain beliefs and certain ideals of conduct. He may or may not label them, but it will not do to just wave his hand in a general way in the direction of uprightness and conformity. That won't do anymore. Unfortunately, it *does* suffice for all too many. As the late Abraham Maslow said eloquently, "The classical philosophy of science as morally neutral, value free, value neutral is not only wrong, but is extremely dangerous. . . . Science itself comes out of human beings and human passions and interests, as Polanyi (1958) has so brilliantly set forth."[22] Maslow goes on to say that just as many psychiatrists and psychologists and biologists now regard practically all diseases as psychosomatic or organismic, so, conversely, one will find as determinants in any physical disease, if he looks far enough, some intrapsychic, intrapersonal, and social variables.[23]

The therapist does not preach or presume to set forth a code of

[22] Abraham H. Maslow, "Toward a Humanistic Biology," *American Psychologist*, 24:724 (August, 1969).

[23] Dr. Philip Rieff, in his book *The Triumph of the Therapeutic* (New York: Harper & Row, 1966), concentrated on the polarity of the gospel of total release ("tell everything," "let it all hang out," "do your thing") and the restoration of a traditional moral demand code. He thinks the Christian Church is oscillating between these two points of view. Certainly psychiatry is. He rejects the popular choice of an ethic of unambiguous release and opts rather for what he calls a therapeutic ethic.

ethics for the patient. He acts as a counselor and exerts his influence to help the patient find a better and less hurtful way to live. He feels his responsibility to his patients rather than to the outside world, but his responsibility to avert evildoing, crime, and self-destruction is itself a moral stance, always present. He, too, must sometimes confront the patient with painful facts and endure his anger without being impatient.

Most colleagues, as I have known them, are upright people. They take seriously their responsibility and they go far beyond the Hippocratic oath.[24] But alterations in the ethical codes of social behavior seem to have involved some colleagues, and reports of sexual and financial exploitation of patients by doctors are very disturbing to all of us. Such transgression of professional ethics has long been a special if rare sin in medicine, and the new morality can scarcely justify it on the sophistry that whatever is seemingly helpful to the patient may be done regardless of the mores. A "treatment" which entails guilt or shame reactions will have ultimate effects which completely erase any temporary "benefits" it confers, and leave the patient with an incurable mental wound.

Seduction is not the chief temptation of psychiatrists, nor is it the only way in which they may depart from moral standards. But how is a patient to know to whom he or she may safely commit his course of treatment?

How indeed is the free-expressing, "confessing" patient to know what tone or zone of life philosophy he is entering? Is he to assume that the standards of mental healthiness and personality equilibrium are the same the world over? Or that they are the same in the minds and hearts of all therapists?

Patients can get a pretty reliable estimate of the therapist's character from members of the medical profession in the community where the therapist practices. The prospective patient can make some very approximate deductions from the same preliminary conferences in the course of which he is appraised. No patient wisely undertakes a course of psychotherapy from a name picked out of the telephone book or heard mentioned in casual conversation. The patient should be definitely referred to a specific therapist by the

[24] See Maurice Levine, *Psychiatry and Ethics* (New York: Braziller, 1972).

patient's own doctor, and that doctor should know the therapist to whom he is referring his patient.

I suspect the most common "sins" we psychiatrists commit are sins of omission. Several colleagues have spoken out forcefully about this of late. "The time has come," declared Judd Marmor of California, "when psychiatry in the name of mental health must find the courage also to challenge the sociosanct values implicit in such institutions as the free enterprise profit system, nationalism and war."[25]

"I am struck," wrote Robert Jay Lifton, "by how little my own profession has had to say about . . . the way in which aberrant *situations* can produce collective disturbance and mass murder. The psychiatry and psychohistory I would like to envisage for the future would put such matters at its center."[26]

Thirty years ago the atmosphere of psychiatric education was strikingly different from today. Psychiatry was a growing medical discipline for the care of a long-neglected segment of the sick. It had exciting new prospects, new ideas in theory and practice, and apparently boundless opportunities! Applicants for training seemed numberless, and institutions for at least minimally acceptable "training" multiplied rapidly. Graduates were sought and besought for many positions such as direction of new community clinics or consultation a few hours a week with a psychologist–social worker staff. They were sought by hospitals, social agencies, industries, stores, courts, schools, prisons, research teams, and medical clinics. A few psychiatrists answered some of these calls; the greater number settled down into a quiet but intense, intimate, lucrative private practice, the bulk of which was psychotherapy or electroshock therapy for the economically fortunate. Once regarded as eccentric asylum keepers and then as wizards and miracle workers, psychiatrists began to gain the reputation of being sleek socialites, affluent recluses, or publicity-seeking courtroom performers reveling in contradictory speculations about the offender on the dock. (This did not describe fairly the rank and file, but it was a trend.)

The clergyman's morally burdened parishioners became the psy-

---

[25] Judd Marmor, "Psychiatry and the Survival of Man," *Saturday Review*, 54:18 (May 22, 1971).

[26] Robert Jay Lifton, "Beyond Atrocity," *Saturday Review*, 54:23 (March 7, 1971).

chiatrist's complex-laden patients; sin became symptom, and confession became psychotherapy. But in this transfer the crying needs of millions of people—disturbed, miserable, angry, depressed, often deluded, and guilt-laden people—continued to go untended. Not that some colleagues did not hear these cries and do their best to respond with services and counsel. But the help was quantitatively inconspicuous compared to the visible need, and the "psychotherapy" remedy was seen as obviously inadequate to the now apparent task. The demands for the services of psychiatrists by groups, institutions, and public agencies continued, and the psychotherapy once monopolized by psychiatrists was increasingly taken over by "subprofessional" personnel. The high repute and public esteem of the psychiatrist began to diminish, as did the number of young physicians electing the specialty.

A few colleagues have lent their efforts to public administration, legal and penal reform, revisions of medical education, and statesmanlike responsibilities. I am proud that my brother Will was able to completely reorganize the method of dealing with psychiatric casualties in the army. But the truth is, as he himself pointed out, this had been well started once before by his predecessors, and then undone (just as his own accomplishments later were).

Within psychiatry everywhere there is a very strong questioning of traditional assumptions. Some practitioners are trying to redefine their role so as to avoid pejorative labeling. Others are concentrating on the study of chronic states of disorganization, formerly labeled "schizophrenic," despite the absurd statement published recently that 60 percent of the population is so afflicted.

Nader's Raiders are said to be about to release a long report on how we psychiatrists are doing and not doing. Although trained to be doctors, we are not "doctoring" the people who have the real psychiatric or medical disorders, it says; we prefer to deal with persons who have nonmedical disease, good patients who speak our language, never telephone us at home, never cancel an appointment, and pay their bills on time.

The trend to become "healers of society" instead of physicians for the sick helps delude the public into thinking that problems caused by poverty, racism, and other social ills can be *treated* and could conceivably lead to the use of psychiatry for social and political control.

Seymour Halleck in *The Politics of Therapy* goes further into this problem. Stress, an excess of which is painful and crippling and may bring one to the psychiatrist, is classified by him as coming from the larger environment, from the more immediate environment (family and social circle abuse or privation), and from personal internal mismanagement or misinterpretation. Stress leads, in Halleck's terms, to oppression—a better word than my word "overstress."[27] Psychiatrists should not continue to assume that all oppression is intrapsychic. Leaders like Halleck, Coles, Marmor, Lifton, Gaylin, and Brown are leading a new front in psychiatry with many anonymous followers.

And So

Out of it all may come a *bonum ex nocentibus*: a good product from an evil source. Beginning with sin and a morality gap, we end up with the idea of a responsibility which each of us has to take, to open our eyes and look at the unpleasant and then go to work.

The editors of *Harper's Magazine* announced that the readers of the December, 1972, issue would find the first few articles very gloomy—cynical discoveries about the FBI, mercenary hospitals, antilibertarian tendencies of the Supreme Court justices, faithlessness in some trusted politicians and a species of journalists, and generals who took unholy boyish pleasure in the Vietnam War.

The editors expect reproach. "Why remind us of the worst?" the letters will ask them. "Why the repetitive chronicle of loss, despair, corruption, betrayal, and defeat? Where is the good news? Where is the bluebird of happiness?"

The bluebird of happiness lies in the existence of magazines like *Harper's*, courageous enough to come out even in the Christmas season with this honest, intelligent, clinical report.

"People who ask such questions [Where is the good news? etc.] apparently cling, like children with their arms full of balloons, to images of cherished innocence. They are willing to concede occasional error, but. . . . *None of them will admit to what the sturdier clergy would identify as original sin* [italics mine]. . . . They prefer

[27] Seymour Halleck, *The Politics of Therapy* (New York: Science House, 1971).

to believe that Americans live in a condition of almost perfect grace. . . ."

And what a great ending to this fine *Harper's* editorial:

"The 'bad news,' so called, is the common soil in which men raise the works of civilization. The bluebird of happiness sings on a compost heap."[28]

The happy ending is, of course, not that these things exist, but that we recognize and deplore them and that we exhort the help of our fellowmen for these things. (You see, I am saying "things" instead of "sins.")

"If *we* had something to do with getting things wrong, then the powers that produce wrong are not wholly beyond us, as would be true if the human predicament came solely from fate, or from a double-minded god, or from a devil who overpowers," wrote Seward Hiltner.

"Even the first statement about sin is, then, a word of possible hope. It pinpoints what needs to be inspected if there is to be improvement. It is a very rough kind of diagnosis. If something is wrong, as it is, look first at yourselves, collectively and individually. However bad it is, we, *you* are involved in it. That should give you hope, not despair."[29]

So there you are, you and I. If we believe in sin—*as I do*—we believe in our personal responsibility for trying to correct it, and thereby saving ourselves and our world. We diminish our long-drawn-out, indirect self-reproach which despairs, but repairs nothing.

Preachers and teachers and doctors and writers and lawyers must join hands and carry on together. They must listen. Hearing confession is not a pleasant process. There are not many to whom one dare confess his worst side. But isn't that one of the reasons for the existence of professions? All of their members may receive privileged communication; why?

We can lean on our brother professionals, the clergy, who have the biggest task of all. They will do their duty best if they are not denied the respect, the affection, and the cooperation of the rest of us. Not every man or woman is strong and brave and intelligent

[28] "Countersigns: The blue bird of happiness," *Harper's*, 245:53 (December, 1972).
[29] Seward Hiltner, "Christian Understanding of Sin in the Light of Medicine and Psychiatry," *Medical Arts and Sciences*, 20(2):35 (1966).

enough to be a minister, a priest, a rabbi. But these are our moral leaders and they must lead. We must follow and help. We're all in this thing together.

We psychiatrists finally demonstrated to the medical world that we know effective treatment for conditions which were formerly ignored or mistreated. But do we not repeat the error if we neglect the availability of help for some individuals whose sins are greater than their symptoms and whose burdens are greater than they can bear?

Bakan cites the three sins listed in the Talmud for which the death penalty was prescribed: murder, adultery, idolatry. Of these, idolatry *was* and *is* the most heinous; Bakan defines it as the worship of the *means* toward the fulfillment of the religious impulse as if it were the end (the fulfillment).

"In both science and religion there is the assumption that the fundamental reality is that which is beyond the manifest . . . the huge world of the unmanifest. If at any stage of development we begin to worship the manifest, or the means whereby we have made some part manifest, then indeed can it be said that we are being idolatrous."[30]

[30] David Bakan, "Idolatry in Religion and Science," paper presented at the Seventh Star Island Conference of the Institute on Religion in an Age of Science, August 1, 1960.

Epilogue
The Displaced Preface

A preface was promised you, and at long last, here it is. Why did I write the book? Why would a psychiatrist presume to write about the categorical imperative and the public state of mind and morals?

Now that you've read the book, I'll tell you why I wrote it.

In 1963 I received the Isaac Ray Award of the American Psychiatric Association for lectures at Columbia University Law School and the University of Kansas. In them I asked listeners if we dared to continue to be as ignorant, indifferent, and self-destructive on this most universal topic—crime—as most of us are. And I made a little more intensive study of it myself, as I expressed later (1966) in *The Crime of Punishment*.

From prisons and punishment and crimes it was a short step to the more general topic of how we control disapproved behavior, our own and that of others. In 1967 I discussed this in the Stone Lecture Series at the Princeton Theological Seminary. The middle chapters of this book are an amplification of what I said there.

One always learns from teaching, and what came home to me from this highly intelligent, idealistic, sensitive audience was the anxious and unsettled feeling among these young clergymen (and some older ones). The role they had chosen as a lifework had seemingly diminished in importance and effectiveness, and some wondered if they might have chosen the wrong profession. The depressed, discouraged mood of the general population had spread even to them.

I began to hear about or observe these phenomena in other places. *"Young clergymen bewildered, disillusioned"* read headlines in the

Chicago *Sun-Times.*[1] "Four out of every ten Protestant and Roman Catholic clergymen interviewed in an opinion survey are considering leaving the religious life."[2] The church is dispirited. Is God dead?

What? A discouraged clergy? Disheartened seminarians? A dismaying note, indeed. Could anything be more paradoxical? The youth of a profession dedicated to moral leadership and inspiration, to ministering to fainthearted, faith-faltering, trouble-burdened sheep, even they, the shepherds, men of faith, hope, and love, disheartened!

And not because their flocks had fled. Not because their God or a God who was too human and got angry, vindictive, violent, vengeful, discouraged, had even been reported dead. Not because they, themselves, had actually lost faith or ceased to feel deep concern for their fellowman.

What, then, indeed? I asked them. Diverse things, they said— inability to communicate, inadequate financial support, lack of interest and devotion on the part of parishioners, disengaged youth, apparent irrelevancy of the church in modern life, the competition of yoga, communism, satanism, groupism, and materialism. These were among the assigned reasons.

Of course I had had some idea of this trend of feeling from the new journals. But it hadn't really come home to me, in spite of my occasional participation in the seminars for clergymen of all faiths at the Menninger Foundation. So I pursued my inquiries further. I visited Carlyle Marney, who conducts the remarkably successful "Interpreter's House" for discouraged pastors at Lake Junaluska. "From some 8,000 laymen and ministers with whom we have conferred, five principal problems emerge: a loss of nerve, a loss of direction, erosion from culture, confusion of thought, exhaustion. . . . They have become shaken reeds, smoking lamps, earthen vessels . . . spent arrows. They have lost heart. But they can be revived!"

One distraction of the modern clergy is the multiplication of methods for dealing with troubled people: psychoanalysis and other psychotherapies, diets and plastic surgery, Zen and yoga, sensitivity groups, and encounter groups. Multiform treatments and magic cures for ills of the body, mind, and spirit seem to leave little for the minister to do, equipped as he is with the "feeble" tools of

[1] April 9, 1971.
[2] By the American Institute of Public Opinion.

preaching, comforting, counseling, intercession, and prayer. Should he not strive to acquire the skills of the treatment art and lessen the pastoral, hermeneutical, and scriptural routines which seminarians have traditionally spent so much time learning?

If nurses, social workers, psychologists, surgeons, general medical men, welfare workers, physical therapists, Christian Science readers, dentists, barkeepers, and housewives can all be enlisted in the army of psychotherapists, why not also the clergy? They have had far more educational discipline than most of those others and they have an avowed purpose in life of shepherding lost sheep. Ministers, priests, and rabbis constitute, after all, a caring profession. Are they being rightly trained for the lifework to which they aspire?

The seminarians did not ask, though well they might have, what tasks remain for the psychiatrists, who took over the field of psychotherapy from the neurologists and who are now being increasingly displaced from their monopoly of it. The seminarians do not realize —or perhaps care—that psychiatric residents, who correspond in educational level to theological seminarians, are also puzzled and discouraged as to their proper future role. One may even say that some are resentful at the dispersal of their onetime magic secret tool among a score of adjuvant professional and subprofessional groups leaving them scarcely more than *primus inter pares.*

Yet psychiatrists enthusiastic about the benefits of this psychotherapy are the first to admit that relatively few of those who could profit by it could obtain it were only psychiatrists to dispense it. If half the world is able and willing to give psychotherapy to the other half, perhaps it can only be for the total good. So the professional dispersal that is occurring is not necessarily to be deplored.

To be sure, bad, false, unhelpful "psychotherapy" may be passed off as the real thing, but the same can be said of friendship (except that the latter is free). And could not psychiatrists lend their help to better functioning of these nonmedical counselors or psychotherapists, *including clergymen?* They could and they do. The Princeton Seminary has been a leader in obtaining this help and giving this training. But there are many others and there are national associations dedicated to that purpose. At the Menninger Foundation the clinical orientation of clergymen has been for more than twenty years a part of the educational program, and the chaplaincy services in the various associated hospitals have been closely associated with the Menninger School of Psychiatry in the training of psychiatrists.

This digression about the members of my own profession was introduced to indicate that psychiatric students are only a little less bewildered and uncertain about their future these days than are seminarians. But the latter seem to be more than confused; they are *discouraged*. They seem to have lost the conviction of their importance, their usefulness. They seem uncertain about their goals and purposes.[3]

In addition to the state of mind of these discouraged seminarians and preachers, I became increasingly aware of the mood of the general public. People are worried. There are almost daily reminders of our environmental sins and the impending consequences made probable by them. The inexcusable slaughter and destruction in Vietnam weighs on our conscience. There is the repeated message that a little stealing and bribing and cheating might as well be overlooked, since it's "being done" everywhere. There is a general depression of spirits which the newspapers profess to be unable to explain.

Meanwhile "confused psychiatrists and clinical psychologists in their hospitals and consulting rooms stand almost as helpless as their functional predecessors and sometime cultural opponents, the clergy," said Philip Rieff.[4] Do they need help? Do we need them? Should more effort be made to support what they are doing, or shall we assume that they will get along, some way, if their belief in God is valid?

About this time I ran across the "morality gap" figure used by Toynbee. It fitted into my observations about the young clergymen.

> There is a great inequality in the degree of man's giftedness for science and technology on the one hand and for religion and sociality on the other, and this is, to my mind, one of man's chief discords, misfortunes and dangers. Human nature is out of balance.
>
> There has always been a "morality gap," like the "credibility gap" of which some politicians have been accused. We could justly accuse

[3] Seward Hiltner has recently reported to me that the sense of discouragement I saw in 1967, though still present, has lessened considerably since 1970. "More of our students now believe that the local church is 'where the action is.'"

[4] Philip Rieff, *The Triumph of the Therapeutic* (New York: Harper & Row, 1966), p. 21.

the whole human race, since we became human, of a "morality gap" and this gap has been growing wider as technology has been making cumulative progress while morality has been stagnating. . . .

The existence of the morality gap and the importance of closing it has been recognized by the world's spiritual geniuses. The teachings of the Buddha do not differ in this respect from those of the Chinese philosophers Confucius and Lao-tse, or the Ancient Greek philosophers Socrates and Zeno (the founder of the Stoic philosophy), or of all the Hebrew prophets from Amos in the eighth century B.C. to Jesus. These spiritual leaders were manifestly on the right track. We ought to follow their lead today. . . .

Science has never superseded religion, and it is my expectation that it never will supersede it. . . . Science has also begun to find out how to cure psychic sickness. So far, however, science has shown no signs that it is going to be able to cope with man's most serious problems. It has not been able to do anything to cure man of his sinfulness and his sense of insecurity, or to avert the painfulness of failure and the dread of death. Above all, it has not helped him to break out of the prison of his inborn self-centeredness into communion or union with some reality that is greater, more important, more valuable, and more lasting than the individual himself. . . .

I am convinced, myself, that man's fundamental problem is his human egocentricity. He dreams of making the universe a desirable place for himself, with plenty of free time, relaxation, security and good health, and with no hunger or poverty. . . .

All the great historic philosophies and religions have been concerned, first and foremost, with the overcoming of egocentricity. At first sight, Buddhism and Christianity and Islam and Judaism may appear to be very different from each other. But, when you look beneath the surface, you will find that all of them are addressing themselves primarily to the individual human psyche or soul; they are trying to persuade it to overcome its own self-centeredness and they are offering it the means for achieving this. They all find the same remedy. They all teach that egocentricity can be conquered by love.[5]

Egocentricity is one name for it. Selfishness, narcissism, pride, and other terms have also been used. But neither the clergy nor the

[5] From *Surviving the Future*, by Arnold Toynbee. © Oxford University Press, 1971. Reprinted by permission.

behavioral scientists, including psychiatrists, have made it an issue. The popular leaning is away from notions of guilt and morality. Some politicians, groping for a word, have chanced on the silly misnomer, permissiveness. Their thinking is muddy but their meaning is clear. Disease and treatment have been the watchwords of the day and little is said about selfishness or guilt or the "morality gap." And certainly no one talks about sin!

I am not attributing any special moral failure to the clergy, nor to my own profession. We all get caught in the waves and currents of popular interests and are as helpless in the cancerous growth of technology as are the parishioners and the patients.

But a trumpet call like that of Toynbee's phrase compels one to stop and reflect. We know that the principal leadership in the morality realm should be the clergy's, but they seem to minimize their great traditional and historical opportunity to preach, to prophesy, to speak out. Spiritual leadership must indeed have intelligent following, so where are the lawyers, teachers, editors, publishers, and others to take up the lead?

Some clergymen prefer pastoral counseling of individuals to the pulpit function. But the latter is a greater opportunity to both heal *and prevent*. An ounce of prevention is worth a pound of cure, indeed, and there is much prevention to be done for large numbers of people who hunger and thirst after direction toward righteousness. Clergymen have a golden opportunity to prevent some of the accumulated misapprehensions, guilt, aggressive action, and other roots of later mental suffering and mental disease.

How? Preach! Tell it like it is. Say it from the pulpit. Cry it from the housetops.

What shall we cry?

Cry comfort, cry repentance, cry hope. Because recognition of our part in the world transgression is the only remaining hope.

The Example of History

Is this presumptuousness on the part of a psychiatrist unforgivable? Will the clergy tell me, a psychiatric cobbler, to stick to my last? And will not my own colleagues perhaps endorse that prescription, with some raised eyebrows about my fall from scientific grace?

I offer, in extenuation, the example of a very good model. It is our most highly esteemed psychiatric leader and prototype, Benjamin Rush, the first American psychiatrist. He was a most remarkable citizen: a signer of the Declaration of Independence and of the first drafts of the Constitution; a founder of the first public school system and the first free (medical) dispensary for the poor and the first colleges for women. He was involved in the first American prison reform movement. He was the first American doctor to profess the specialty of psychiatry and one of the founders of our American Psychiatric Association. And in spite of this great attention to public affairs and social problems he had a very busy private practice.

Withal, Benjamin Rush was a stern moralist. In June, 1788, having worked hard and traveled much to get the new Constitution ratified by enough states, he sat himself down and took pen in hand to dash off an open letter to the clergymen of all faiths *on the subject of American morality.*

He condemned many current "sins," among them smoking, drinking, the popular election of judges, the country (*sic*) fair ("a temptation to extravagance, gaming, drunkenness and uncleanness"), horse racing, cock fighting, dining at men's clubs, and enjoying oneself on the Sabbath by swimming, sliding, and skating.[6]

My distinguished forebear felt it his duty to counsel the clergy, to exhort them, encourage them, spur them on. It was a responsibility beyond his professional preoccupations. But he acted upon his convictions. I may do no less. Some will regard my present long letter to the clergy as amateur theology. Perhaps it is.

Tillich said that anyone who had a degree of ultimate concern was a theologian. One's life is, after all, an expression of all his 'ologies, including his private theology. And at its heart, as Frederick Buechner has well said:

> Most theology like most fiction, is essentially autobiography. Aquinas, Calvin, Barth, Tillich, worked out their systems in their own ways and lived them in their lives. And if you press them far enough, even at the most cerebral and forbidding, you find an

[6] David Freeman Hawke, *Benjamin Rush: Revolutionary Gadfly* (Indianapolis: Bobbs-Merrill, 1971).

experience of flesh and blood, a human face smiling or frowning or weeping or covering its eyes before something that happened once . . . maybe no more than a child falling sick, a thunderstorm, a dream, and yet it made . . . a difference which no theology can ever entirely convey or entirely conceal.[7]

The Great Riddle

Nearly fifty years ago I was associated with a brilliant and charming colleague, Dr. Logan Clendening. We officed together; we taught at the same medical school, and we spent many hours talking together. At about the same time we each wrote a book, *The Human Body* (Clendening) and *The Human Mind* (Menninger). They were kindly received by the reading public.

I proposed one day that together we write a third book, this one to be entitled *The Human Soul*. Clendening was intrigued with the idea and we even sketched some of the chapters. But time passed and our ways separated; we never got that book written.

Maybe I am still trying to write it—a book describing the confluence of the streams of our knowledge about health. Neither theologian nor prophet nor sociologist, I am a doctor, speaking the medical tongue with a psychiatric accent. For doctors, health is the ultimate good, the ideal state of being. And mental health—some of us believe—includes all the healths: physical, social, cultural, and moral (spiritual). To live, to love, to care, to enjoy, to build on the foundations of our predecessors, to revere the constant miracles of creation and endurance, of "the starry skies above and the moral law within"—these are acts and attitudes which express our mental health.

Yet, how is it, as Socrates wondered, that "men know what is good, but do what is bad"?

[7] Frederick Buechner, *The Alphabet of Grace* (New York: Seabury Press, 1970).

Index

Abolition, 127
Abortion, therapeutic, 213–214
Abuse. *See* Child Abuse
Acedia, 146–148, 189
Addiction
   drug, 42, 65, 70–71
   masturbation and, 34
Adler, Alfred, 39
Adler, Herman, 43
Adolescents, masturbation and, 34–35
Adultery, 139–140
Affluence, 148–156
Aggression, 19
   consequences of, 181
   personal responsibility for control
      of, 176–179
   rationalized, 184–186
   symptoms and, 85
   violence and anger, 143–146
Aggressive behavior, 23
Aggressive energy, absorption of, 178
Air pollution, 128–132
Alcohol, 42, 68–69
Allnatt, R. H., 32
American Bar Association, 204n
American Pyschiatric Association, 103,
   229
   Isaac Ray Award, 223
Amsterdam, Anthony, 53n
Anger, violence and aggression, 143–
   146
Animals
   cruelty to, 163–166
   extinction of, 121–122
Antisocial behavior, 46
Anxiety, cardiac distress and, 83–84
Aquinas, Thomas, 134n, 135, 138n
Architectural sins, 21–22
Arendt, Hannah, 100n
Armies, group guilt and, 99

Assassination, 185
Atlanta *Constitution*, 211
Atonement, 180–182
Atrocities, in prison, 63–64
Attica Prison riot, 143
Attitudes, toward sin, 173–177
Auerbach, Jerold, 204n
Autoerotism, 31–37
Automobiles, pollution by, 122
Avarice, 148–156
Avicenna, 83
Avoidance, of sin, 14–18

Bakan, David, 167n, 221
Barbellion, W. N. P., 90
Barber, David, 211
Bard, Morton, 207
Barnes, Peter, 129, 151n
Battered child syndrome, 167
Beeson, Trevor, 10n
Behavior research, pioneers in, 79
Bennett, James V., 52n
Berheim, Hippolyte, 38
Bertalanffy, Ludwig von, 86n
Biofeedback research, 77–78
Blake, Eugene Carson, 200
Bollinger, Richard, v
Bombing
   destructiveness of, 7
   guilt feeling re, 15–16, 99, 105–106
Boniface, William R., 88n
Boorstein, Daniel J., 9
Born, Max, 179
Boulding, Kenneth, 203n
Braid, James, 38
Briggs, Vernon, 43
Brinker, Berenice, vi
Bromberg, Walter, 52n
Bronfenbrenner, Urie, 159
Brown, Bertram, 219